THE DOWNFALL OF THE AMERICAN ORDER?

THE DOWNFALL OF THE AMERICAN ORDER?

Edited by Peter J. Katzenstein
and Jonathan Kirshner

CORNELL UNIVERSITY PRESS   ITHACA AND LONDON

First published 2022 by Cornell University Press

Library of Congress Cataloging-in-Publication Data

Names: Katzenstein, Peter J., editor. | Kirshner, Jonathan, editor.
Title: The downfall of the American order? / edited by Peter J. Katzenstein and Jonathan Kirshner.
Description: Ithaca [New York] : Cornell University Press, 2022. | Includes bibliographical references and index.
Identifiers: LCCN 2021040011 (print) | LCCN 2021040012 (ebook) | ISBN 9781501762970 (hardcover) | ISBN 9781501762987 (paperback) | ISBN 9781501763007 (ebook) | ISBN 9781501762994 (pdf)
Subjects: LCSH: Liberalism. | World politics—1945–1989. | World politics—1989– | International relations. | United States—Foreign relations—1945–1989. | United States—Foreign relations—1989–
Classification: LCC JC574 .D69 2022 (print) | LCC JC574 (ebook) | DDC 320.510973—dc23
LC record available at https://lccn.loc.gov/2021040011
LC ebook record available at https://lccn.loc.gov/2021040012

In memory of John G. Ruggie

Contents

Preface

The erosion of the American order is a subject that has troubled us at least since the disastrous war that America waged in Iraq and the financial crisis of 2008. Despite Donald Trump's defeat in 2020, his presidency made it clear, at least to us, that with the end of that order global affairs have reached a turning point. Looking backward, this book seeks to understand the character of the American order that is passing before our eyes. Because we both share a healthy respect for uncertainty in world affairs, we are cautious in our prognostications about what comes next.

This book engages issues that touch core themes of our research interests. Going beyond purely intellectual matters, we acknowledge fully that we also embarked on this project for selfish reasons: as a goodbye present to ourselves. After we had shared offices across the hallway for more than twenty years, Jonathan Kirshner decided to join the political science faculty at Boston College. We had spent innumerable hours bantering in each other's offices about this and that. But we had never done a project together. This book, among other things, is a way of celebrating our extended, deep intellectual friendship.

This is a book of essays, not of scholarly papers. We have encouraged all of our authors to write in a way that is accessible to a broader audience and to challenge our conventional understandings as best they could.

To reach that objective we decided to run two lecture series, one at Cornell University and the other at Boston College; Mark Blyth generously hosted one of these talks at the Rhodes Center at Brown University. With the exception of the two editors, all authors were thus given an opportunity to develop their arguments in front of a live audience while presenting us with early drafts of their chapters. Rewritten chapters were discussed in three Zoom meetings in May 2020. Our discussion was much improved by Peter Hall, Eric Helleiner, and Erin Lockwood, who provided outstanding critical commentary and constructive suggestions to help all authors in their final rewrites. The book then went through a review process at Cornell University Press with two referees offering extremely helpful suggestions for further improvement.

We are grateful for the financial support of the Einaudi Center, the School of Industrial and Labor Relations, the Law School, the Program of Ethics and Public Life, and the Walter S. Carpenter Chair in international Studies (all at Cornell University); and of Boston College.

We would like to thank Colin Chia and Aditi Sahasrabuddhe for their expert research assistance.

John Ruggie died after this book was completed. His life had two missions. He was the leading theorist of his generation who influenced cutting-edge work in all parts of the world. He was also immensely successful in pushing for positive change in world politics. Witnessing with dismay the dis-embedding of liberalism by liberals in various countries, he had the chutzpah to make the re-embedding of liberalism at the global level one of his life's main purposes. Few academics had his encompassing vision. Finally, he remained a life-affirming *Mensch*, ready to chuckle at the absurdities he encountered, as he traveled the long road from Graz to Harvard. At the very end of that road he treated his ideas, and ours, with utmost seriousness while enlivening our discussions as this project took shape. We dedicate this book to his memory.

Peter J. Katzenstein, Ithaca, NY
Jonathan Kirshner, Newton, MA

THE DOWNFALL OF THE AMERICAN ORDER?

Introduction

Jonathan Kirshner and Peter J. Katzenstein

Everything comes to an end.

—Carmella Soprano, *The Sopranos*

In 1945, the United States, in concert with Britain and other affiliated states, set the foundations for an international economic order and mechanisms of global governance. Present in the minds of the creators of that new order were the ruins of the old. The 1930s had exposed the failures of capitalism left to its own devices, and the international economy descended into closure and chaos, contributing to the cataclysm that was World War II. As President Franklin D. Roosevelt observed in his 1945 State of the Union Address, although the war was approaching its successful completion, victory would leave still much left to accomplish. "In our disillusionment after the last war we preferred international anarchy to international cooperation with nations which did not see and think exactly as we did," he lectured. "We gave up the hope of gradually achieving a better peace because we had not the courage to fulfill our responsibilities in an admittedly imperfect world. We must not let that happen again, or we shall follow the same tragic road again."[1] After a dismal thirty years—war, depression, and war—the architects of a new order, with these memories fresh and haunting, sought to build something different, resilient, and durable. From the vantage point of those moments of creation in the late 1940s, the American-led order, despite its visible and often profound blemishes, was successful to an extent that would have been far beyond the most wildly optimistic hopes of its founders. And now, it looks to us, this all might be over.

Distinctive of the American order was a tight coupling of political and economic liberalism. After 1945 many states supported economic liberalism. But

1

they were unwilling to sign up for political liberalism. American hegemony and widespread support for the United States' "empire by invitation" in western Europe made the coupling of political with economic liberalism the defining trait of the Atlantic world.[2] A generation later, in the 1980s, Japan as America's looming rival subscribed to the main tenets of political liberalism. As was the case in Sweden, this one-party-dominant system shared many more traits with political liberalism than with any of the other models in the Second or Third World.[3] By 2020, as the importance of the Atlantic world recedes and a multiregional, global system emerges, the end of the American order points to a return to the looser coupling of economic and political liberalism that characterized the years immediately following World War II.

Embedded and Neoliberal American Orders

We define the American order as the international system largely orchestrated by the United States from 1945 to 2020. Forged by the United States in the global ruins of World War II, the American order was improvised at its origins and far from coherent, and it retained domestic and international elements that were antithetical to liberalism, often profoundly so. We nevertheless describe that order as a liberal one, if necessarily bearing the untidy and idiosyncratic markings inherent to both economic and political liberalism. Stretching across three-quarters of a century, the American order unfolded in two different phases, each marked by different political contexts and distinct material and ideational underpinnings, interrupted by an interregnum lasting from the early 1970s to the mid-1980s.

The first American order flourished for a quarter of century after 1945. Even as the United States exercised far-sighted global leadership, and, especially from the late 1940s through the early 1960s, cheerfully bore a disproportionate share of the burdens of international leadership, long-standing and enduring instincts of isolationism and unilateralism remained part of the American disposition. Recall, for example, the failure of the US Senate to agree to the originally envisioned International Trade Organization, or the considerable strength of the isolationist wing of the Republican Party in 1952—it was only with the Party's nomination of Dwight Eisenhower that America's bipartisan, internationalist consensus was fully formed to support the first American order.

The first order gave way to an untidy interregnum lasting about fifteen years from the early 1970s to the mid-1980s). The first order unraveled during the stagflation of the 1970s, marked by rampant inflation, increasing unemployment, low economic growth, two oil shocks, and the American abdication of the Bretton Woods international monetary regime. At the time many observers saw in all this the end of US hegemony, because it was attendant with the apparent rise of Soviet military power and foreign policy assertiveness and the spectacular growth of the Japanese economy.[4] Others emphasized continuity in the extraordinary attributes of the American colossus, though admitting that it was limping through a difficult decade. As Susan Strange observed, "To decide one August morning that dollars can no longer be converted into gold was a progression from exorbitant privilege to super-exorbitant privilege."[5] President Richard Nixon suddenly slammed shut the "gold window," but the world still ran on dollars.[6] The United States had simply shrugged off the modest constrains that had accompanied its position as the issuer of the world's currency while transferring state control over currency values to market forces. Nevertheless, from the early 1970s to the mid-1980s the American order was adrift. It was also the period when the postwar practice of "Keynesianism" was largely discredited. It mattered little that this widespread delegitimation, as Raymond Aron observed at the time, tended to overlook the fact that "the ideas derived by postwar governments from [Keynes's] *The General Theory* were only vaguely attributable to the author of that book."[7] A shift back toward pre-Keynesian economic orthodoxy was a crucial development in these hinge years, buttressing a more conservative politics and economics.

The second American order emerged in the early 1990s in the wake of the collapse of the Soviet Union, the end of the Japanese miracle, and the resurgence of the US economy. This order was characterized by its embrace of unrestrained market fundamentalism and the aggressive promotion of globalization— especially in finance. The consensus for that disposition was not as strong as during the 1950s, the initial decade of the first order. In the 1990s the right posed repeated challenges, as the end of the Cold War left uncertain as to what the purpose of American power could and should be in its aftermath. (The first post– Cold War US presidential election, in 1992, witnessed the rise of the nativist, insurgent candidacies of Patrick Buchanan and Ross Perot.) And by the end of the 1990s the Left was increasingly opposed to some of the policies that helped support the American order, as international competition placed new pressures on traditional, labor-intensive sectors of the US economy. But the center held as the Democratic Party, loser of five of the previous six presidential elections, lurched rightward and propelled the second American order. In the twenty-first century, the hollowing out of American society through the trauma of two long, unsuccessful wars, a global financial crisis and its grueling aftermath, and the ever-widening gaps between the wealthy and the rest, led to a resurgence of the populist backlash that had bubbled to the surface decades before. It is possible to protest that the election of Donald Trump as president in 2016 was a fluke.

But his nomination, steamrolling through the establishment of the Republican Party while articulating positions that trampled on its core principles was clear evidence of a sea change in American politics heralding the end of the second American order. So was the fact that a fringe candidate, an obscure Socialist from Vermont, nearly wrested the Democratic nomination from the formidable, party-backed candidate. Similarly, despite Trump's loss in the 2020 presidential election, there is little evidence to suggest that anything short of a tectonic shift has taken place in the American domestic political disposition, and one that will shape the nation's prospects for international leadership and engagement.

This book's primary focus is on different forms or economic liberalism. Classical economic liberalism refers to the nineteenth-century notion of unrestrained market forces. We associate the period from roughly 1947 to the early 1970s with the practice of "embedded liberalism." This is a reference to a seminal article by John Ruggie.[8] The institutions of the postwar economic order were designed to encourage a thriving and growing international economy, but with buffers that were intended to permit various domestic social practices and purposes. The "liberalism" of Ruggie's embedded liberalism was thus classically defined—the play of free market forces—which, however, were not totally unrestrained but were embedded (or reembedded, if Karl Polanyi is to be believed) in varieties of local social purposes.[9] In this volume the phrase "embedded liberalism" refers to both domestic and international arrangements from 1947 to the early 1970s.[10] In this first era the influence of John Maynard Keynes was at its peak. Keynes helped design the postwar international institutions that aspired to steer a middle course between the unfettered play of free market forces that led to disaster in the late 1920s and the often authoritarian and state-centric experiments of the 1930s.

"Neoliberalism" refers to a turn toward the market understood in classical economic, "liberal" terms. With roots extending back to the 1930s and foreshadowed by some policies of the Carter Administration in the 1970s, it emerged full blown in the 1980s and is most notably associated with the reigns of Ronald Reagan in the United States and Margret Thatcher in the United Kingdom. But it endured well into the 2000s. In different states and markets it arrived at different moments and took different forms. It affected both domestic and international politics. The erosion of the embedded liberal order was accelerated, as Ruggie anticipated, not by real economic changes but by the unraveling of the normative consensus that supported it. The neoliberal turn was facilitated by the deregulation of global finance, just as Keynes feared (and would have predicted). Thus, in terms of economics, the first American order reflected the principles and practices of embedded liberalism; the second order reflected those of neoliberalism.

These different American orders, spanning seventy-five years, were, in broad brush, liberal.[11] Liberalism, of course, is a contested and perhaps inherently contestable political concept that lends itself to a wide range of views. This volume does not impose a uniform definition or interpretation on its authors. According to most familiar conceptions of the term, political liberalism includes dispositional tolerance, wariness of concentrations of public and private power, freedom of expression, and the primacy of law over leaders. Of course, the behavior of the United States commonly fell far short of these aspirations. It is certainly the case that in practice, the United States engaged in ghastly illiberal conduct: its wars in Vietnam and Iraq, intimate political relationships with unsavory and even neofascist regimes, and the endurance of profoundly illiberal, racist policies at home, to name a but few. Liberalism, like all politics, cannot escape from dirtying its hands.

Nevertheless, we choose to characterize the American order against plausible counterfactual worlds—what came before, what might otherwise have been, and what might emerge in the future—as opposed to judging it against an idealized vision of the what liberalism aspires to be. By that more modest metric, the American postwar order was indeed a liberal order. And as that order ends, it cedes the stage to a more diverse international system increasingly populated by varieties of authoritarian nationalisms. In this new global order, what will be the balance between political and economic forms of liberalism and other alternatives? And on which side of the scale will America put its considerable weight?

Preview

Jonathan Kirshner details in chapter 1 Keynes's search for a distinct "middle way" between laissez-faire and collectivism. Keynes himself was neither a traditional liberal nor a man of the left. He wrote that in a class war he would fight on the side of the educated bourgeoisie. Sharing many Hayekian philosophical positions, he was a reluctant planner.[12] The "new order" he helped build differed dramatically from the nightmarish one the Nazis attempted to fashion in the 1930s and 1940s. In an uncoordinated fashion, Keynes's ideas helped restart the engine of capitalist growth in war-torn Europe after 1945 and helped build an eventually thriving international economy. "The purpose of embedded liberalism," writes Kirshner, "was to permit the practice of the middle way."[13] Of central importance were the taming of finance and national control of destabilizing movements of speculative capital. In addition, Keynesianism was helped along by the horrific memories of the 1930s and 1940s, America's economic exceptionalism in the 1950s and 1960s, and the restraining influence of the Cold War on the predatory instincts of the money-making classes. The weakening of these conditions over time, the sour experience of the stagflation of the 1970s, and the fantasy of an economy characterized by risk, not uncertainty (nourished by the ascendance of clever but hollow rational expectations theory) initiated the era of uncontrolled capital movement and financialization that collapsed in and was resuscitated after 2008. What comes after the total rupture of 2020 nobody knows. Even if Keynes, Keynesianism, and the middle way will not reappear in anything like the form we encountered them before, the radical uncertainty that he recognized as constitutive of much of economic life continues to be with us. Kirshner's chapter introduces two of the key themes that many of the chapters touch on. Was embedded liberalism sustainable? And did its erosion contribute to the political backlashes that Keynes's middle way had been designed to resist?

The creation of what Mark Blyth calls in chapter 2 the first American order looks preordained only in hindsight. It was, in fact, a jerry-built, accidental arrangement that could have easily failed in its first decade. American interests dictated final outcomes on issues such as a global currency and provisions for liquidity in times of need. If there was a driver in all of this it was not the farsighted policies of a benevolent hegemon but security policy and anticommunism in an intensifying Cold War. Improvisation[14] and an "anti-anarchy struggle" defined the early years of the Cold War.[15] Not so in domestic politics. By 1948 the American version of embedded liberalism had been installed and was supported by an array of political forces enjoying a win-win game.

With Kirshner and Abdelal, Blyth situates the second American order as a reaction to the perceived failure of the first as manifested by the calamitous 1970s. The partial decommodification of labor under a full-employment regime created a backlash by social forces favoring greater reliance on market forces. Keynesian ideas gave way to monetarist dogma. The social purpose of the second order shifted from promoting full employment to disciplining labor, creating price stability, and restoring returns on capital investment and the capital/labor share of the gross domestic product that had slipped since the 1960s. Eventually, the success of these policies favoring capital brought about the financial crisis and the Great Recession. Since 2008 reforms have remained modest and partial, falling well short of creating a new social purpose. Instead, a massive influx of public liquidity stabilized the second order without addressing any of its underlying dysfunctionalities. Trumpist populism and the explosion of the Black Lives Matter movement during the COVID-19 epidemic in the spring and summer of 2020 set the stage for the emergence of something new, the contours of which remain indistinct. Blyth argues that "nationalism with loose money" may come to replace "globalism with tight money" as one feature of a new pluralist and neonationalist order serving a variety of social purposes. That order, Blyth claims, will remain American because of the continued, pivotal role of the dollar in the international economy, not because of the articulation of a new social purpose in and by America.

In chapter 3 Peter Gourevitch fleshes out the political story of the foundation of the European welfare state. Embedded liberalism was a set of complex compromises more than a cause. Akin to Blyth, who insists on historical contingency, Gourevitch insists that the terminology of embedded liberalism is a shorthand for compressing into a single phrase a multiplicity of complex political processes. In the late 1940s and early 1950s the pivotal political force in western Europe was Christian democracy, personified by Konrad Adenauer in Germany, Robert Schuman in France, and Alcide de Gasperi in Italy. With the support of other democratic forces, including social democracy, these three leaders sought to restabilize Europe socially and economically under the banner of conservative Christian democracy. In the nineteenth century the Catholic Church had been actively involved in what was then known as the Social Question through papal edicts, such as Quadragesimo Anno, and through Catholic-run or state-assisted social work bureaucracies. Clerical fascism before World War II was one result; Christian democracy after World War II was another. With Europe reduced to physical rubble and spiritual wasteland after 1945, the aim was a resurrection of sorts of Lotharingia, part of Charlemagne's empire, in modernized form.[16] With one exception, despite deep-seated hostility and suspicion on both sides, Christian democracy's opposition to unfettered liberalism, fascism, and Marxism made it a de facto comrade in arms for social democrats seeking to build a welfare state. On the question of European integration, however, and in contrast to Christian democracy social democrats were divided. Some joined their communist colleagues in seeing the European Union (EU) as a thinly concealed clerical-fascist plot designed to undermine democratic capitalism. Others saw it as a bulwark against Stalinist-style communism. The historical compromise between center-left and center-right suppressed but did not eliminate various resentments: the working class's resentment of capitalism; the working and middle classes' resentment of collaborators with fascists, national socialists, and occupying forces during World War II; former fascist and communist activists' resentment of the democratic order; and various groups' resentment of US domination after 1945.

In contrast with Gourevitch, who stresses the role of coalitional bargaining and varieties of capitalism in emerging postwar Europe, Sheri Berman emphasizes the underlying tensions between economic and political liberalism—that is, between capitalism and democracy. In chapter 4 she holds that embedded liberalism is a "misnomer" especially for its domestic pillar. "'Liberal,'" Berman writes, "is not merely inaccurate, it also obscures what it took to finally make democracy work in Europe."[17] After 1945 the relationship between states, markets, and societies was transformed. The state became a guardian, protecting society against the economic dislocations wrought by capitalism and furthering a "communitarian gemeinschaft."[18] This was the type of order social democrats had been fighting for since the late nineteenth century—against liberals, right-wing parties, and others on the left. In the second half of the twentieth century, this social democratic order succeeded where liberalism, Marxism, fascism, and National Socialism had failed, finally making democracy compatible with capitalism and social stability. Sweden was the exemplar of the victory of social democracy, and so was, in a different manner, Germany's social market economy. But despite scoring an important victory in terms of principles and values, a refashioned democratic capitalism did not always bring political victory to social democrats. Too many leftists continued to cling to outmoded ideologies, and too many nonleftists moved quickly to appropriate central social democratic planks.

Francis Gavin in chapter 5 homes in on the interregnum between the two American orders, crucial hinge years for the concerns of all the chapters in this volume. He shows how California's dreams and nightmares turned real, creating a new center of capital accumulation and wealth that affected states and peoples in every corner of the world. California created Silicon Valley, invigorated commerce with Asia, and shaped many other aspects of human life ranging from bodies and sexuality to popular culture and cuisine. California altered individual identities and capabilities on a massive scale. It changed the pace and direction of technological innovations, the financial modalities that support them, and models of entrepreneurship that seek risk and accept failure. The Golden State Warriors are emblematic of a transformation that profoundly affected not only the game of basketball but also traditional conceptions of warfare and welfare. Most importantly, for better and for worse, California changed America's and the world's actual and aspirational way of life, from start-ups to wines, movies to social media, fashion to sexuality, and stand-up comics to health clubs. California thus elevated the soft power of America that helped shore up the declining legitimacy of the hard power of the United States. Not all change was for the better. Environmental degradation, social and economic inequality, mass incarceration, and the ruinous effects of social media on public debate and politics belie the notion that the Golden State has brought us only gold. But that does not deny the magnitude of a historical shift that Gavin argues has been as disruptive as the first and second industrial revolutions.

Rawi Abdelal argues in chapter 6 that the legitimacy crisis of globalization encapsulates a story about a recurring cycle of learning and forgetting that has marked the history of the international political economy since the late nineteenth century. The first globalization in the decades leading up to World War I taught the leaders of Europe the growth benefits of an open international economy with a free flow of goods, services, capital, and people. The interwar period, characterized by financial crises, collapsing national incomes and trade flows, virulent populist backlashes, and finally World War II shredded that pre–World War I consensus. Articulating a theme touched on by several chapters, he notes how, after 1945, a new learning cycle took into account the disasters of the 1920s and 1930s and led to the compromise of embedded liberalism. A generation later, intellectuals and policymakers had forgotten those disasters as they confronted the dreadful record of the 1970s, which brought stagflation and rising unemployment. Thus, they shifted back to unfettered markets and the policy approach of the first globalization period. The reactionary politics of the 1980s learned from the 1970s while forgetting the 1930s. What will be the next cycle of learning and forgetting now that the second American order is coming to an end?

Abdelal argues, counterintuitively, that the creation of neoliberalism was not the work of neoliberals. Instead, the second American order of the 1980s and 1990s was a European creation. Americans had no interest in creating a multilateral order. They were more interested in using power bilaterally in the interest of making money. By contrast, France wanted rules for capital markets, and rule-conscious Germany was intent on spreading capital mobility through Europe and the entire world. This was the second coming of an adage with a lot of historical baggage: *am deutschen Wesen mag die Welt genesen* (German ways will heal the world). Neoliberalism brought prosperity in swaths of the Global South, and in the North it generated technological innovation, economic inequality, financial volatility, and a loss of dignity among those frozen out and left behind. As Keynes had feared, the convergence of the center-left and center-right in support of this order inevitably invited the rise of populism on the right and the left that has hollowed out the transatlantic consensus and impaired the domestic legitimacy of many democracies. By the 2020s, the wheel of history is turning back to the 1920s and 1930s and their disastrous rebellion against the first, pre-1914 era of globalization.

Unlike most of the other contributors, Ilene Grabel sees a silver lining to the erosion of the American order, because (perhaps ironically, as this was the objective of embedded liberalism) it creates opportunities for varieties of national policy experimentation (as opposed to the rigid *diktats* of neoliberal orthodoxy). In chapter 7 she characterizes the current state of affairs as a post-American interregnum marked by incoherence that has both destructive and productive features. This may be disconcerting for social scientists searching for order, predictability, and the uncontested reign, real or imagined, of single "isms" that marked the first and second American international economic orders. Economists in particular, Grabel writes, are too partial to eliminating uncertainty and messiness. They prefer certainty and coherence, which are not on offer. Not all, of course. Grabel draws on the work of Albert Hirschman, inveterate pragmatist, opponent of all "isms," and champion of localized experimentation and possibilism.[19] She describes a layering of regimes—democratic, authoritarian, kleptocratic, populist—seeking to rebuild a measure of social embeddedness, often in terms of rhetoric, sometimes in terms of policy. James Rosenau's concept of "fragmegration"[20] aptly summarizes the fragmentation, experimentalism, resilience, and incoherence that Grabel highlights in her discussion of contemporary global financial governance. At this particular juncture in history, and reinforced by massive public programs seeking to stabilize markets in the era of COVID-19, patchiness helps open up spaces for policy experimentation in which some of the values and practices associated with a long-discarded embedded liberalism can be rearticulated, at times under the auspices of what Grabel calls "embedded populism."[21] These experiments tolerate a thin, permissive globalization in a world marked by deglobalizing and reglobalizing impulses. Put differently, the fracturing hegemony of the American model has created productive spaces for innovations that may eventually extend well beyond the financial sector, on which Grabel focuses. What is true for policies holds also for the productive incoherence of disparate, overlapping institutions. They, too, point to the possible emergence of a more complex, pluripolar financial and monetary system in a post-American world.

Given that no one can ever step in the same river twice, patchiness and incoherence in policy and institutional arrangements cannot resurrect the welfare state and Keynesian instruments of embedded liberalism. But it might offer a collage of social protection for actors and groups who for decades have been harmed or put at risk by neoliberal ideas and policies. By 2020 the terms of social protection had become the site of fierce political conflicts that pit progressive populists (favoring the most vulnerable groups and individuals through universal protections) against right-wing populists (favoring exclusive constituencies, defined by pressing needs and lost privileges, that share national, racial, or other identities). Despite the myriad risks of the current environment, Grabel is not nostalgic for either of the American orders. Instead, her eyes are trained on the possibilities created by the aperture and agency previously unavailable in more scripted environments.

John Ruggie, fittingly, revisits the limitations, tensions, and dilemmas of embedded liberalism that motivate the puzzles central to this volume. In chapter 8 he considers the limits of the vision of disembedded liberalism and tracks important ongoing reforms. An understudied driver of these reforms are multinational corporations that have prospered mightily since 1945. The global production chains they have forged cannot easily be scaled back to national territories, as the Trump tariff wars have illustrated. Central as multinational corporations were to the disembedding of liberalism, Ruggie shows that their interest in globalization also makes them stakeholders in a partial reembedding of markets and states in emerging transnational norms and evolving standards. This is no small matter. Well over half of international market transactions occur within multinational corporations. This generates dynamics quite unlike the arms-length interactions between governments. Specifically, the United Nations (UN) Global Compact and the UN Guiding Principles reflect and have contributed to a modest though noticeable shift in corporate identities, resulting in firms engaging with some of the broader environmental and social challenges of our times. Corporate identity, conceived in terms of shareholder property or social purpose, yo-yoed throughout the twentieth century. The UN Compact and UN Guiding Principles indicate that at the outset of the twenty-first century, corporations' social-purpose identities are making a comeback. In an era of rampant inequality and urgent environmental challenges, this makes again conceivable what in the neoliberal era was deemed impossible: a partial and inchoate reembedding of capitalism in a broader social order. Corporate social responsibility is neoliberalism's response to the social and environmental problems that unregulated markets have greatly intensified. It has become far more strategic over time and has generated soft-law and even some hard-law standards. In themselves, Ruggie concedes, new corporate initiatives will not be enough to rebalance the dysfunctions of the global economy. But they moderate some of them and thus encourage governments to increase political efforts to put people and planetary concerns center stage, mitigating the harmful consequences of maximizing shareholder values.

Finally, in chapter 9, Peter Katzenstein argues that the end of the American order is not coterminous with the end of liberalism. The history of liberalism points to its multiple traditions and political forms as well as its great resilience. The paradoxical antinomy of liberalism is that its endings have always been periods of new beginnings. In an uncertain world of pluralizing power centers much will depend on America itself. Will American liberalism limp along in some form of sustainable decadence for a few more years or decades, experiencing intermittent crises at home and abroad while being sustained mostly by the weakness, incoherence, incompetence, corruption, and brutality of its international and domestic inheritors or rivals? Or will American liberalism offer a revived, reconfigured, dynamic, and just form of liberalism that can reinvigorate legitimacy in America and inspire hope around the world?

Uncertain Futures

The early 2020s are defined by cascading uncertainties about American politics, America's position in the world, the international order, and environmental issues pressing governments, all illustrated and underscored with renewed urgency by COVID-19 and the attendant stunning display of American dysfunction. Where will this lead? Our keen interest in anticipating the future is tempered by a profound respect for the consequences of uncertainty.

World politics is full of the unexpected. The end of the Cold War, the 9/11 attacks on the World Trade Center and the Pentagon, the financial crisis and its aftermath, the Arab Spring, Brexit, the election of Donald Trump in 2016, and COVID-19 were unexpected thunderbolts. Insider information and in-depth knowledge help us little in such moments. Our impatience is insatiable as we crave unobtainable knowledge from God or Science. More than three thousand years ago, the Delphic oracle would fathom the unknowable from the mumbling of a priestess sitting inside the Temple of Apollo, inhaling intoxicating fumes that induced a trance-like state to convey the god's riddles and cryptic remarks. In the twenty-first century, retired politicians and pundits respond to the same craving with no better results in our ever-expanding mediascape. We want to be power walking into the future "when in fact we are always just tapping our canes on the pavement in the fog."[22]

The changing fault lines of American domestic politics lay down important markers for the course that the United States charts in world politics. Contemporary American politics reflects bone-shattering uncertainty. This marks the individual lives of tens of millions of Americans who are confronting unsettling vulnerabilities in their health, their economic sustenance, and their aspirations for racial justice. America is balancing on the knife's edge. Will it become a populist semiauthoritarian presidential system that can no longer represent the will of the majority of the population, or will it initiate a new cycle of reformist policies designed to enhance equality and inclusiveness?

Uncertainty also marks America's position in the world. Admiring, loathing, and fearing America have been complemented by something unexpected and new: pitying America. The Trump administration's retrenchment from the international stage, its efforts to undermine multilateral institutions and global governance efforts, its lack of clear strategies, its attack on traditional allies, and its admiration of authoritarian regimes all increased the inherent uncertainties in world politics. These changes cannot be undone—there is no going back, only moving forward, with world politics, as always, influenced by the looming shadow of the relevant past. With the defeat of Trump in 2020, some might be tempted to suggest that his presidency was an aberration and that the United States could return to some version of business as usual, jettisoning its brief and regrettable flirtation with ham-fisted America Firstism and diplomacy characterized by mercurial, personalist dealmaking. But this is both wrong and naive.

The Trump-as-fluke fable was perhaps a comforting one for many to murmur to themselves after the general election of 2016, but as noted, this fails to account for Trump's steamrolling through the Republican Party during that year's nominating process, an astonishing upheaval against the establishment that was paralleled by the almost successful insurgent candidacy of Bernie Sanders on the Democratic side. The ease with which Trump seized the Republican Party defies reassuring post hoc rationalization. Both outsiders tapped a powerful and deeply disenchanted undercurrent. Trump and Sanders did not agree on much, but they both hated the Trans-Pacific Partnership (or at least what it seemed to represent). Secretary of State Hillary Clinton had painstakingly negotiated this trade pact, and at that time it enjoyed widespread support in the Republican Party. Clearly, and indisputably since 2016, the American taste for engaged internationalism has diminished greatly, and there is no evidence to suggest that it might rebound.

Moreover, notwithstanding the outcome of the 2020 Presidential election, that contest actually underscored Trump's robust political strength. Despite innumerous, often bizarre, and commonly norm-shattering episodes and ethical scandals that surely would have ruined the political fortunes of any previous president, not to mention the Trump administration's horrifying, almost delusional mishandling of the COVID-19 pandemic that took the lives of hundreds of thousands of Americans, Trump nevertheless received more votes in 2020 than in 2016. Seventy-four million people voted for his reelection (nine million more than in the "fluke" election of 2016)—the most votes ever cast for a Republican candidate for president. This is not a transient interlude. The center of political gravity in the Republican Party has shifted dramatically and it is likely to remain a nativist-nationalist (and some would argue increasingly antidemocratic) one. Other countries will readily understand this profound shift while assessing their future relationship with the United States.

It is true of course that President Joe Biden received eighty-one million votes in 2020. But Biden operates under severe restraints. Although he is easily recognizable as a well-schooled internationalist, he will has limited degrees of domestic political freedom within which to operate. Biden's mandate is circumscribed. He was elected primarily on the basis of not being Trump, which was sufficient glue to hold together a large and winning coalition. But his congressional majorities are slim and vulnerable. Many in the opposition recite the fiction that his was a stolen election. And his own party is notably divided, often along generational lines between its left-leaning and centrist wings. The young left is not easily described as internationalist, and Biden, with a pressing domestic agenda, is unlikely to spend precious political capital (or complicate delicate efforts to hold his fragile coalition together) fighting for unpopular elements of his foreign policy agenda.

The consequences of these domestic political facts are not to be underestimated. And even if US domestic politics somehow become more functional in the coming years, the world cannot unsee the still relevant past. At a Los Angeles press conference in 1966, a reporter asked George Harrison how the image of the Beatles had recently changed. "An image is how you see us," Harrison responded, "so, you know, only you can answer that." And so it is for countries. The image of America abroad has changed. It is perhaps hard to remember now, but well into 2016 the notion of a Trump presidency was so beyond the pale of the plausible that the prospect was not taken seriously (possibly not even by the candidate himself). But the unthinkable is now more than thinkable. And to this must now be added the abetting of the insurrection of January 6, 2020 by prominent members of the Republican Party. These events will now become part of any assessment of the American prospect; its democracy can produce these outcomes. In fact, the robustness of American democracy itself must now be reevaluated. This affects friends more than foes, who must now hedge their bets and anticipate that US foreign policy might again turn nativist, nationalist, deeply wary of multilateral cooperation, suspicious of traditional allies, and short-sighted and zero-sum in its mentality. Indications are that this new wariness will be hard to shake.[23]

And it is not simply US allies that will view both America and the emerging the world order or disorder with new eyes. The fascination and preoccupation with China's rising power conceals the broader regional contours that have defined world politics since the end of the Cold War. The United States was the major player in all of the world's regions without dictating outcomes in any of them. No other state has played such a multiregional role. The foreign policy of the Biden administration will seek to resume playing that role, to the extent that pressing domestic problems permit. China's rise poses a new challenge for American diplomacy to maintain or build up its political position in East, Southeast, and South Asia. But not only there. In Africa, Latin America, Europe, and Central Asia China's growing importance is readily apparent in a variety of regional orders.

But neither the United States, nor China, nor their cooperative and conflictual duopoly will rule over international politics. Nor will a small handful of major powers. The growing importance of nongovernmental actors, transnational social movements, and global mediascapes prevent a return to nineteenth-century great power politics. Instead, world politics will be shaped by the encounters and engagements of the United States, China, and other states in regional meshes open to national and global political processes.

A world of encounters and engagements is a much bigger territory than conventional theoretical maps can capture. Explanations focusing on structural constraints and incentives operating in a putatively anarchic system inhabited by identical actors differentiated only by their relative capabilities give us limited insights into the dynamics of world politics. The same can be said for approaches that focus on abstract models of bargaining behavior between individuals and groups that are assumed to exclusively pursue narrowly conceived material interests.[24] Instead, emerging patterns of world politics are best explained with proper attentiveness paid to regional and civilizational elements.[25]

Notably, as many eyes turn to China, it needs to be recognized that China's domestic politics, like those of the United States, are experiencing a basic transformation. For decades the Chinese leadership adopted a strategy of creative muddling through with outcomes that nobody, including the leaders themselves, could foresee. The self-control that China's traditional system of collegial leadership imposed is now gone. With President Xi Jinping adopting dictatorial power and following harsh and hard-edged polices at home and abroad, China's future course becomes even more unpredictable—just as the heterogeneity and unruliness of American society creates unpredictabilities of its own. In contrast to China's state-owned enterprises and regimented civil society, social, economic, and political surprises are hardwired into America's dynamic society. Following Walt Whitman, America is large and contains multitudes and contradictions creating plenty of uncertainties about future developments.

Because the prospect of the United States in the world is uncertain, so is the future of the international order. With the United States stepping back from its central position in world politics, will China and other states step forward and fill the role that the United States is no longer willing or able to perform? Perhaps they will purposefully rebuild the international order along traditional nationalist lines, protecting national sovereignty and shunning multilateral governance arrangements. Perhaps they will muddle through to novel arrangements reflecting the intersection of new global, regional, and national challenges. Will an overarching order give way to a multiplicity of regionalized orders that exist side by side? Or will global issues, such as public health and the environment, compel states to develop new approaches to cope with impending catastrophes, now that COVID-19 has given the world a taste of what lies ahead? Any answer to these questions touches cherished memories and vested interests. Some remember the past as a rule-governed multilateral order presided over by a benevolent United States as the leader and defender of the free world. Others remember the past as traditional power politics, with the United States using multilateralism to achieve its preferred national objectives. Conventional readings of what the past was like inform analyses of what the future might become. Memories and interests, however, are no match for the uncertainty that is shrouding the future filled with possibilities that yield no clear picture.

KEYNES AND THE ELUSIVE MIDDLE WAY

Jonathan Kirshner

Morally and philosophically I find myself in agreement with virtually the whole of it; and not only in agreement with it, but in a deeply moved agreement. . . . Your greatest danger ahead is the probable practical failure of the application of your philosophy in the U.S. in a fairly extreme form.

—John Maynard Keynes to Friedrich von Hayek, on *The Road to Serfdom*

"The Compromise of Embedded Liberalism," the felicitous phrase coined by John Ruggie in his seminal article articulating the purpose with which the post–World War II economic order was forged, is often associated with Karl Polanyi.[1] In *The Great Transformation*, Polanyi argued that laissez-faire capitalism was unsustainable and incongruous, and he did indeed situate the notion of embeddedness at the heart of the matter: "Instead of economy being embedded in social relations, social relations are embedded in the economic system."[2] But the economic philosophy of embedded liberalism is a distinctly and fundamentally Keynesian conception. It is an attempt to embrace and harness the essential engines of capitalism and an expanding international economy in order to provide the means to prosperity, while at the same time insulating national economies from unmediated, often destructive market forces so that they might enjoy the autonomy to pursue a variety of domestic social purposes.

The Great Transformation was published in 1944 (based on a series of lectures that Polanyi delivered from 1941 to 1943), and it was motivated to dismiss capitalism, not domesticate it.[3] Whereas Keynes, who similarly renounced laissez-faire (in a dramatic break, as he had been raised firmly within the faith—he had taken it "with his mother's milk" from its most revered high priests), in the dozen odd years from 1925 to 1938 struggled to develop a "middle way" that would save capitalism from itself. And the postwar order was forged, under the profound intellectual influence of Keynes, to facilitate the practice of the middle way.[4]

Keynes's break with orthodoxy in 1925 was a watershed moment, heralded by his essay "The End of Laissez-Faire" and its declaration, "The World is not so governed from above that private and social interest always coincide." This disenchantment would grow still more pointed in the depths of the Great Depression: "[Laissez-faire capitalism] is not intelligent, it is not beautiful, it is not just, it is not virtuous—and it doesn't deliver the goods." Yet in the same breath Keynes also observed, "When we wonder what to put in its place, we are extremely perplexed."[5] Keynes's disposition and his profound opposition to collectivist economic and political ideologies meant that he rejected the revolutionary answers that many were reaching for in the 1930s. Thus emerged his search for a middle way between the unpalatable extremes of unfettered capitalism and authoritarian collectivism. This was Keynes' project, and it was, for a time, wildly influential.

Keynes was one of the architects of and the principal intellectual influence on the institutions designed to oversee the international order after World War II. Even more important, he was, despite his early death in 1946, the most influential touchstone of economic thought in the postwar decades. Thus, Keynes's articulation of a middle way deeply shaped the economic practices in the quarter-century that followed the war. Varieties of national economic policymaking in these years were not necessarily "Keynesian" (as defined by the American neoclassical economists who imagined they were his disciples). Nevertheless, in the 1950s and 1960s the practice of capitalism looked much more like an embrace of embedded liberalism than like the then discredited, neo-Dickensian unfettered capitalism associated with the robber-baron abuses of the 1890s and the horrors of the Great Depression.[6]

This chapter draws on Keynes's writings to consider his articulation of the middle way, as well as the broad (if, as envisioned, varied in practice) embrace of that philosophy after the war and its subsequent erosion in favor of less socially constrained capitalist practices. With a focus on the United States, I consider some of the key causes of the long retreat from Keynes's vision: the possibility that only exceptional circumstances permitted the practice of embedded liberalism in the first place; the unhappy trip from Keynes to "Keynesianism" and the unraveling of the latter in the dismal 1970s, which allowed for the ascension of anti-Keynesian economic theory (most notably, rational expectations theory) and economic practices antithetical to the middle way; and the rise of bare-knuckled "shareholder value" capitalism. And in particular, I emphasize how the great financial deregulation project of the 1990s that heralded the emergence of a second postwar American order was incompatible with the practice of the middle way. This point cannot be overemphasized. The middle way, and the postwar order as envisioned, depended on the taming of finance and the control of capital flows. Capital controls permit the practice of independent monetary policies; and as early as 1926, still groping toward a coherent vision, Keynes understood that "It is not an accident that the opening stage of this political struggle, which will last long and take many different forms, should centre about monetary policy."[7] And ultimately, as Keynes would have anticipated (and feared), the permissive financialization of the American economy led to widening inequality, the global financial crisis of 2007–08, and from those the widespread rise of virulent populism and personalist authoritarianism. Keynes was right to fear the consequences of Hayek in practice, and the great dangers it would unleash.

Establishing the Middle Way

The Keynesian revolution in macroeconomics would culminate with the publication of *The General Theory* and its immediate aftermath. As Keynes explained plainly, that revolution was founded on two fundamental departures from orthodoxy: (1) an economy, once stuck in a rut, could remain in a rut; (2) actors in the economy made decisions in an environment characterized by uncertainty, not risk.[8] But the middle way was much more than a macroeconomic theory—it was an economic philosophy. And its development was a slow burn that emerged from the mid-1920s, after the publication of *A Tract on Monetary Reform*— an excellent and still valuable book, but one written by a brilliant, inquisitive, insightful, but still largely mainstream economist.[9]

Keynes's writings have been broadly interpreted over decades, but a basic and central attribute of the middle way was that it was indeed, importantly and unambiguously, a middle way, inspired by a renunciation and scathing indictment of unfettered capitalism, but tempered by an abject horror of collectivism. Despite his definitive repudiation of laissez-faire, Keynes never much wavered from most of what we now call microeconomic theory (the foundations of which can still be found in Marshall's *Principles of Economics*, first published in 1890): "A large part of the established body of economic doctrine I cannot but accept as broadly correct. I do not doubt it."[10] Moreover, philosophically, Keynes placed an enormous premium on individualism and celebrated the diverse, idiosyncratic choices afforded by the decentralized market; by disposition (and in accord with his emphasis on uncertainty and thus the unforeseeable consequences of rash measures) he could be well described, at least with regard to proposals of economic policy, as cautious. James Meade, emerging from a meeting once quipped "Keynes on the rate of interest showed himself in a typical mood: revolutionary in thought and very cautious in policy."[11]

Thus, although Keynes defined the challenge of the ideal society as how best "to combine three things: economic efficiency, social justice, and individual liberty," the solution was not to be found in the extremes: "The abuses of this epoch in the realms of government are Fascism on the one side and Bolshevism on the other." Sensing the need, perhaps, to avoid any ambiguity, he immediately added, "Socialism offers no middle course."[12]

Keynes was under no illusions about the horrors of fascism (unlike many of the British right, who were content to avert their eyes), and had no taste, fashionable in many left-leaning Western circles of the day, for the Soviet experiment. A visit to Russia with his new bride in 1925 yielded the following observation: "Red Russia holds too much which is detestable . . . I am not ready for a creed which does not care how much it destroys the liberty and security of daily life, which uses deliberately the weapons of persecution, destruction, and international strife."[13] (This, is should be noted, was a full ten years before the show trials of the 1930s and thirty years before Khrushchev rendered finally undeniable the full range of the Stalinist terror.) Keynes was repulsed by collectivist authoritarianisms, but more to the point, he feared them. In particular, he feared that the great mass of people, unwilling to bear the increasingly bitter portions served by laissez-faire capitalism, would turn to these alternatives. And so he set out to save capitalism from itself: "The authoritarian state systems of to-day seem to solve the problem of unemployment at the expense of efficiency and of freedom. It is certain that the world will not much longer tolerate the unemployment which, apart from brief intervals of excitement is associated—and in my opinion, inevitably associated—with present day capitalistic individualism. But it may be possible by a right analysis of the problem to cure the disease whilst preserving efficiency and freedom."[14]

As noted, Keynes was not simply providing a new way of conceptualizing macroeconomics, he was articulating a philosophy of political economy. And for a discussion of embedded liberalism and its prospects, the specific technicalities of the former are for the most part less central than the overarching vision of the latter. In *The General Theory*, he phrased it this way: "The outstanding faults of the economic society in which we live are its failure to provide for full employment and its arbitrary and inequitable distribution of wealth and incomes."[15] Thus on offer is more than a means to achieve full employment. The basic questions of "What's fair?" and of "Who should get what, and why?" are also squarely on the table—and once again, the free market, left to its own devices, is found more than wanting.

Unfortunately, Keynes was frustratingly vague on the specifics of the distribution of income. For both positive and normative reasons, he strongly favored a more equitable distribution of income. As a technical matter, Keynes put much emphasis on the "marginal propensity to consume" and the fact that poorer and working-class people spend more of their income on consumption simply because they have more basic needs to urgently fulfill. Thus, wealth transfers from rich to poor boost aggregate demand. "If capitalist society rejects a more equal distribution of incomes," he wrote in 1937, "then a chronic tendency towards the underemployment of resources must in the end sap and destroy that form of society." Keynes also favored robust estate taxes and higher taxes on large incomes.[16] Beyond these admonitions, however, he was vague, and he routinely tempered his enthusiasm for redistribution with the qualifying notion that some significant degree of income inequality was essential to provide the impetus for progress and the incentive structure necessary for a market economy to function.[17]

This knot is rather easily untied, however, as Keynes's concern for income distribution, once that murky middle ground has been reached, is rooted not in a mathematical formula but in an emphasis on a broadly shared sense of economic justice, a core Keynesian theme which can be traced to his earliest writings. Keynes's enduring wariness of inflation, for example (a characteristic many of his critics overlook), was more philosophical than material—and deeply informed both his conception of the middle way and, as I will argue, the consequences of its unraveling. High levels of inflation are especially dangerous because they bring about an "arbitrary arrangement of riches," Keynes wrote in 1919, which "strikes not only at security, but at confidence in the equity of the existing distribution of wealth." This matters profoundly because, as he subsequently observed, "No man of spirit will consent to remain poor if he believes his betters to have gained their goods by lucky gambling." Even the "pre-Keynesian" Keynes stressed this point: "The business man is only tolerable so long as his gains can be held to bear some relation to what, roughly and in some sense, his activities have contributed to society." Capitalism cannot be sustained if it is viewed as inherently unfair.[18] (It is jumping ahead to note that the aftermath of the global financial crisis of 2007–08 left very few outside a well-heeled community of insiders retaining the view that the system was in any way fair, contributing to the understandable but dangerously misguided tear-it-all-down populism of both the left and the right.)

Finally, no discussion of the middle way and its contemporary implications would be complete without emphasizing another strand of Keynes's philosophy: his anti-economism.[19] Keynes, first comfortable and later wealthy, nevertheless saw something unclean in the pursuit of wealth for its own sake. He opposed the overvaluation of pecuniary criteria in shaping personal and social decision-making beyond what was necessary to attain necessities and satisfactory comfort. Ultimately, capitalism had no soul. This was another reason why he feared communism, despite its economic incoherence and political insidiousness. He thought it might appeal by providing social purpose, which people crave. Capitalism, in contrast, was vacuous, "without internal union, without much public spirit," and often, though not always, "a mere congeries of possessors and pursuers."[20]

As Keynes wrote in his memoir, "My Early Beliefs," which Robert Skidelsky properly described as "a key document for understanding his life's work," Keynes concluded that it was "the Benthamite calculus, based on an over-valuation of the economic criterion," that was "the worm which has been gnawing at the insides of modern civilization and is responsible for its present moral decay." Similar sentiments informed his better-known essay "Economic Possibilities of Our Grandchildren," in which he famously declared that the purpose of economics was to solve the economic problem, so that people would no longer need to organize their lives around the empty chase of money and instead have the freedom to pursue their varied, idiosyncratic interests that would allow them "to live wisely, agreeably and well."[21]

Before turning to the forging of the Keynesian-inflected postwar order and to the opening and closing of the window that permitted the possibility of the practice of the middle way, it is worth underscoring how essential this philosophical grounding is (especially as that philosophy was quickly shed by the neoclassicals who sought to domesticate Keynes and was subsequently rejected by the free-marketeers who would usher in a new era of unabashed economism that was, as Keynes had feared, vulnerable to dangerous backlash.) "Capitalism was in some ways repugnant to him but Stalinism was much worse," Joan Robinson summarized. "He hated unemployment because it was stupid and poverty because it was ugly. He was disgusted by the commercialism of modern life" and "indulged in an agreeable vision of a world where economics has ceased to be important and our grandchildren can begin to lead a civilised life."[22]

Making the World Safe for Embedded Liberalism

Nothing is more certain than that the movement of capital funds must be regulated.

—John Maynard Keynes, 1941

The founding of the Bretton Woods institutions is a familiar story often told.[23] The general frameworks of international economic governance that would characterize the American-led postwar order were hashed out over a series of meetings and multilateral conferences during and immediately after World War II. The principal architects of those institutions were Britain and the United States, with Keynes (who with his tireless efforts essentially worked himself to death) as the principal representative of his government and Harry Dexter White serving as the point man for the Americans. Negotiations were often difficult—as was, at times, Keynes, who could be less than diplomatic in rebutting arguments he found unsatisfactory. In the haggling over various "Keynes Plans" and "White Plans" history properly records that the end results were much closer to those proposed by the Americans, as would be expected given the dramatic gulf in the balance of bargaining power between the two partners.[24]

Occasionally overlooked, however, is that the negotiations took place entirely in what could be called a "Keynesian space." Although it is certainly the case that Keynes wanted and did not get, among other things, a much more capacious International Monetary Fund (IMF) and better terms for the Anglo-American loan, the influence of Keynes's ideas on the overarching conceptualization of the postwar order was so profound that the similarities of the plans were much more consequential than their differences. And the aim of that shared purpose and vision was to avoid the catastrophes of the interwar years: the failure of laissez-faire capitalism and the murderous backlash that failure engendered—that is, to forge an international order that would permit the practice of the middle way.[25]

Crucially, this would only be possible if states were permitted to deploy various forms of capital control. Thus, the rules of the IMF were written explicitly with the practice of capital controls in mind. On the centrality of these points Keynes could not have been clearer: "Control of capital movements, both inward and outward, should be a permanent feature of the post-war system." This is easily misunderstood. Keynes did not argue that capital should be prevented from moving across borders—such flows were welcome and essential. Rather, he recognized that not all capital movements were productive. Indeed, much capital movement was intensely unproductive, as illustrated by the havoc of the interwar crises, and the foundation of good governance rested with policies and mechanisms that were able to distinguish between productive and unproductive capital flows, to encourage the former and inhibit the latter.[26]

Keynes had long wrestled with the issue of capital mobility, and concluded—and all subsequent empirical evidence supports this contention—that completely unrestricted capital flows are suboptimal from an economic perspective. There were three principal reasons why some mediation of capital flows were essential for Keynes—and for the practice of the middle way: free capital prevents states from pursuing appropriate domestic macroeconomic policies; it has a deflationary bias and skews the burdens of adjustment inefficiently and unfairly; and it greatly increases the likelihood of wildly destabilizing financial crises.

A principal theme of *A Treatise on Money* (1930) focused on the dilemma of any international monetary system: the desire to obtain some stability in a country's external monetary and financial relations while preserving adequate autonomy over domestic macroeconomic policy. Completely unrestricted capital flows, unfortunately, undermine policy autonomy. They create pressures for conformity across macroeconomic policy postures, because "credit is like water"— that is, it will seek out its natural level, flowing toward the highest rate of expected real interest. This caries an implicit deflationary bias, and, worse, creates a situation whereby "everyone must conform to the average behavior of everyone else." But states experience distinct national circumstances and asynchronous business cycles—not to mention varied national practices and purposes (the preservation of which was the purpose of embedded liberalism). Thus, heterogeneity rather than homogeneity of macroeconomic policy orientations across nations is appropriate. For this to be achieved, some sand must be thrown in the gears of international finance.[27]

Wholly unfettered finance is also suboptimal in practice because "it throws the main burden of adjustment" on debtor countries, as "the process of adjustment is compulsory for the debtor and voluntary for the creditor," given that the former must act when reserves run dry, but the latter can choose to passively accumulate balances. As surplus and deficit are simply two sides of the same disequilibrium, an ungoverned financial system is thus not only inefficient, imparting a deflationary bias, it is also unfair. The process of downward adjustment involves economic distress, and, if debtors are relatively small, the attendant misery falls disproportionately on the most vulnerable. (This is why Keynes wanted a more capacious IMF—one that would nudge more burdens toward creditors—than the cash-rich Americans would accede to.)[28]

Finally, liberated capital is dangerous because it both contributes to and exacerbates financial crises. The understanding that financial crises are endogenous, that is, naturally occurring and to be expected, especially in moments when finance is left ungoverned, is associated with the contributions of Charles Kindleberger and Hyman Minsky. But this understanding is rooted in Keynes, and, again, his emphasis on uncertainty. Keynes's investors are essentially rationalist creatures, but they are governed not solely by cold calculations but also by "animal spirits," and are also often left groping in the dark, especially in unfamiliar situations (and financial disturbances). Always but especially when pressed, they fall back on conventional wisdoms, rules of thumb, and, crucially, not just guesses about what will happen next but guesses about what other actors collectively are guessing about what will happen next. (Again, Keynes singled this out as one of the foundations of his dissent from classical economics: "The orthodox theory assumes that we have a knowledge of the future of a kind quite different from that which we actually possess.") And because financial flows can move so fast, mobile capital is little more than fuel poured on the fire of individually logical choices that yield collectively irrational stampedes. A global economy governed by free finance is one that will be plagued by financial crises.[29]

In sum, the purpose of embedded liberalism was to permit the practice of the middle way. This required some form of capital control—that is, the imposition of rules to rein in the dysfunctional aspects of capital flows. Such rules were largely in place in the 1950s and 1960s.

But Was It Sustainable?

The halcyon days of the compromise of embedded liberalism—roughly speaking, the quarter of a century from 1948 to 1973—was a golden age of capitalism. And then it was gone.[30] What happened? Before turning to a key argument of this chapter, the crucial role of the great Keynesian forgetting, another prospect must be acknowledged: that the real puzzle is not why embedded liberalism atrophied, but why it was ever possible in the first place. In the United States, four exceptional factors permitted the practice of the middle way: the great chastening, economic exceptionalism, the Soviet challenge, and the taming of finance. All of these factors faded over time.

The Great Chastening. The founders of the postwar order were eager, even desperate, to learn the lessons of the past and to not repeat, for example, the catastrophic mistakes that followed the end of the Great War, where narrow conceptions of short-sighted self-interest were favored over enlightened self-interest, that is, concerns for systemic stability.[31] In addition and even more important, the Great Depression—the catastrophic failure of laissez-faire capitalism—left few eager for a return to those practices; if anything, there was the looming fear that without the war to stimulate the economy, it might slip back into depression. (Note that the conference that led to the international trade regime was called "the international conference on trade and *employment*.") And the war itself was a national experience of shared sacrifice, which contributed to a mindset that yielded policies like the G.I. Bill, which in turn contributed to the rise of the middle class. All of this, then, reflected a distinct culture of capitalism, in which the captains of industry practiced self-restraint with regard to their treatment of workers—and their own compensation. Both anecdotal evidence and descriptive statistics support the notion that attitudes about how executives should be paid (and how they should, or, more to the point, should not flaunt their wealth) were different in the 1950s than they were in the 1920s—or the 1980s. In the 1950s, the CEO of a large company earned about 20 times the salary of an average employee; that pay gap widened to approximately 50 times in 1993, reaching multiples of a hundred times in 1993, and 278 times in 2018. It is exceedingly unlikely, to say the least, that increases in relative productivity can account for these changes.

In fact, uninhibited capitalism does *not* appear to apportion rewards commensurate with marginal productivity. Notably, in the United States a divergence between worker pay and worker productivity emerged in 1971 and widened into a yawning gap across each succeeding decade through the 2010s. This suggests, crucially, that compensation is less about rewarding marginal productivity—a foundation of the philosophical justification for laissez-faire and its economic appeal—and more about the ruthless extraction of what can be taken. This is also suggestive of a cultural change in the practice of capitalism, not one rooted in the dictates of economic logic and efficiency, but in a bare-knuckled fight over how the profits of enterprise will be shared, with outcomes determined by relative economic and political power.[32]

Economic Exceptionalism. As it turned out, the middle-way postwar economy, with its high taxes, powerful unions, and varied regulations, did not fall back into depression but was associated with explosive growth. It was also a period, well into the 1960s, when the US economy was an unprecedented colossus, and faced little in the way of meaningful international competition. Such an environment could not but help take the edge off domestic distributional conflict (and thus create space for ambitious domestic policy initiatives), but such a setting could not be expected to endure indefinitely.

The Soviet Challenge. To a significant extent, the existence of the Soviet Union encouraged the practice of the middle way, both at home and abroad. To the extent that the compromise of embedded liberalism was facilitated beyond US shores via American leadership of international institutions, we likely have the Soviet Union to thank for that—it is considerably less certain that the bipartisan internationalist foreign policy consensus could have emerged short of that perceived urgency. Moreover, however impossible this may be to conceive many decades later, in the 1950s and 1960s the Soviet Union presented an economic and ideological challenge to American capitalism. In the late 1950s in particular, there were concerns that Khrushchev's boasts of "burying capitalism" were not empty rhetoric. The capitalist and communist models competed to capture the imagination of what was then called the "Third World"—and, again, this had a tempering effect on capitalist practice. Given the Soviet portrayal of capitalism as a miserable, worker-crushing dystopia, the United States had every incentive to demonstrate that capitalism was in fact philosophically appealing, just, and functional. Concerns for national image during the Cold War were a positive externality that influenced public policy—they contributed, for example, an impetus to the federal government's receptivity to the civil rights movement.[33]

The Taming of Finance. Finally, the golden age of capitalism in the United States was exceptional in that the financial sector was heavily regulated, supervised, and more or less boring. It was not a booming sector of the economy;

rather, it essentially served its intended role, to support the real economy by acting as a coordinating intermediary between savers and borrowers. How did this come about? As Barry Eichengreen argued, the economic catastrophe of the Great Depression in the 1930s was "an implosion so complete" that the political mandate for fundamental reform overwhelmed the opposition of the (then somewhat smaller) financial sector, which was still smoking in ruins. From this emerged the New Deal regulations that ushered in a half century of financial stability, including the Glass-Steagall Act and a panoply of other rules and oversight bodies. (This of course contrasts with the relatively modest and swiftly eroding reforms that followed the 2008 financial crisis, when better public policy in the heat of the moment prevented a complete financial meltdown and second Great Depression—and took the wind from the sails of much-needed reforms.)[34]

All of these special circumstances are long gone. Growth rates are more sluggish than in the golden age and competition is global and fierce. The notion of chastened capitalists is a virtual oxymoron. The 1930s and 1940s are long forgotten, buttressing the emergence of a new culture of capitalism defined by shareholder value—the ultimate caricature of robber-baron capitalism, and one that no longer has to look over its shoulder at the prospect of a competing economic ideology. The shift to "shareholder primacy," as Ruggie emphasizes in his chapter in this volume, has weakened "the provision of public goods, social cohesion, and broadly shared prosperity that were the aim of the "embedded" part of the postwar compromise." This transformation was abetted and exacerbated by the liberation of finance, which, risen from the ashes, dominates the American economy. In addition to its other pathologies, footloose capital shifted the balance of bargaining power away from labor, as Mark Blyth notes in this volume (and which was still another reason why Keynes was so wary of unlimited capital mobility—because of its deleterious effects on inequality).[35]

The Long Goodbye:
From Keynes to Keynesianism

I want to argue, however, that a principal cause of the unraveling of the compromise of embedded liberalism was the postwar departure—in a process that started from the very beginning—from Keynes' vision of the middle way. As noted, Keynes died in 1946, which meant that what would become known as "postwar Keynesianism" was developed entirely in his absence, primarily by a new generation of American economists. Prominent among them was Paul Samuelson (a student of leading American Keynesian Alvin Hansen), whose mathematical models of economics derived directly from Newtonian physics and whose textbook would introduce economics to two generations of college students. (Keynes, of course, forcefully and explicitly rejected the notion of drawing analogies from physics to explain behavior in the social sciences in general and economics in particular.[36]) More generally, a cohort of brilliant young American economists advanced a dramatically distilled, simplified, and, especially, domesticated interpretation of some of the arguments found in *The General Theory*. Commonly dubbed "the neoclassical synthesis," (the moniker alone should give any close reader of Keynes considerable pause), it drew on John Hicks's influential attempt to reconcile *The General Theory* with elements of the old orthodoxy in his article "Mr. Keynes and the Classics" (subsequently elaborated by Hansen). From this flowed the IS-LM model—the specifics of which I will not engage, but simply note that it provided some of the basic policy levers for the practice of postwar Keynesianism that appropriately earned it the nickname "hydraulic Keynesianism." (Keynes's student Joan Robinson, characteristically blunt, preferred the term "bastard Keynesianism.") Ultimately, hydraulic Keynesianism—a far cry from Keynes—foundered because it was vulnerable to basic theoretical critiques and ultimately crashed on the rocks of the dismal 1970s. A decade later it would be reconstituted as something called "New Keynesianism," still further removed from the original—indeed, so far removed it is well described as "Keynesianism without Keynes." The emergence of New Keynesianism reflected a broad consensus in macroeconomics that abetted the policy prescriptions that contributed to collapse of the middle way, and with it brought about many of the dire consequences of liberated finance and unfettered capitalism that Keynes so feared. But this runs ahead of the story, the details of which merit closer attention.[37]

Keynes saw this coming. In 1944, the day after dining with American economists in Washington, DC, he remarked to a friend, "I was the only non-Keynesian there."[38] As Robinson subsequently observed, the hydraulic Keynesians rejected and jettisoned the two core elements of the Keynesian revolution, viz., his skepticism of the self-correcting market (that an economy, once disturbed, would naturally trend back toward equilibrium), and, centrally, his shift from "the problems of rational choice to the problems of decisions based in guess work and convention." That shift from risk to uncertainty and the resulting importance of psychological aspects of decision-making (all disregarded or assumed away by the bastard Keynesians), meant that, for Robinson, "all these pretty, polite techniques, made for a well-paneled board room and a nicely regulated market, are liable to collapse."[39]

Keynesian fine tuning was in vogue in the 1960s, but toward the end of the decade it came under powerful intellectual fire, in particular from Edmund Phelps and Milton Friedman, each of whom argued that in practice, the benefits of such techniques were illusory, dependent on ever-increasing levels of inflation, which their practice would invite. With the inflation of the 1970s (actually rooted in the undisciplined macroeconomic practices of the Lyndon Johnson and Richard Nixon administrations, which slammed into the hard realities of dramatic supply shocks, especially of oil and food) these critiques seemed vindicated, and the Keynesians beat a hasty retreat.[40]

This in turn led to the three-headed monster that would discredit and chase from the scene the notion of (overt) Keynesian practice: the deep recession associated with Paul Volcker's crushing of American inflation; the rise of conservative governments (in America, a backlash clearly visible by 1978 and culminating with the election of Ronald Reagan in 1980) as electoral punishment for the broadly perceived failures of the left; and, within economics, the rise of rational expectations theory. Each of these had indirect but profound consequences. Whether Volcker's deflation was worth its heavy price paid is still disputed, but the cycle of inflation and severe recession was in any event a generationally formative lesson. And it was a lesson overlearned, contributing to an overreactive anti-inflationary hypervigilance. The electoral thumping handed to the Democrats in three presidential straight elections (1980, 1984 and 1988—actually four out of five when the landslide of 1972 is included) sent the party lurching toward the center, as heralded by Bill "the era of Big Government is over" Clinton and his embrace of the supercilious, libertarian Federal Reserve Board chairman Alan Greenspan. (Notably, this was essentially the opposite of the political setting that secured the foundations for the broad, postwar middle-way consensus.[41]) And the rational expectations revolution that swept through the mainstream of the economics profession—to the extent that, in something of an intellectual oxymoron, even so-called New Keynesian models assumed rational expectations—took as a basic point of departure that markets, left to their own devices, always got it right.[42] Tragically, however, rational expectations theory, with its supremely sophisticated and elegant models that were more than suggestive of a return to the old, pre-Keynesian orthodoxy (its intellectual founders fancied themselves "New Classical" macroeconomists), turned out to get it all quite precisely wrong. But not before the damage had been done.

Learning the Wrong Lessons: Rational Expectations and Capital Deregulation

The widespread embrace rational expectations theory stamped out whatever modest embers of Keynes's macroeconomics had managed to survive its bastardization over the years. The approach assumed that all actors quickly, dispassionately, and efficiently process all available relevant information—and, crucially, assumed that they processed that information though the same more or less correct underlying model of how the economy functioned. Following these radical assumptions, any errors in forecasting such actors might make would be randomly distributed around the "correct" prediction. Of course, Keynes assumed anything but such so-called rational expectations (a term more powerful as a marketing ploy than as an applicable theory).[43] Mervyn King, governor of the Bank of England, highlighted the folly of this dubious, foundational assumption: "No economist can point to a particular model, and honestly say 'this is how the world works,'" he admonished. "Our understanding of the economy is incomplete and constantly evolving." And not surprisingly, despite spreading like wildfire throughout the economics profession, when rational expectations theory was finally subjected to empirical scrutiny, it failed test after test, even those conducted by its most ardent advocates, and especially when it was applied to questions pertaining to financial markets.[44]

Unfortunately, the mainstream of the macroeconomic profession processed the empirical failure of rational expectations theory with a talk-to-the-hand response that amounted to "tests, schmests." Macroeconomists of all ideological stripes converged around "Dynamic Stochastic General Equilibrium" models. Rooted in rational expectations, these models assumed that the macroeconomy was best understood as a largely tamed beast occasionally buffeted by random shocks that would nudge it away from an equilibrium to which it would naturally be restored.[45] Sustained downturns and things like financial crises were assumed out of existence. From rational expectations theory also flowed the efficient markets hypothesis—that asset prices always and everywhere reflected their correct underlying values, and thus could be safely left to their own devices, unregulated and unsupervised.

The long goodbye from Keynes (and its consequences) can be summarized in two sentences, uttered twenty-eight years apart. "At research seminars, people don't take Keynesian theorizing seriously any more—the audience starts to whisper and giggle to one another," a triumphant, extremely confident Robert Lucas crowed in 1980. Decades later Robert Skidelsky would offer this rejoinder: "But these giggling economics students became the architects of the policy that led to the great crash of 2008."[46]

Of course, economists recommending financial deregulation in the 1990s were pushing on an open political door. The liberation of capital had its roots in a variety of factors that can be traced to the early 1970s.[47] These trends accelerated during the Reagan 1980s, when deregulation and a policy shift that favored "free markets" accelerated and was extended to the financial sector. (This all coincided, not coincidentally, with the first major financial crisis in the United States in a half century—the Savings and Loans crisis—and the stock market crash of

1987, which featured the then largest single-day drop in American history.) But the full collapse of financial regulation would take place in the 1990s, with the bear-hug embrace by Clinton's New Democrats of Wall Street. (Rawi Abdelal describes a similar convergence of center-left and center-right in Europe, with similar consequences, in his contribution to this volume.) In addition, and not to be underestimated, was the replacement of old school, systemic-risk wary, cop on the beat Paul Volcker with the gee-whiz, free market cheerleading Alan Greenspan as the nation's top financial regulator. With Greenspan's enthusiastic support, late in that decade the Gramm-Leach-Bliley Act shattered the Depression-era financial firewalls imposed by the Glass-Steagall Act, and the Commodity Futures Modernization Act assured that exploding markets for derivatives and financial exotica would be free from government scrutiny. None of this was accidental. In the 1990s, a second postwar American order was forged. In contrast to the first order—a Keynes-inflected embedded liberalism designed to facilitate the practice of economic policies that reflected diverse social purposes—this new order, aggressively pursued abroad (unchecked by the tempering presence of the now vanished Soviet Union), was rooted in market fundamentalism, the belief that there was one set of correct policy practices appropriate for all settings, and the sharp-elbowed promotion of financial globalization.[48]

Unbounded Financialization and the Embrace of Economism

By the turn of the twenty-first century the American economy had a new structure, and a new culture, both of which were profoundly anti-Keynesian. Most obviously, unleashing finance was not just a mistake, but a catastrophe waiting to happen. In the United States, finance, freed from its last shackles, became the largest and fastest growing sector of the economy. From 1980 to 2002 it leapt from 14 percent to 21 percent of gross domestic product; on the eve of the global financial crisis, finance accounted for 47 percent of all US corporate profits. Finance also became the place to make money. From the 1930s through the 1970s, compensation in finance tracked generally with remuneration in other parts of the private sector, before galloping ahead after 1980 (by 2007, the average pay for someone working in banking was double that of other participants in the economy). There were spectacular amounts money to be made on Wall Street, and from a young age, and especially at the very top.[49]

Such incentives are powerful, and graduates from elite universities increasingly flooded into the financial services sector, at the expense of more productive endeavors (at Princeton's School of Engineering and Applied Science, in the midst of this frenzy, operations research and financial engineering became the most popular undergraduate major). Old Keynesians sounded the alarm, but nobody was much interested in listening. James Tobin lamented, "We are throwing more and more of our resources, including the cream of our youth, into financial activities remote from the production of goods and services, into activities that generate high private rewards disproportionate to their social productivity." Robert Solow reached a similar conclusion. "God created the financial sector to help the real economy, not to help itself," he noted, following good Keynesian (and good economic) logic. "I suspect," he added, "[that] the financial services sector has grown relatively to the point where it is not even adding value to the real economy. It may be adding compensation to its members but it is not improving the efficiency or productivity of the real economy."[50]

Or consider this remarkably prescient warning by a young economist writing in 2006:

> Speculators may do no harm as bubbles on a steady stream of enterprise. But the position is serious when enterprise becomes the bubble on a whirlwind of speculation. When the capital development of a country becomes a by-product of the activities of a casino, the job is likely to be ill-done. The measure of success attained by Wall Street, regarded as an institution of which the proper social purpose is to direct new investment into the most profitable channels in terms of future yield, cannot be claimed as one of the outstanding truimphs of *laissez-faire* capitalism—which is not surprising, if I am right in thinking that the best brains of Wall Street have been in fact directed towards a different object.

Actually, that wasn't written in 2006. It was written seventy years earlier, by Keynes, in *The General Theory*.[51] No young economist would have written that in the early twenty-first century—when was the last time a graduate student in an elite American economics department was assigned to read a word of Keynes? Yet Keynes was right, then and now.

It goes without saying that Keynes was not always right. Notably, with regard to a key element that informed his philosophy of political economy, he appears to have been quite wrong, namely, in his assumptions about human nature. Apparently insatiable materialist cravings are the rule, not the exception. That someone who earned $1 million a year would look wistfully at another making $10 million who would in turn envy the billionaire, with each striving to accumulate still more—this would have been incomprehensible to Keynes. Rather, writing in 1930, he thought that "the economic problem" could be solved in perhaps two generations. By then most people, at least in the societies on which Keynes focused his attention, might have achieved the level of material comfort that would free them to pursue more fulfilling interests than chasing money. As he put it, "The love of money as a possession—as distinguished from the love of money as a means to the enjoyments and realities of life—will be recognised for what it is, a somewhat disgusting morbidity." Indeed, the emptiness and purposelessness of capitalism, its utter lack of a motiving ideology that could remotely be described as ennobling, was, as far back as the 1920s, an attribute of laissez-faire that Keynes did not just disdain, but feared. He thought such ideational vacuousness threatened to handicap the liberal West in its struggle with totalitarian collectivism, which, though odious, offered at least the illusion of a social purpose around which people (especially aggrieved people, it should be noted with trepidation for both then and now) could rally.[52] "It seems clearer every day," he wrote, "that the moral problem of our age is concerned with the love of money, with the habitual appeal to the money motive in nine-tenths of the activities of life."[53]

Keynes believed that although capitalism provided essential economic efficiencies and wealth-creating engines that no other system of economic organization could offer, it nevertheless had "extremely objectionable" attributes. Ultimately, again, the search for a middle way beckoned with the challenge "to work out a social organisation which shall be as efficient as possible without offending . . . notions of a satisfactory way of life." More generally, economism—the notion that all social decisions should be left to the whims of the purposeless, amoral market mechanism—was little short of madness. A passionate supporter of what is now called "landmark preservation," for example, Keynes viewed architecture as "the most public of the arts." This was no idle invocation, as engagement with the arts more generally was an essential part of a life well lived. (Keynes founded a theater in Cambridge, among numerous such private and official endeavors.) And without public support of such activities, he warned, we risk reducing "the whole conduct of life . . . into sort of a parody of an accountant's nightmare," where every potential course of action is judged by its financial results: "We destroy the beauty of the countryside because the unappropriated splendours of nature have no economic value. We are capable of shutting off the sun and the stars because they do not pay a dividend."[54] This has literally come to pass in New York City, with the proliferation of ugly, supertall skyscrapers along "billionaire's row" on West Fifty-Seventh Street. These lifeless, looming structures, springing up one after another, are largely unoccupied by their plutocratic owners (as the city endures a middle-class housing crisis), and throw shadows across the cherished public space of Central Park (a desecration of the public good once fiercely and successfully resisted).[55] Such is the culture of contemporary American capitalism.

The Sum of All (Keynes's) Fears

Ultimately, the shift back toward a culture of capitalism that prioritized shareholder value over shared purpose had exactly the consequences Keynes would have anticipated—a four-decade experiment during which the rich got much richer and most everybody else increasingly struggled to get by. The high priests of economic orthodoxy would have us assume that companies operate on the precarious margins of profitability and do not have the luxury of rewarding factors of production one penny more than their value added to the company. In the real world, however, most going concerns make profits, and social norms (and asymmetries of economic and political power), not irresistible natural laws, shape how the fruits of enterprise are distributed. The new face of capitalism can be seen in companies like Amazon, whose proprietor, Jeff Bezos, is worth more than $100 billion. What does he want? Contra Keynes, still he wants, in a word, more, and in 2020 he added to his collection of homes a 13,000-square-foot, $165 million Beverly Hills mansion and adjacent estate. In that same year, Amazon warehouse workers, who are expected to inspect and scan 1,800 parcels per hour, earned an average of $15 an hour.[56]

Finance unbound also yielded exactly the pathologies Keynes anticipated it would, generating massive amounts of wealth for the casino's high rollers—and a sector increasingly riddled with systemic risk. The question was when, not if, a massive crisis would occur. When it finally arrived in 2008, it was, in Ben Bernanke's estimation, "the worst financial crisis in global history, including the Great Depression." The chair of the Federal Reserve estimated that "out of . . . 13 of the most important financial institutions in the United States, 12 were at risk of failure within a period of a week or two."[57] There was no choice but to take the emergency measures necessary to save the financial system from completely melting down, and that achievement is to be lauded. But in their joint, self-congratulatory memoir of the crisis, Bernanke, Tim Geithner, and Hank Paulson obtusely and repeatedly express frustration that regular folks don't seem to understand that the bailouts were ultimately paid back, and thus did not come at the expense of the average taxpayer. What they seem to overlook is that those who caused the global financial crisis bore few if any costs, and soon returned to business as usual, whereas average American families were left to endure the long, difficult Great Recession. Or as Martin Wolf put it, more pointedly and more accurately, this is a system in which "well-connected insiders" are "shielded from loss but impose massive costs on everybody else."[58]

As Keynes cautioned, capitalism is only compatible with liberal civilization if it is generally perceived to be fair, and, as he warned Hayek, the practice of unfettered capitalism would likely cultivate a dangerous backlash. The bitter harvests of soaring inequality and reckless finance were finally reaped in 2016. What is remarkable about that year is not the outcome of the general election, but the nominating processes of each political party. Brewing and widespread anger and revulsion at the governing elites, festering during decades of middle-class difficulties, reached a fever pitch of increasingly virulent populism not at the site of the global financial crisis, but in its grueling aftermath. And so in 2016, in the Democratic primaries, an obscure fringe candidate—a socialist from a tiny state who wasn't even a member of the party—came very close to toppling the formidable and seemingly irresistible Clinton political machine; in the Republican primaries, a vulgar, inexperienced game show host blew away a broad field of establishment competitors, despite his own intermittent party membership (and few fixed principles, other than a small handful that were the opposite of what the party had embraced for three generations).[59] And as discussed in the introduction to this volume, the election of 2020 did little to alter these stark new realities; indeed in some ways it reinforced them, in particular by brightly illuminating the fundamental transformation of the Republican Party.

The middle way was designed to save capitalism from itself; the compromise of embedded liberalism was intended to permit the practice of the middle way. But the grand postwar understanding, eroding for decades, has been finally shattered. And the United States, now flirting with plutocracy, risks veering toward the extremes of governance by distraction (nativist nationalism) and varieties of burn-it-all-down radicalism. Keynes, ever the pragmatist, would be again searching for a course of action that would navigate between these two dystopian destinies.

THE END OF SOCIAL PURPOSE?

Great Transformations of American Order

Mark Blyth

This book is based on an observation and a distinction. The observation is that the American economic and political order that has served as the framework for domestic and international policy choices since 1945 is having its owl of Minerva moment. What happens next, after the American order, is what we are all trying to figure out. Some contributors to this book, such as John Ruggie, and from a different vantage, Ilene Grabel, see this as a moment of possibility. For Ruggie, international firms rather than states are now the standard bearers of liberal rights, and that is to the good in a globalized world. For Grabel, the fracturing and fissuring of the American order opens up possibilities for a more pluralist and potentially reformist set of global actors, especially in global finance. Other contributors, such as Sheri Berman and Peter Gourevitch, situate the fracturing not in the global, but in the European-local, as the social forces and political bargains that made postwar social democracy possible in Europe fell apart. Here the space for future possibilities is much more constrained because that version of social democracy was based on a set of historical circumstances that no longer exist.

My account takes a different tack. Like all of the contributors to this project, I view the American order as having two versions. A distinction should be made between the first American order, what has become commonly known as the "embedded liberal" order, and the second American order, the neoliberal order, because the two regimes had dramatically different social purposes—full employment in the former and price stability in the latter. The question I want to answer follows from this distinction. Why did these orders vary in this way, and what does the answer to that question tell us about the current moment?

My answer to that question is neither hopeful nor pessimistic. Nor does it depend on the agency of social democratic politicians. It is based on viewing capitalism as a computer and economic ideas as the software for running it. As the hardware evolves and the software matures, bugs buried deep in the source code eventually crash the system. This is an ongoing process that drives orders forward. The current moment is, then, the working out of the long system crash of 2008–16, which was itself a function of the bugs built into the neoliberal software. To see why this is the case, we need to go back to a small town in northern Scotland in the early 1980s, just as the owl of Minerva was abandoning, as Kirshner puts it (in this volume), "Keynes's middle way," in that country, and around the world.

Economics as Politics: Social Purpose and Change in Orders

One evening when I was thirteen years old, I watched a face-off between macroeconomic models live on television.[1] In one corner was everyone's idea of a stuffy old professor, complete with a patched tweed jacket and beard, hawking the virtues of a Keynesian macro model with hundreds of equations. I recall that he was from Manchester. In the other corner was a young man in a very nice suit. I recall that he was from the London Business School. He had a monetarist model that had barely a dozen equations. The host of the program, game show style, then asked the professors to input various shocks into their models to see what happened. In almost every scenario the monetarist model gave clear results, and tax cuts were usually the optimal policy. I may have been thirteen, but I knew politics when I saw it. Observing this use of economics as a political intervention made me wonder why anyone took economics seriously. To answer that question, I went to university in 1986.

Sixteen years later I published my first book, *Great Transformations: Economic Ideas and Institutional Change in the Twentieth Century* (hereafter *GTs*).[2] That book took economics very seriously—not as a correspondence theory of the world that seeks to explain it, but as a thing in the world that has a specific politics attached to it and that seeks to shape that world. Years before Donald McKenzie recovered Milton Friedman's idea of financial theory being "an engine not a camera," I was telling the same story for macroeconomics.[3] I argued that economics is always and everywhere a political project that has a uniquely potent language of power attached to it. Control the grammar of the economy, define what is efficient or natural, and you will get quite far along in shaping who gets what in that economy. That, in a nutshell, was the thesis of *GTs*. Its theoretical underpinnings may have stressed such things as decision-making under conditions of Knightian (nonprobabilistic) uncertainty as constituting those moments when the politics of economic ideas are most important. But at base, the simpler claim was that economics was politics by other means. I got that idea from the best thing I read in graduate school, which was John Ruggie's article on embedded liberalism.[4]

I see the contributions of Ruggie's piece as two-fold. First, it brought Karl Polanyi's concept of the "Double Movement" into general usage in American political economy.[5] Polanyi contended that any attempt to create, as he called it, "one big market" through the commodification of everything, especially labor, is doomed to fail, because labor is the one commodity that cares about its own supply price. It likes it going up and hates it going down. So, when you design an international monetary order, a gold standard for example, where open financial flows tied to gold dictate adjustment through downward pressure on wages, you are asking for trouble. I liked that idea so much that I not only read Polanyi but I also reworked his title and his Double Movement thesis to frame my own book.

The second contribution of Ruggie's piece was more subtle, but arguably deeper still, and it brought me back to one of my first experiences as an undergraduate. I went to university in Scotland in 1986. If you studied economics at that time you might remember something odd about the textbooks of the period. The macro chapters were split into two. One half was Keynesianism, and one half was monetarism, bolted on to a weak version of rational expectations theory and efficient markets. The schism then apparent in the field of economics was honestly reflected in the textbooks of that day—at least the ones that I had to use.[6]

What Ruggie's article opened my eyes too was the fact that the macroeconomy is not a timeless set of markets, constituted by microfoundations and coordinated by prices. Rather, it is a distinct set of price and nonprice institutions, politically bonded together to produce an economic order with a distinct social purpose. When I read that, it brought me back to my bifurcated textbooks. I realized fully for the first time that the rival models were vying not just to define what the macroeconomy is but also what social purpose it serves.

Consider the following. The simplest way of writing down the social purpose of a classical liberal regime (or of the contemporary neoliberal one, for that matter) is to write down the quantity equation $MV = PQ$, where (M)oney times its (V)elocity equals all the stuff made (Q) and the (P)rices that denominate it. What gives this tautology a social purpose is the operationalizing assumption that V is constant. This turns the tautology into a causal statement; M is causal and

M is the province of the state, so bad things like inflation and (occasionally) deflation, are all the fault of the state manipulating M. Hence, the state should not manipulate M.

This is less a theory than a morality play, and all morality plays have heroes. If you break the above equation out into investment and consumption functions, the heroes in this story are the entrepreneurs and merchants beloved by (neo)liberals who bring things (Q) to market. Workers are the mere necessary adjuncts closing the supply loop as per Say's famous law that supply creates its own demand.

Now consider in contrast what Keynes did with the national income equation, simplified to $Y = C + I + G$, and what social purpose this served. In this world of aggregates there are neither Schumpeterian entrepreneurs nor Smithian merchants. Rather, the level of national income (Y) is a function of aggregate (I)nvestment and (C)onsumption, such that C drives I via I^*—investment expectations—which are decidedly nonrational and short term. Given shocks to the economy, shortfalls in I will occur because of the collapse in I^* that results, and so I^* needs to be boosted by the (G)overnment via spending to increase C, given that that system has no natural tendency to settle at a full-employment equilibrium. This is also a morality play. Its moral is that the market will fail you, and thus its heroes are quite different than those of the monetarist morality play.

The heroes are the millions of joint consumption decisions made by well-paid citizen consumers. In a Keynesian world, demand drives supply, which promotes investment to enhance productivity, which was very much the design behind the first American order. This was its social purpose: to maximize consumption at full employment, thereby driving wages higher, which would force the productivity increases needed to pay for such high levels of consumption. Workers, not merchants, were best served by this social purpose, and that was by design, given the realization that the Depression, and the war that it fostered, could not be allowed to repeat. It was of course, ironically, that prolabor bias that *GT*s saw as the order's greatest weakness.

Placing the framework of *GT*s in the context of the stresses and strains that the neoliberal order has suffered since 2008 reveals a simple truth—that Polanyi was, and is, still right. As the latest attempt to commodify and make market exchange the *sine qua non* of human experience, the second American order—the neoliberal order—was equally bound to engender a backlash by labor as the inequality and instability it generated proved too much to contain within the formally representative institutions of neoliberal capitalism. This backlash has gathered momentum to the point that we can see the end of this second American order coming fast. Indeed, we are probably present at the birth of a third, different, order. But how different will it really be?

To put this discussion of orders in some kind of order, I sketch them out sequentially. The first American order (1945–73) was built from the Polanyian reaction against the social purpose of the prior gold standard order, which collapsed in the 1920s and 1930s. As noted by Ruggie, this first American order had as its social purpose the creation of an "embedded liberalism"—that is, a liberalism that had full employment at its core to ensure that the international financial balance never again dictated the domestic political balance of forces.

The second order (1985–2008), as laid out in *GTs*, was a second Polanyian reaction.[7] Just as any attempt to fully commodify labor creates a backlash against the market itself, so any attempt to sustain such a high level of decommodification of labor that labor gains while capital loses risks a backlash by promarket social forces. The second, neoliberal American order, had its own social purpose, which was to restore the real value of capital, discipline labor, and create price stability after both the returns to investment and the capital/labor share turned against capital by the late 1960s.

GTs stressed the power of economic ideas in both of these orders to act as institutional blueprints in moments of uncertainty and as weapons in the political combat needed to shape the future. That is still the case. But I would now argue that economic ideas also act as the software that defines the social purpose of a regime.

The first American order drew on and developed Keynesian ideas of full-employment stabilization that constituted the first half of my introductory textbook in 1986. The second American order was built around the ideas of monetarism and rational expectations macroeconomics that formed the second half of that same textbook.[8] The first order stressed attaining full employment. The second sought price stability. That second order, built in the 1980s and 1990s, was massively successful in achieving that goal. But precisely because it was so successful in increasing the returns to capital it endogenously destabilized, crashed, and burned in the financial crisis of 2008.

A true third American order, which could have been built in the moment of uncertainty fostered by the 2008 financial crisis, could have again made full employment the regime's social purpose, restoring the labor share. But this third order was stillborn. Instead, because of what one might call the great "hardware mod" of the second order—the rise of independent central banks,[9] the neoliberal order was rebooted through a massive influx of public liquidity.[10] That reboot brought the second order back to life, but without dealing with any of its underlying pathologies. This has predictably given rise to the latest Polanyian reaction against this order, the populist revolution that I have called elsewhere "Global Trumpism."[11]

This set of social forces directly challenges the social purpose of the neoliberal regime, moving it from a policy frame of what might be called "globalism with tight money" to one of "nationalism with loose money," and in that regard it has already gone quite far. Party systems throughout the developed democracies have been transformed over the past decade, with populist parties and their agendas challenging both the social purpose of rebooted neoliberalism and, piece by piece, the institutions that make it possible.[12]

The extent to which these new partisans can fully transcend the second American order remains limited, however. What we are witnessing is the transformation of the America neoliberal order into what I would characterize as a pluralist neonationalist order with a variety of different social purposes. This pluralist neonationalist order will, despite what most observers assume, remain an American order, for reasons to do with the structure of the global economy.

The First American Order

It is easy to forget, especially when teaching the foundations of the first American order, that what was constructed at the Bretton Woods conference of 1944 was a jerry-built compromise that could have failed at any moment in its first ten years. As the work of Eric Helleiner and others has shown, the conference ranged over territory far beyond what it has come to symbolize, such as a more thorough inclusion of the Global South in the postwar order.[13] It was also more conflictual than is often portrayed, with compromises and failures, such as the defeated attempt to establish the Bancor or a similar global currency, that at the time stressed American interests over any general social purpose.

Moreover, the institutions set up in 1944, such as the modified gold standard at the heart of the Bretton Woods exchange-rate mechanism and the International Monetary Fund (IMF), designed to add liquidity when countries' balance of payments got out of whack, were essentially moribund for the first ten years of their existence.[14] Again, as Helleiner has detailed, following capital flight out of Europe in 1946 and 1948 that eviscerated investment in Europe and resulted in the Marshall Plan as a bailout to those European divestors, convertibility between the dollar and the rest of Europe was suspended from 1948 to 1958.[15] This is also when those European economies experienced their greatest growth spurts.[16]

Keynes had wanted capital controls to be "double ended" to, as he put it, "above all, keep investment local." But despite capital's flight from Europe, these controls were built "single ended," and by the time convertibility was established—at the same time as the Eurodollar markets blossomed—they were increasingly ineffective. The World Bank funded developmentalism in the Global South, to be sure. But as far as the American order as a whole was concerned, such activism was rare. Trade and tariffs, so central by the 1960 Tokyo round of the GATT were hardly an issue in a world where the everyone was short dollars and the only way to earn them was to export to the United States.[17]

What overcame these fragilities and gave these so-called Bretton Woods institutions stability in this early period was the security politics that drove much of what we still identify as "the American order" today. The various blockades of Berlin and the incorporation of Poland, Czechoslovakia, East Germany into the Soviet Bloc as satraps encouraged intense alliance building by the United States to contain communism under the auspices of NATO (the North Atlantic Treaty Organization), SEATO (the Southeast Asia Treaty Organization) and a host of other regional orders. The defense buildup that began under President Harry Truman and accelerated under President Dwight Eisenhower made Cold War liberalism a reality. But containing communism was only one part of the American order's social purpose. For the rest, we need examine US domestic politics and its expressions found elsewhere. This is also where contingency and leadership mattered.

The Domestic Politics of American Social Purpose

The dominant presence of Franklin Roosevelt during the Depression and World War II belies how weak and torn the US Democratic party was at the time of his death. The Republicans had regained much of their swagger and, tired of wartime restrictions, the public in 1946 elected a Republican-dominated "sweep clean" Congress that promised to sweep away New Deal regulations and policies.[18] The previous year, a weak and unpopular Harry Truman had come to power, in part because of Democrats' fears concerning how far Roosevelt's vice president, Henry Wallace, would drag the party to the left. A four-time failed haberdasher and machine politician from Missouri, Truman was never expected to defeat the Republican presidential nominee Thomas Dewey in 1948. Indeed, he nearly didn't. Had Truman lost, he would not have been able to launch his Fair Deal proposals as a way to (successfully, as it turned out) distract the Republicans from dismantling the core of the New Deal order.[19]

Truman and the Democrats in Congress were pretty much alone in defending this emerging domestic bargain. The Democrats' main partner, organized labor, effectively adopted a strategy of political neutrality and accommodation with business, which culminated in the so-called Treaty of Detroit in 1950. This accommodation was driven by the 1947 Taft-Hartley Act, which clipped of labor's political wings, and by the prior failure of the 1946 Murray Bill (the Full Employment Act of 1946) to mandate a full-employment target as government policy. Truman's feints against the Republican Party in the Fair Deal period were in fact the only available means of consolidating the domestic order that was the counterpart of the international order sketched above. But he succeeded. And by the end of the Truman administration a distinct institutional form of embedded liberalism with a distinct social purpose had taken root in the United States.

First, domestic banking was siloed and international banking became heavily restricted through capital controls on speculative flows.[20] These policies forced high levels of investment at home, just as Keynes had said was necessary for full employment. Second, labor was decommodified in the sense that collective bargaining was made legally secure, despite the Taft-Hartley Act. Industry-wide bargaining that tied pay increases to productivity increases, COLA (Cost of Living Adjustment) contracts, became the norm, stabilizing labor and product markets. These institutional innovations forced firms to invest in productivity enhancements in order to survive and profit, which in turn allowed further real wage growth.[21] Third, the fiscal authority of the state, under the guise of military Keynesianism and the Cold War, opened up highways, rebuilt railways, and invested in airports, infrastructure, electrification, and education. Fourth, welfare rights for unemployment and disability became federal mandates for states to fulfill, and though this was in large part predicated on the continued exclusion of agricultural workers, most or many of whom were African Americans, the mechanization of agriculture in the 1950s led to the great northern migration of African Americans to better paid factory jobs and a greater—albeit still partial—inclusion in the post-war settlement we are sketching out here.

Finally, though the Federal Reserve regained its independence in the Treasury-Federal Reserve Accord of 1951, it did not seek to use its power, as had the Bank of France and the Bank of England in the 1920s and 1930s, to thwart the government's prolabor agenda.[22] Rather, it remained supportive, pausing only, in the words of then Federal Reserve chair McChesney Martin, to "take away the punch bowl when the party got going." Bipartisanship reached its zenith in Congress and across the world as talk of "the mixed economy" and the "welfare state" as permanent features of politics became normalized everywhere. In short, this was not just an American story. At an international and domestic level, this order was generalized.

It's actually quite breathtaking how much institutional engineering was achieved with so little opposition across so many countries. This occurred partly because opposition forces had been either destroyed, in the case of fascism, or neutered by containment, in the case of communism, but also because both labor and capital were able to both able realize positive gains within these new institutions at this particular historical moment.[23]

The spread of Fordist technologies, plus the revolution in energy wrought by the opening up of the East Texas basin and Middle Eastern oil, made possible a virtuous circle of cheap and stable inputs, large productivity gains, high profits, high wages, and high taxes and transfers. And at the core of all of this was the commitment that the Murray Bill had failed to legally establish, but that nonetheless became enshrined as the social purpose of the internationalized American order—the pursuit of full employment.

There could now be no return to mass unemployment and destitution. How one got to that target varied, but by making the social purpose of the regime full employment, this new global order demanded a Keynesian understanding of how the economy worked. There was no other way to achieve that purpose.[24] A purpose that focused on the singular importance of sustaining adequate demand and keeping capital at home to force investment and hence provide the productivity increases needed to pay for constantly rising real wages and high levels of transfers.

In the United Kingdom, given the dominance of the City of London and the external constraint of sterling as a now-weakened reserve currency, such a policy goal created domestic dislocations as increasing wages drove up inflation, which hit the currency, which in turn led to interest rate increases and credit restrictions to maintain the currency's external value. So-called stop-go policies were the result, and the United Kingdom's growth lagged in comparison to that of its European peers. Nonetheless, in this period the United Kingdom built 1.5 million houses, real wages still rose, and in 1957 the then UK prime minister Harold MacMillan could boast that Britons "had never had it so good." And he was quite possibly right.

Despite the devastation of war and the partitioning of the country, the Germany economy turned the corner in 1951, and by 1958 the Wirtschaftswünder was well under way. In Sweden, the economists Gøsta Rehn and Rudolph Meidner found an entirely supply-side way to get to full employment, using active labor-market policies and wage compression to force inefficient firms into bankruptcy while pushing efficient ones further along the technological frontier.[25] Even Japan regained its exporting and engineering prowess and rejoined the fray.[26] By the end of the 1950s, not only had the Brits "never had it so good" but the Italians also had "Il Boom," while the French were just beginning to enjoy the second decade of "les Trente Glourieuse."

There was unfortunately, to use the computer analogy, a set of three bugs deep inside the software running the first America order that were just about to start derailing the train of working-class prosperity. The first was using the Bretton Woods exchange-rate mechanism. The second was the consequences for capital, as predicted by Mikhal Kalecki in 1943 of running sustained full employment for twenty years.[27] The third was the generalization of Fordism beyond the United States in a context where states were no longer simply recovering or rebuilding their capital stocks.

Bugs in the Software: Bretton Woods, Kalecki's Warning, and Oil Shocks

It's worth remembering that Bretton Woods only went live in 1958. Until that time there was restricted currency convertibility within Europe and between European economies and the United States. By the time that the Bretton Woods exchange-rate mechanism became fully operative, much of Europe's recovery had taken place. The recovery created incentives for American firms to move abroad to take advantage of new markets and engage in regulatory arbitrage to avoid controls on finance at home.[28] This in turn encouraged the growth of off-shore dollar deposits that would eventually bring volatility to the fixed value of the dollar itself.[29] However, what really destabilized the system, as Michael Brodo notes, were three bugs buried deep inside the Bretton Woods software.[30]

First was the adjustment problem, whereby a dual commitment to full employment and (relative) capital account closure meant that balance-of-payments deficits would produce unemployment rather than downward wage adjustments as imports closed down local competitors. Second was the confidence problem, whereby external US liabilities eventually outweighed US gold reserves, threatening a bank run on the key currency, the dollar. Third was the liquidity problem, whereby reversing US deficits would deprive the world of dollar liquidity and crash the export economies that depended on it.

What made these bugs into critical flaws, argues Brodo, were the accommodative monetary policies of the Lyndon Johnson administration, which led to ever-greater balance-of-payments deficits in the United States and ever-greater surpluses elsewhere. The orthodox response to balance the system would have been to rein in US deficits, but that would have made the liquidity problem chronic for the rest of the world. So instead, the United States decided to push the costs of adjustment onto other states while refusing to be bound by the rules of the system, which demanded that the issuer of the key currency not run an inflationary policy that undermined the dollar-gold peg. If you do exactly that, the peg has to go, and go it did in 1973.

These bugs in the software at the international level were compounded by different but equally destabilizing bugs in the domestic-level software of running a full-employment economy. Even before the architects of the first American order gathered at Bretton Woods a Hungarian economist exiled in London issued a warning in 1943 that attempting to run a full-employment regime on a permanent basis would lead to that regime's demise. Mikhal Kalecki wondered about "the political problems of full employment" in a seven-page journal article that predicted the breakdown of the first American order before it was even built.[31]

Recall that all the different national versions of the American order around the world in the first order have full employment as the policy target because, in the context of limited capital mobility, aiming for that target forces firms to invest in productivity enhancement in order to survive. Doing so creates an environment where greater productivity drops marginal cost, which in the face of strong demand, leads to expansion and further employment. Demand creates supply, as Keynes predicted, which in turn, creates a labor market where labor has all the power.

In such a permanently tight labor market, marginal workers can move costlessly from job to job, bidding up the median wage as they go. The effect for skilled workers will be even stronger. This will lead to a breakdown in labor discipline, and Kalecki predicted that strikes would rise in frequency and intensity. To pay for these ever-increasing wage demands, firms will push up prices, leading to a spiral of cost-push and demand-pull inflationary dynamics beyond what productivity can pay for. This, in turn, will reduce future profit expectations, which will lead to a fall in investment via investment expectations (I^*) and thus lower growth. This will lead firms to lay off labor, which encourages more militancy, while producing inflation, or more correctly, stagflation, as the government stimulates the economy to compensate while I^* collapses.

The inevitable result, as Kalecki put it, was the formation of "a powerful block . . . between big business and the rentier [financial] interests . . . [who] . . . would probably find more than one economist to declare that the situation was manifestly unsound. The pressure of all these forces, and in particular of big business, would most probably induce the Government to return to the orthodox policy of cutting down the budget deficit."[32]

With the United States pinned down in South East Asia with 500,000 men under arms and another 2.5 million in support roles, these dynamics hit especially hard in the US labor market in the late 1960s and early 1970s, and an accommodative monetary policy at the Federal Reserve made them worse.[33] With inflationary forces rising and profits falling, a crisis of capital formation was declared by the leading agents of capital and the drumbeat for a return to orthodox polices, last heard in 1937, grew louder. But for these forces to reach a tipping point, one more blow to the regime was necessary, and that came in the form of oil.

The Arab oil shocks of 1974 and 1979 are often, and correctly, blamed for producing much of the inflation of the period. But these one-off shocks did not do all the damage, nor did the recycling of the petrodollars that these crises produced. Rather, the deep bug lay in the production architecture of the first American order: how its firms were organized and the Fordist model of mass production that underpinned it.[34]

In brief, in the early postwar period, different national versions of full-employment capitalism could coexist because they each made more or less similar things that they occasionally traded with each other. As European and Japanese economies went beyond recovery to expansion, technologically challenging the United States in many areas, a fallacy of composition cropped up in Fordism. Although any one country could be Fordist, insofar as the social bargain that underpinned it required stable prices, a stable wage share, increasing productivity growth, and stable inputs, that could only happen in a world in which the United States was the price setter and the rest of the world were price takers. But if the model was generalized, if West Germany and Japan became serious exporters and the rest of the world joined in, then those stable input prices would disappear and the positive-sum politics of single-state Fordism would give way, as it did, to a zero-sum view of competition, with each country bidding up the prices of key commodities.

Thus, by the time the oil shocks hit in the 1970s, inflation was well and truly baked into the proverbial cake at the same time as states' ability to keep capital at home to force investment was obviated. The oil shocks simply provided the energy to tip the system into a critical mode. And when it disequilibrated, there was no way to tip it back into equilibrium, given the endogenous changes that were well under way at the same time (as detailed by Francis Gavin in this volume). A new equilibrium had to be found. Doing so meant, above all, changing the social purpose of the regime once again—rewriting the software, if you will. In the face of an inflationary crisis, this new social purpose unsurprisingly focused on a set of ideas based around attaining price stability.

The Second America Order: Building a New Social Purpose

The core of *GTs* details the construction of this second order in the United States and Sweden. Space prevents a full retelling here. But I want to stress how the ideational and political battles of the period were based around solving the inflationary crisis of the 1970s and the shift in ideas and institutions that this necessitated. Whether one focuses on Paul Volcker's decision to ration bank reserves and force a recession in the United States in 1980, the IMF's prior bludgeoning of the United Kingdom's budget in 1976, or Margaret Thatcher's monetarist turn in 1981, the first-order target was the same—to restore the real value of capital and the discipline of the market which became the new social purpose of the regime. Once capital was freer to move, as it was after 1976, when all attempts to restore the Bretton Woods system were abandoned, two obstacles still prevented it from doing so at a domestic level—organized labor and the political control of the economy. Both obstacles had to be removed.

For capital this struggle over labor power and political control was no minor adjustment. It required a fundamental rebuild and reboot of the system. Regardless of the particular form of national capitalism or the contingency of events, the whole point of capitalism is to realize an expected real rate of return. It's about profits—period. Inflation plays havoc with this expectation and thus future investment. In short, if I invest in a business or a financial transaction and expect a real return on investment (nominal minus inflation) of 5 percent, and inflation is 3 percent, I need to make 8 percent. But if inflation rises to 10 percent or beyond, then my profits will evaporate and my incentive do invest, along with actual investment, disappears. As Kalecki warned, Keynes's I^* in such a world, collapses.

Add to this mix the prospect of militant labor sequestering an investors' assets and limiting their freedom to invest, and the situation becomes intolerable. One simple fact bears this out: how capital's war against labor was waged. Labor's share of gross domestic product peaked in 1973 at 65 percent of GDP and fell thereafter to a current (2021) low of 55 percent as capital restored its share. Given that 95 percent of active US labor-market participants are wage earners rather than capital earners, that's an astonishing turnaround and an incredible redistribution upward.[35] Capital did this, in part, by decoupling pay and productivity. To do that, capital had to break organized labor and collective bargaining.

There were multiple ways to do this and all were tried. Direct confrontation of the type seen in the United States and United Kingdom, with Professional Air Traffic Controller's Organization (PATCO) in 1981 and coal miners in 1984, respectively, was one way. A more subtle approach was to maintain the shell of agreements while devolving to lower levels of bargaining and/or expanding investment to multiple locations and then playing them off of each other, as occurred in Sweden and Germany.[36] By the mid-1990s these effects had reduced the power of organized labor everywhere. In the United States, states such as Wisconsin lost one-third of their manufacturing plants and employment to "right to work" states in the US South, then to Mexico, and then to China. In Germany, formally strong organizations tolerated more than a decade of wage freezes, knowing that globalization started sixty kilometers outside Berlin with the option to move production east under the auspices of the European Union's (EU's) single market.[37]

Globalization and European integration together furthered these dynamics. Adding eight hundred million workers to the global labor pool while freeing capital from almost all restraints produced massive deflationary pressure that pushed down core country wages and pushed up profit margins as input costs fell as global supply chains expanded.[38] Technology abetted this, as just-in-time production abetted zero-hours contracts and a gig economy pushed wage deflation further.[39] The pressures, once again, were all on labor. The profits, once again, were all with capital. The system worked exactly as it was meant to. Polanyi's Double Movement was bound to reappear eventually.

The second obstacle that capital overcame was political control of the economy. Democratic input into the investment function had to be neutered, given that majoritarianism meant that the preferences of labor would win out by dint of simple electoral arithmetic. This is where the real ideational work was done. One part of this struggle took place on the elevated plane of intellectual debate. The neoliberal turn in economics spawned a huge literature, first, on the monetary origins of inflation, and second, on the need for conservative central bankers to control money because politicians supposedly suffered from "time inconsistent preferences."[40] These developments were turbocharged by the success of real business cycle theory in macroeconomics, insofar as its ability solve by sidestepping the microfoundations problem inherent in Keynesian models by building so-called representative agent models. This allowed a new generation of more neoliberal-minded central bankers to ditch those clunky Keynesian models and thereby make a grab for control of the economy with so-called Dynamic Stochastic General Equilibrium macroeconomics.[41]

In short, the software for running the second American order—the economic ideas underpinning it—was rewritten. This in turn necessitated the great hardware modification of the period: the devolution of power to independent central banks that were able to enshrine monetary stability—or even active disinflation— as the new social purpose of the second American order. Again, this was not just as American story. As Juliet Johnson details, by the late 1990s this institutional transformation had affected policymaking throughout the developed—and most of the developing—world.[42]

Democratic politicians went with the flow. After spending the 1980s trying to defend a social purpose that had already been abandoned by capital, labor and social democratic parties began to mirror the policies of the right.[43] As Stephanie Mudge exhaustively details, the shift from in-house Keynesian economists to external finance-friendly economists and political strategists as the key policy actors in such parties led them to embrace the core neoliberal position on state involvement in the economy.[44] Basically—you can't do it, you shouldn't do it, and if you try it you will pay an electoral price.

Over the next decade the parties that had invented and defended the old bargain abandoned their traditional constituencies and moved to capture richer (older) median voters, changing their policy stances in doing so.[45] They increasingly narrowed their policy offers to the public, rejecting any real role in steering the economy. The result was the self-abnegation of state competencies and a retreat from state responsibilities for economic outcomes such that by the time the 2008 crisis hit, states were both blindsided by the crisis and terrified to use the fiscal tools that they still had to confront it.[46] Indeed, they indulged in austerity budgets that made their political situations worse and increased the pressures on their populations, especially the most vulnerable, in doing so.[47]

With politicians abdicating their responsibilities, central banks, as the only game in town stepped up to the plate in their stead, violating everything that that supposedly stood for in terms of promoting price stability as the primary policy goal (at least after Mario Drahgi became European Central Bank chief).[48] The four big central banks poured a total of 17 trillion dollars, euros, renminbi, and yen into everything from liquidity support and distressed asset purchases to cushioning recession effects and quantitative easing, deliberately producing massive price *instability* to stimulate economies.[49] But the fundamental problems generated by the second order—the bugs in this version of the software—remained untouched. These problems were wage stagnation, ever-increasing income inequality, increasing asset concentration, a reliance on debt financing (especially in the private sector) to spur growth, and a cosmopolitan attitude to immigration that was increasingly contested by native populations.

The result of this massive exercise in volatility suppression via turning on the liquidity pumps of the state was unsurprisingly the collapse of those parties, especially on the left, over the next decade that had made neoliberal virtue their calling card. This gave rise to what Rawi Abdelal (in this volume) usefully calls "the entrepreneurship of contemporary populisms," which fed on this new Polanyian reaction and has been weaponized as nationalism across the globe. Those political parties that have failed to adapt to this new world, such as the German Social Democratic Party, are all but dead, replaced by the Alternative for Germany on the right and the Greens on the left. Those that have adapted, such as the UK Conservatives or the Danish Social Democrats, seem to be tearing up the neoliberal rule book, opting for old-fashioned gambits such as industrial policy, regional policy, increased government spending to spur domestic innovation, and immigration controls. The United States elected Donald Trump, a neoliberal populist, and India elected Narenda Modi, a neonationalist populist. Eastern Europe, meanwhile, has elected parties that manage to traverse both

TABLE 1   Contrasting American orders and their social purposes

AMERICAN ORDER 1 (1945–80)	AMERICAN ORDER 2 (1980–2008)	AMERICAN ORDER 3 (POST 2008)
Social purpose: Full employment	Social purpose: Price stability	Social purpose: Inchoate
Policy outcomes	*Policy outcomes*	*Policy outcomes*
Positive inflation	Secular disinflation	Activist central banks and more active legislatures
Labor's share of GDP increasing	Capital's share of GDP increasing	Emergency reactivation of fiscal policy (COVID-19)
Corporate profits low or stagnant	Wages low or stagnant	Wages low or stagnant
Inequality low	Inequality high	Inequality high
Finance weak and immobile	Finance strong and mobile	Partial de-globalization
Central banks weak and politicized	Central banks strong and independent	Central banks strong but politicized, labor still weak
Strong economic role for legislatures (fiscal dominance)	Curtailment of legislatures' fiscal role (monetary dominance)	Disintegration of national party systems and the embedding of populisms

Source: Adapted from Mark Blyth, "Policies to Overcome Stagnation: The Crisis, and the Possible Futures, of All Things Euro," *European Journal of Economics and Economic Policies* 13, no. 2 (2016): 220.

stances at the same time. The transformations of the second American are summarized in the following table, with the third column detailing the moment in which we find ourselves. In 2021 the third order is not yet fully with us, but its outlines are becoming clearer.

A New Order with What Purpose?

What would the theory behind *GTs* tell us about the current moment? To be honest, I'm not sure it would be of much help. The focus on Knightian uncertainty in *GTs* was there to suggest that when standard models fail, policymakers may be more open than usual to new ideas and the new politics that they make possible. Such a focus worked well for the 1940s, really well for the 1970s, but perhaps not as well for 2008, and especially not well for the early 2020s. There may be a great deal of uncertainty, but there seem to be no new ideas, and especially in this historical moment a failure of agency—a general hesitancy in the political center to try to find new ideas. The reason why is quite clear. Whereas contingency and leadership came together to establish the first American order, both characteristics are conspicuous by their absence this time around, for very simple electoral reasons.

Resuscitated neoliberalism serves the top 20 percent of any country's income distribution very well indeed. And as the work of Martin Gilens and many other studies have shown, that's the part of the income distribution that politicians legislate for.[50] As far as mainstream parties are concerned, central banks rebooted the system in 2008 and saved the assets and incomes of that top 20 percent, so mission accomplished. Despite the COVID-19 shock, politicians are still afraid of being accused of fiscal activism, or are bound by rules, such as those in the EU, that despite much heralded financial packages still seek to legislate permanent austerity.[51]

Two sets of people recognize the underlying bugs in the software. The first set is, ironically, the leaders of the central banks, who keep asking for more fiscal activism even as they warn governments about their debt burdens. The second set is the populists of the left and the right, who broadly agree on the problems, but differ massively on the solutions. Does this auger the final end of the American order as the disintegration of the neoliberal model is compounded by a divergence of rival social purposes? Only partially. The order will remain American because of the centrality of the US dollar, but it will become increasingly diverse in the social purpose(s) that it enshrines.

Key here is a problem identified by Keynes at Bretton Woods that led him to argue, unsuccessfully, for a global currency—the Bancor—to offset the deflationary bias of surplus countries on the system as a whole. We didn't get a Bancor, but we did get the dollar. And despite the end of Bretton Woods and the breaking of the gold peg, the US dollar has become more central than ever to international trade, contract settlement, payment systems, currency reserves, and commodity denomination.

The first-order reason is simple: What's the alternative? When China thought about internationalizing the renminbi to challenge the dollar, loosening capital controls in 2015, nearly a trillion dollars left the country, which is hardly a signal of confidence in the contracts and assets of a society.[52] The euro is a 'one size fits none' currency that is choking off growth in its periphery so that its core can run an export surplus against the rest of the world.[53] The main reason it survives is because you cannot exit it without destroying half of your own national savings in the devaluation that would come with a new currency.[54] The lack of any reasonable alternative to the US dollar gives the dollar extraordinary power as the de facto Bancor in the system. To see why this is the case, let's go back to the general point that Keynes made in this regard at Bretton Woods—that too many states running an export surplus creates a dangerous deflationary dynamic in the system as a whole. This is relevant to the current moment because it is precisely what has been going on globally since 1999.

After the East Asian financial crisis of 1997–98 forced otherwise solvent countries to go cap-in-hand to the IMF for a punitive bailout, East Asia as a whole decided to run an export surplus against the rest of the world in order to build up reserves so that it would never have to go back to the IMF again.[55] Ten years later the global financial crisis caused Europe to play the same trick. Its fiscal hands tied by its ordoliberal rulebook and mired in self-imposed debt-deflation, the EU also started to run a surplus against the rest of the world.[56] That left one part of the world—broadly, the Anglosphere—running the corresponding deficits. As Herman Schwartz has shown, the sum of the current account surplus of the East Asian and European exporters almost perfectly matches the current account deficits of the Anglosphere countries. Moreover, such a system creates a banker's dilemma that embeds dollar centrality still further.[57]

Any exporter by definition receives dollars in return for its exports. Depositing those dollars in the local banking system creates an asset-liability mismatch, which is resolved by buying US Treasuries bonds. Doing so forces down US interest rates, which encourages more US consumption, which encourages more imports, and hence yet more dollar accumulation by exporters. The structure of the global economy—too many exporters—makes this inevitable.

This constant external accumulation of dollars in turn encourages huge amounts of foreign borrowing in dollars outside of the United States. When those loans get into trouble—as foreign currency borrowing inevitably does—the home central banks of these borrowers and lenders cannot bail them out because they do not print dollars. All of this makes the US Federal Reserve the de facto global central bank, as seen in the swap lines of 2008 and in the same lines being activated during the COVID-19 crisis.[58] The US Fed's ability to produce both safe assets for surplus countries and "outside money" (money not dependent on asset sales in a crisis) to solve liquidity crises is the real and continuing source of American power.[59] So what does this mean for the order that is appearing before our eyes? It means we will have an American order that runs on American dollars, but without American leadership or even American norms.[60] In short, the emergent order will be a US dollar standard run by the US Fed. In that sense it's still an American order. It's an American order in terms of the financial plumbing that holds it together. But this order now enshrines no definitive social purpose and allows a multiplicity of such purposes to flourish.

The United States in the has over the past several years alternated between nationalist populism with belligerent bilateralism under Trump and a return to multilateralism that has probably passed its sell-by date under Biden. Unlike in the first and second orders, where the generalization of a social purpose—full employment and then price stability/restoration of profit—was central, in the current moment no such singular purpose emanates from the United States. Talk of a paradigm shift in the United States remains largely talk while in Europe the debate over the fiscal rules at the heart of the EU isn't even a debate.

One could argue that the emergent social purpose is national economic preservation, given the ruptures of the past decade. Whereas the first American order served labor and the second one served capital, the emergent third order is trying to serve both by turning away from globalization via a neonationalist economic settlement that benefits domestic labor and capital. But even if that is the case, it compels no internationalization of that social purpose. The preservation of democracy abroad is no longer a US imperative as it was in the first order. The restoration of capital, which has now been achieved to the point of detriment, is nowhere under real threat. So there is no impulse to generalize a social purpose coming from the United States. Biden's victory augurs no return to the policies of the past. Nor are the traditional allies of the United States likely to pick up the burden of providing any alternative future. The United Kingdom remains mired in the years-long distraction called Brexit. The EU manages to talk a good game on human rights while cooperating with China. Meanwhile, Poland and Hungary carve out exclusionary ethnonationalist political regimes in the midst of the EU's democratic framework.

Outside of these cases, a state within such an open order can prioritize the interests of domestic labor if it wishes to do so, or it can prioritize local or global capital. It can try to find a third way that takes the emerging green economy seriously, as many small, open economies, such as Denmark and Ireland, seem to want to do, or it can engage in xenophobic nationalistic denialism, as Russia and other carbon exporters—perhaps including the United States itself—seem to want to do. In short, the third American order, insofar as it will allow a multiplicity of social purposes that continues to rest on the centrality of the US dollar, will effectively have none, nor will it argue for none.

THE CONSTRUCTION OF COMPROMISE AND THE RISE AND FALL OF GLOBAL ORDERS

Peter A. Gourevitch

History is a projection of the present into the past. Not always, but often. We are interested in the embedded liberalism, as John Ruggie named it, of the postwar years, or the "historical compromise," as many Europeans called it, as we see those arrangements under substantial challenge in the early twenty-first century.[1] We care not just to describe but to explain, to amend, and to preserve. We seek to understand in order to protect the features we like and change the ones we don't. Understanding origins, development, and crisis may offer ideas for these trajectories.

Many of the explanations of the current crisis see issues according to the following logic, which we can call the standard interpretation of the postwar consensus. The acute class and regional conflicts that stoked nationalism before World War II were solved by a big, largely economic bargain to provide a welfare floor to the masses and to contain allow market forces and private enterprise to manage the economy in restricted ways.

There is considerable truth to this interpretation, but it distorts, in my view, description for causality. It describes the bargain and infers the cause from the contents of the description. The construction of the bargain itself involved issues, arrangements, and compromises that went beyond the content of the economic exchange expressed by the label of embedded liberalism. A number of noneconomic issues had to be worked out in order for this bargain to come about.

"Working out," or constructing a bargain, means compromise, subordination, or repression of some kind. It means giving something up to get something else—making priorities. It is not costless. In a well-ordered democracy, the people have accepted the bargain's costs and trade-offs. Even so, there is some element of resentment among the people. To some degree these wishes are sublimated, but they can resurface. If a democracy is not well ordered, these resentments can be simmering grievances, where the deal is all the more resented because it was imposed.

The compromise model of change contrasts with a movement model of change. In that frame, a mass of people adheres to a vision of society and rallies behind a leader or an organization that provides them with the support needed to realize that vision. The vision is a more unitary an ideal than occurs in the compromise model. The opposition or enemy to the ideal is also seen as more unitary than with the compromise model (the bourgeoisie, the billionaires, capitalists, or the radical agitators, the Jews and Roma, the foreigners).

Embedded liberalism did not occur through a movement model, but through a bargaining/compromise model. A consensus was constructed. Several groups, led by identifiable leaders, worked to build agreements, to make trade-offs, and to accept some parts of their ideal and give up others.

Europe faced a number of conflicts to be resolved or accommodated. These issues included defining a national identity and membership in it, a position in the world, and a relationship to the Soviet Union on one side versus the United States on another. They included the formation of social solidarity or hostility, that is, formation of social order and relations among members of a national community. They involved consideration of religion. Which religions? What authority and support should they have? What should be their relationship to schooling and taxation? They included the division of authority between central and regional governments, as many countries had movements seeking regional autonomy. Who would live together under one flag and how? After the white-hot furnace of depression, war, bombing, armies, and death and destruction, Europe was in deep moral crisis. How to order society, how to live together, how to construct a nation-state, around what bonds to reconstruct society—these were burning questions. So were issues of identity, culture, international relations, security, class sector, economic justice, economic productivity, and civic and cultural freedoms. A number of competing ideas were at play. It took politics, leaders, and events to work them out. Leaders had to develop a broad vision, what Gérard Bouchard calls a "collective imaginary," to justify the challenges ahead: taxes, hard work, and collaboration.[2] After the bitter conflicts of the previous years, a common framework was needed.

Constructing a Consensus: Enabling Embedded Liberalism

Hitler's defeat in 1945 opened the door to a debate over how to replace the pre-war order and the fascism of the war years. European political space was fragmented into multiple poles of political representation, as political activities both reflected and sought to articulate various cleavages.[3] Class divided people as workers, managers, or white-collar professionals. Through each of those categories ran another divide, based on religion—Catholic, Protestant, or anticlerical. And through those differences ran yet another disagreement, regarding attitudes toward the market. How much regulation or state ownership should there be? To what extent should the economy be market-centered. And to those disagreements others must be added: regional divides in some countries that generated claims about language and culture and demands for regional autonomy; political settlements about the institutions and processes of democracy and constitutionalism; and finally, disagreements over international order, such as what to do with Germany in the space between the United States and the Soviet Union, and how to provide peace and security acceptable to each of the parties.

These cleavages sliced through each other, so that many combinations, and therefore many outcomes, were possible.[4] A socialist could share a Marxist tradition with a communist and yet have sharply different views of the Soviet Union and democracy; a Christian democrat might support a European consortium more than a nationalist coreligionist would. Workers split into three categories of trade unions: communist, socialist, and Catholic. The boundary between domestic and international politics was impossible to draw, as people lined up for or against Moscow or Washington.

In this confusing situation, with many possible combinations, leadership mattered. A decisive driver toward the historical compromise came from the Christian democrats, the Catholic, central swing leaders in the continental democracies. Konrad Adenauer of Germany, Robert Schuman of France, and Alcide De Gasperi of Italy were all leaders of the Christian democratic movements of their respective countries. Adenauer was the chancellor of his country, and leader of the Christian Democratic Union; Schuman was prime minister and foreign minister, as well as leader of the Mouvement Républicain Populaire (MRP), a centrist Catholic party; and De Gasperi was prime minister and leader of the Italian Christian Democrats.

These leaders imagined an integrated Europe, bound by common ties of Christianity and values of family, community, and society, in which the nations would integrate harmoniously. They shared a long-standing desire of progressive Catholics to form a natural order based on a community of organic bonds of labor, capital, families, and church, cutting across boundaries, reestablishing what nationalism had torn asunder, but based on strong local and regional institutions.

The ancestral home of Christian democratic leaders' imagination was Lotharingia, a piece of Charlemagne's empire that lay between modern Germany and France when he divided his empire among his sons. Back then, Lotharingia was no less authentic than its neighbors, but over the centuries it was carved up by the emerging monarchies of France and Prussia. The coal fields of Belgium and northeastern France and the iron pits of the Rhine area formed the foundation of a "natural economic" community of exchange, knit socially by bonds of common religion on top of the older historic ties of dynasty. Otto von Bismarck integrated a piece of this area into Germany by force when he took Alsace and Lorraine from France, but he created deep enmity by doing so. He also imposed a penalty on France as a defeated country of 5 billion gold francs, as large, proportionally, as the penalties imposed on Germany at Versailles. France paid it and rebuilt its economy, contradicting the complaint of the Germany nationalists in the 1920s and 1930s that the penalties from Versailles were ruinous to the German economy. Hitler's march to a continental German empire marked the most extreme negation of this communitarian vision.

The postwar years represented a moment for the progressive Christian views to burst forward. For a century or longer progressive Christian groups had been at the margins of political life—active in many places, but rarely in command. Their views had long battled conservative and reactionary visions of a Catholic Europe, of hierarchy, and of absolutism; the Syllabus of Errors and the infallibility of the pope dated from the late nineteenth century, the same period when democracy and industrialization emerged in much of Europe and South America. In the lean years, they had developed political parties, trade unions, and cultural organizations of varying political outlooks, but had been marginalized by their conservative colleagues. Now they could operate with the extreme right and left contained.

They had for many years advocated a moderated democracy mixed with a tempered capitalism: a managed market economy and regulated free enterprise that would provide a safety net, security, and stability, to integrate individuals into families and stable Christian communities. This meant job security, pay, health care, schools, and social and cultural networks. Catholic and Protestant groups had provided such networks and private insurance for many years. With much of society in ruins, they now advocated that the state do this.

On top of the domestic understanding, the Catholic viewpoint extended to an international one, a consortium of European powers bound by international agreements and institutions. The first step was the European Coal and Steel

Community, built in 1951, which then evolved into the numerous structures that led to the European Community.

Adenauer, Schuman, and De Gasperi provided a key political bond that cut through the many divisions within national borders. They were joined by a significant number of socialists and social democrats who were anti-Soviet and anticommunist, as the Cold War and communism split the left deeply. To fight the Soviet Union and the communists, the Section française de l'internationale ouvrière (SFIO) in France and the Social Democratic Party in Germany formed a vital political bond with prewar enemies.[5] Kurt Schumacher in Germany and Guy Mollet in France were among the key leaders. Socialists shared many values with the Christian democrats, though with more tension over working with capitalist bosses. Many socialists shared the communitarian sensibility of the Catholicism, its desire to overcome national hostilities, and its sense of local bonds and local work. Socialists were divided into a decentralized view and a statist one. Those who held the latter view often went to the communists, leaving the socialists with the community-minded able to build bridges with the Catholics. The socialists strongly supported the welfare-state formulations that would provide security and solidarity to the working masses, protecting them from the disruptions of market forces.

Communists and nationalists of various kinds were against this coalition for the postwar compromise. The communists argued against the capitalist order, the movement to contain the Soviet Union, and the alliance with the United States. Nationalists, most notably the Gaullists in France, argued against the subordination of the sovereign nation to the new supranational institutions of Europe. The communists had a very strong strategic position, especially in France and Italy. As leaders of the resistance to fascism, they attracted considerable loyalty to their vision of the future. The far right was discredited by fascist collaboration and prevented from engaging in political activity by US troops backing up the national anger.

Older resentments remained in place: defiance of authority, dislike of the social order, the sense of being taken advantage of, anger about domination by traditional social and business elites and subordination to the *patronnat* (the bosses). These are grievances of long standing throughout most of Europe. And in Europe regional and religious cleavages by no means disappeared and remain potent as focal points for discontent.

The standard portrayal of the historical compromise has stressed the economic elements of the bargaining at the expense of the identity elements. It has been used in the political economy narrative to stress the origins of the welfare state and its relationship to the relatively open economy that was constructed among the participating countries.[6] And yet, strong elements of disagreement and protest on identity issues remained in political life. As conditions changed and the historical compromise came under pressure, the repressed elements remained available. They would return in different forms and symbols to express discontent.

Thus, embedded liberalism was not a cause of the postwar compromise but rather itself a complex compromise involving policies and bargains that cut across many issues, held together by partial agreement on a collective imaginary, of which embedded liberalism was a part. As the compromise cracked, its pieces emerged and the constructed bargain faced new challenges.

Development to Crisis: Seventy Years

The system created in these postwar period worked for an impressive number of years, and now it is in crisis. What happened? Of course, over a seventy-year period, there are many variables. Here I will focus on two variables from the system's founding years as they confronted two variables in the later years. At the founding, two elements, closely intertwined differed in the countries of Europe and North America and Japan.

One has to do with the corporate governance system, a label I use to evoke a type of market economy; the other has to do with the level and nature of the welfare state. These two variables pose special interest for calling attention to the microeconomic elements of political economy, whereas the traditional Keynesian culture emphasized the macro dimension. Many decades later, these countries faced extensive changes in the world economy (globalization of production) and extensive social change (immigration from eastern Europe, the Middle East, and Africa). The crisis appeared among the micro variables, posing intellectual and policy challenges over how these interacted with the macro ones. This led to a series of crises which surprised and often paralyzed decision makers and politics, all contributing to the recent populist surge: the financial crisis of 2008, the Greek bankruptcy crisis of 2015, the ongoing migration crises, the Brexit crisis, the trade disputes, and so on.

The strong institutions set out in 1945, with the added energy of postwar reconstruction and new technologies, expanded productivity. They generated what in French is called *les trentes glorieuses*: strong, steady growth, full employment, and rebuilt cities and houses. They also generated a new society. The lower classes of workers and farmers were included in a new order with some cross-class and cultural accommodation and higher degree of social peace than Europe had previously known. Income grew, as did social mobility, standards of living, and the emergence of middle-class life.

Yet contradictions were developing. The first of these, as noted above, involved corporate governance.

Comparative Capitalism: Corporate Governance and the Welfare State

In the shifting dynamics of the late twentieth century, corporate governance differences among the capitalist models mattered considerably and were perhaps underappreciated. The comparative literature had come to understand that there is more than one capitalist model at work. Researchers focused on two ideal types: an Anglo-American, neoliberal, decentralized market type, and a German-Japanese, coordinated, regulated, interconnected type. Peter Hall and David Soskice's book, *The Varieties of Capitalism*, became one of the most well known of these books on comparative capitalism. It used the labels "liberal market economies" (LME) and "coordinated market economies" (CME), supplanting an earlier, important book, Andrew Shonfield's *Modern Capitalism*.[7] Michel Albert described Rhenish capitalism, and Ronald Dore elaborated on the cultural foundations of the difference between the British factory and Japanese factory.[8] Other work stressed government-state relations; Chalmers Johnson wrote of the role of MITI (Ministry of International Trade and Industry) and the Japanese miracle, and Peter Katzenstein wrote of the German state-centered model.[9] These authors argued that the state in Continental Europe and Japan were more involved with their economies than were the United States and the United Kingdom. In the bureaucratic-leader model, the state led, with bureaucrats guiding businesses, picking winners, selecting technologies and companies, and developing national champions.

Alternatively, the state could be seen as a coordinator or a broker rather than as a leader. In this rival view, the state favored a system of corporate governance that privileged networks of firms, banks, and producers. It is these networks that made the key decisions on technology and products. The networks of relationships were protected by a web of regulations on corporate governance, which shaped governing boards, stock acquisitions, management, and employment. These regulations did a number of things: they severely limited mergers and acquisitions, takeovers, competition; they privileged elite workers, so that lifetime employment went to the top workers in the system, not the distant subcontractors; and they generated a system of suppliers in several tiers into which it was difficult for outsiders to enter, even Japanese ones. The regulations restricted foreign competition, subsidized technology, suppressed domestic consumption in favor of savings steered to businesses, and allowed interlocking directorates that protected firms from hostile takeovers. The state was very important, but as a protector of the networks, a supplier of capital, and a promoter of trade and for-eign relations of networks preferences, setting standards that favored producers and excluded foreigners. The state served the networks. It articulated and helped formulate their interests, but did not by itself lead the networks or go deeply against their wishes. The state was "a web with no spider," as one specialist put it, generating a lot of controversy.[10]

Corporate governance lay at the core of what made the capitalist system dif-fer. The interdependent pieces of the production system, for Wolfgang Streeck, lay with the labor apprentice system, which was situated in the large intercon-nected institutions of the German system, not with the dominant state.[11] And for Streeck, therefore, each piece was neither easily transferable nor changeable.

There were patterns of difference in adjustment to trade; the US economy got out of the old and into the new faster than Germany and Japan. So at crisis moments, the United States seemed in worse shape because of its weak welfare state, but then it adapted faster and moved ahead.[12] The United States built inter-national value chains quickly, shedding labor and capital investments at home, to pick up on lower cost factors of production around the world. So the United States adapted quickly to the new economy of electronics and highly articulated value chains while Germany and Japan modernized much of their traditional economy to become the world's leaders in precision engineering equipment and products.

These trends built up. Trade agreements increasingly liberalized the world economy. At that same time, within that liberalized external trade regime, reg-ulations within countries were often left in place—protectionist measures that favored financial interests, corporate managers, and existing relationships among management, labor, and community. Sweden and Switzerland, for example, often rated as open economies, were not so when it came to foreigners seeking owner-ship control and minority shareholder protections. Chile, after carrying out the liberalizations advised by the Chicago boys during the Augusto Pinochet years, remained a closed economy when it came to control and ownership.[13]

In these years, other regulations were loosened that allowed a shift in power in the United States and the United Kingdom. Managers sought to preserve compa-nies and their relationships among all the suppliers, distributors, and workers in the supply chain. Now the emphasis was on maximizing returns at the expense of these relationships. Power shifted to finance (both inside and outside firms), to financial institutions, and to traders. The ideology justifying all this was share-holder primacy, a shorthand for managerial autonomy to maximize the rate of return to themselves.

The assumption was that optimizing shareholders returns would be in every-one's interests, so making managers shareholders would bring incentives in line.

The classic problem, as Berle and Means articulated it, was that the incentives between managers and shareholders were out of alignment. The solution by convergence proved illusory. Divergent interests arose among types of shareholders. Managers who held a lot shares acquired an incentive for risk not shared by the ordinary owner, who preferred long-term stability of return and price. Mergers and acquisitions severed the goals of specialized clientele, and undermined the stable relationships of members of the larger stakeholder network: workers, suppliers, distributors, communities, neighborhoods, and localities.

These differences were of long standing. In the 1970s, their impact accelerated. In the United States and the United Kingdom, a considerable expansion of stock investment in retirement savings took place, in sharp contrast with the continent, where pensions remained in government or banking hands, a step removed from the savers.[14] The ERISA legislation encouraged pension fund development so that employee savings flowed increasingly into the stock market, and in many cases into accounts over which employees had some voice through their union or employer pension funds. Financial institutions played an important role, in ways that had a substantial impact. Public employee funds such as CALPERS had a direct managerial role. The owners of private sector ones (such as Fidelity and Merrill Lynch), centered their goals purely on profit. Vanguard was an unusual case; it was private sector but wholly owned by its savers, with no layer of separate owners. TIAA-CREF was similar, owned by its savers. The employee owned institutional investors increasingly pushed for managerial responsiveness to employee concerns, whereas the purely private one continued to side with management.[15] Organizations like the Council for Institutional Investors became activists for reform in defense of shareholders over managers, and lobbied around the world for financial reform to encourage minority shareholder protection. The collapse of 2008 created the politics that enabled the Dodd-Frank Act, which finally compelled Fidelity-style firms to declare how they would vote their proxies, thereby setting off another round of controversy of over what shareholder pressure would mean and the role of institutional investors.[16]

The shift to the market-shareholder approach in the United States helped destabilize the economy. It happened along with an extensive push for deregulation, which occurred in many sectors of the economy, from airlines, to shipping and trucking, to banking and finance. The deregulatory free market attitude led to appointments that placed people into regulatory positions who discounted risk in favor of innovation and change. A particularly striking example concerns derivatives. These innovations were allowed not only to spread unregulated but to be used as components of the core reserves of banks, so that when the crisis hit instability would magnify. Bundled mortgages meant no accountability, as they were too complex to unbundle. In estimating risk, it was assumed that the regions of the US mortgage market had never declined at the same time—but the baseline of the comparisons was 1945, as if the Great Depression had never happened. And in the cleanup after the 2008 crisis, the banks were bailed out, providing stability, but little was done for mortgage holders and not enough for the unemployed.[17] Famously, no one went to prison from the group that caused it all, the titans of finance and mortgages. The title of Reed Hundt's book *A Crisis Wasted* expresses a view of many progressives in the current period critical of the Barack Obama appointees Timothy Geithner and Lawrence Summers.[18]

This contributed substantially to erosion of the postwar consensus. Many ordinary people felt that whereas elites were helped, they were abandoned. David Autor and coauthors showed how strongly the vote for Donald Trump corelates with the impact of Chinese trade after 2000. Is this evidence for the economic side of the argument about populism's rise, or is it also evidence for a cultural argument—a sense of abandonment by the powerful, including the Democrats who claimed to represent ordinary people, especially workers. The shift of parts of the union vote in key blue-collar states is striking. At the same time, there was a drop in Democratic party turnout in 2016 and a resentment toward Hilary Clinton as a member of the elite financial interests who benefited from globalization and the financialization of the economy and failed to do enough to share the benefits with society as a whole.

The Welfare State

Differences in capitalist organization are mirrored in differences in welfare-state systems. These came to be described as social democratic, Christian democratic, and liberal models. The first group, notable in Scandinavia, covered all people as individuals, not as members of a family or as employees. Thus, one was covered regardless of loss of job or change of family status and the benefits were paid by high taxes raised by levies on income and sales taxes of the valued-added kind.[19] In the Christian democratic or central European model, benefits flowed to heads of family, who were overwhelmingly male, and were connected to those individuals' employment. The levels were generous and were paid through employment as well as though general taxes. They covered many areas, from unemployment to health and education. This system tied people closely to the family and the male breadwinner. The liberal model, characteristic of the United States and the United Kingdom, gave benefits to employees, whoever they were, male or female, independent of marital status, through the employment connection. Benefit levels were relatively low, as were taxes.[20]

These models of welfare do align with the corporate governance models, though by no means perfectly. The CME model rewards close connections among members of an economic linkage. The company sits and the center of this linkage, which includes the supply chain, the banks that finance the company, the employees, and the schools that train them. These are all interdependent pieces. They fit each other and reinforce each other.[21] Their tight interconnection made them difficult to lift from one society to another, as the disciples of best practice often urged be done.

These systems were both integrated into an open world economy, but in different ways. In the LME model, big pieces of the production system were exported long distances to follow cost advantages. In the CME model, pieces of the supply chain were exported nearby to preserve pieces of the supply system in the core countries. The CME model stressed seems strong preservation of higher value-added improving the production of familiar products, whereas the LME model provided more rapid transfer of resources from old economic activities to new ones.[22]

The difference appeared in conflicts over international trade and financial coordination, which sharpened in the trade disputes of the last decades of the twentieth century and burst open in the financial meltdown of 2008. In the trade disputes, the United States accused Japan of favoritism when its US-based manufacturing plants bought material from the same suppliers they used in Japan. The Japanese responded that they used these suppliers for efficiency reasons; they had developed cost and quality reductions through the just-in-time networks that required close and continuous relationships among manufacturers, final assemblers, and suppliers over long time periods.[23] Over time, US manufactures learned to do similar things, giving some support to the efficiency argument, or at least separating it from the evident protectionism that came from specialized rules like requiring special skis on the grounds that Japanese snow was different, or health rules on the grounds of different Japanese body metabolism, or more plausibly, giving advanced notice about specifications to Japanese companies before non-Japanese.

A second round of disputes between capitalist systems took place during the next decade over responses to the financial meltdown of 2008. This meltdown produced the sharpest economic downturn since the stock market crash of 1929 and compelled policy makers to respond quickly. The Americans pursued substantial demand stimulus with large government deficits. They urged European allies to do the same, and swiftly. Germany, the largest European economy, resisted. Germany was known for preferring strict money policy. This has often been attributed to a fear of inflation stemming from the hyperinflation of 1923. The hyperinflation is often used to explain Hitler's rise to power, as it wiped out the savings of many small savers. Aside from the historical fallacy—a new German mark stabilized hyperinflation in 1924–25, and the Nazis did poorly in elections until unemployment spread after 1929 to over a quarter of the population—this interpretation underplays the role of contemporary institutions in explaining the aversion to inflation. The tight interconnections among economic actors make them all acutely sensitive to price signals; they prefer careful calibration of wages and prices increases limited to productivity increases.[24]

German decision makers told their US counterparts that Germany was already spending substantial sums fighting the recession because its welfare levels were higher. These should be counted as a form of stimulus, and not just as the levels of the budget deficit itself. Later in the crisis, the US Fed began a policy of monetary easing, which the Germans and Dutch opposed. After a few years of greater stagnation in Europe, the European Central Bank came to adopt that policy after sharp internal disputes. European banking attitudes again reflected structural differences in the relationship of banks to economic institutions that shaped the determination of wages and prices.

Yet another area of dispute came up in 2015 over the Greek financial crisis. The strict money people in Germany and the Netherlands insisted Greece repay fully its enormous debt. A very large chuck of this was owed to German banks. The German argument was Greece should extensively reform its structures to be more productive—thus, to look more like Germany in many social ways. Other countries, especially from southern Europe, resisted this, arguing that it was an unfair imposition of one society's forms on another.[25]

Economic structure, welfare levels, and fiscal and monetary policy all interacted in these crises. They were not autonomous areas to be understood separately, as frequently had been done in debates over economic and social policy. There is considerable variance to be found among the industrial countries in their policy behavior, which can be linked to their corporate governance and welfare-state models. This makes it hard to generalize into broad patterns of historical stages of an economic policy story, as Mark Blyth does in this volume, however compelling it is to seek patterns. It becomes all the more difficult when we add the sociocultural variables, as in the section heading immediately following.

Social-Cultural Roots of Crisis: Migration, Values, Economic Shocks

With the economic erosion of the postwar compromise have come strong social-cultural challenges to the partial consensus of the social contract forged in the late 1940s: urbanization, education, changing job structures and experience, tourism, transnational European institutions, and the collapse of the Soviet Union and its model. Most notable have been waves of migration from outside national or regional boundaries: eastern and southern Europe, the Middle East, Africa, and

South and East Asia. People have arrived to flee economic hardship, political oppression, and social turmoil.

In many places the immigrants have been demonized by politicians as threats to the domestic social order who displace natives from their centrality in national life and supplant them in jobs, or appear to. What is fact and what is fiction? How do we speak of a cultural reaction as fiction? How much of this can be attributed to insecurities arise from vulnerability, which is itself affected by economic precariousness, be it from jobs, health, or housing?

Some insight can be obtained by looking at levels of welfare-state support and other forms of economic support. A simple test would be to examine whether higher levels of welfare-state support yield lower levels of populist backlash of a nativist kind. The measurable indicators on one side of the relationship are welfare-state provisions of income, health, job security and retraining, and housing. On the other side lies support for populist parties that direct criticism against immigrants as the cause of threats to security and culture and the source of crime. A materialist interpretation of the trends would suggest that the stronger the welfare-state support, the lower the populist vote. A more culturalist interpretation would challenge the adequacy of this viewpoint, stressing the autonomy of the cultural threat variables.

Research provides support for each argument. Welfare-state levels are quite high in Scandinavia. Denmark and Finland provide extensive assistance to all manner of people, the safety net in those countries is wide, and populist support does go down with welfare-state support.[26] In Sweden, workers with high economic insecurity were more likely to support the populists, and in France lower-income voters with higher housing insecurity and more precarity were more likely to support Marine Le Pen than were people of similar Social Economic Status (SES) who had more stable situations. We see continuous evidence of the interaction of the cultural resentment with economic change; one enables the other.

For many writers, the nationalist right has grown because the social democratic parties have failed to play their proper role as defenders of workers interests.[27] They have not listened to the concerns of the working class faced with the stresses of globalization. People like Bill Clinton and Tony Blair moved the Democrats and Labour to the center. In the financial meltdown of 2008, Barack Obama relied on centrists like Geithner and Ben Bernanke and undertook only modest reform of the financial sector, helping to bail out financial institutions, sending no executives to jail, and providing very limited help to mortgage holders.[28]

The culturalist argument sees the discontent as having to do with cultural psychological issues regarding decenteredness, a challenge to the status location in nation and dislike of immigrants and foreigners. This argument sees the level of protest as connected to the levels of immigration, and to some degree to the nature of political organization and the activities of politicians and the press in nurturing resentments.

Despite high levels of welfare supporting those facing economic dislocation, a substantial nativist protest vote has arisen in Scandinavia, focused primarily on reaction to immigration from eastern Europe, Africa, and the Middle East. Protesters like the support they receive from the state but don't want the benefits to go to "outsiders." They do not rally for neoliberal solutions to society's problems, but for the activist state to help the native population. We see the emergence of a welfare state linked to the right, to the "real" Finns, Swedes, or Danes— a nationalist version quite contrary to what was expected and observed earlier within a center-left embedded liberalism.

An important line of research finds identity threat not correlated with class but with increasing anxiety regarding the engines of change in growing domestic diversity and globalization. Diane Mutz writes that "financial hardships affect the daily lives of working class Americans, but . . . how they respond is based on cultural beliefs that may lead them to scapegoat minority groups."[29] Arlie Hochschild writes vividly and brilliantly about people in Louisiana who resent minorities "cutting in line" ahead of them, though she provides no explanation for why they have these feelings and the history of racism that enables.[30] The importance of framing is widely recognized by many authors, notably George Lakoff.[31] "When salient, immigration has the potential to mobilize otherwise left-leaning voters in a right-leaning direction."[32] When people perceive a threat, they move against immigrants, and left and centrist voters move right. Is it the lower-skilled people who are threatened, or does education capture differences in tolerance, ethnocentrism, cultural capital, sociotropic assessment, or political correctness? Several decades ago, John Goldthorpe and David Lockwood showed that French and British workers interpreted quite differently the meaning of identical improvements in their living situations. For the French worker, the acquisition of a TV was forcibly extracted from the jaws of the reluctant owner/boss; for the British worker, the TV was the result of the ongoing collective bargaining process between union and employer.[33]

The Contemporary Crisis: Forming New Bargains and the Struggle for Defining National Identity

The formation of a postwar consensus embedded liberalism involved an economic agreement located in a compromised national project of the collectivity.

The recent elections in Europe and the United States involve a challenge to the collective imaginary, to the nature of the consensus, and to the definition of the protest itself. In this view, it is not new issues redefining politics, but the rearticulation for older resentments and grievances toward authority, inequality, class, and domination. The same areas of France that once voted for the Communists now vote Le Pen. What is missing in political representation after the demise of the Communists, that induce people to turn in that direction? How do we interpret the weakening of the social democratic parties across Europe? Why do Communists or Socialists not shift to La France Insoumise, the most assertive on the left of the major parties, led by Jean-Luc Mélenchon, rather than to Le Pen's nationalist, anti-immigrant National Front? Why is the label "real" used as a weapon against the left—"Real Americans, Real Finns, Real Danes"—to make a distinction against foreigners? This is a familiar trope in the politics of industrial societies; the right competes with left for loyalty, fighting over the definition of nationhood.

The older left parties embraced a protest against the established order, the elites who dominated politics, the economy, education, and culture. Large numbers of people felt excluded. The decline of fascism and communism did not mean that the resentment of exclusion disappeared. The old left failed to be the alternative that made sense. It ceased being the expression of resentment. It taught integration into the institutions of France, or Italy, or the other established countries, and into the international institutions they supported: the EU and the global trading system. In the face of migration, climate change, and new issues they had less to say. They proposed an international accommodation, which did not assuage resentment. The economic distress explanation certainly captures an important theme. Those whose skills allowed them paths in the new economy were drawn into it, able to develop new identities. Those excluded did not; they were left with resentment and a changed issue space surrounding them. They shifted to new options.

An analogy can be found in the literature on cleavages by S. M. Lipset and Stein Rokkan. Mattei Dogan wrote of a region in France that had a left-right divide in the mid-twentieth century.[34] As he studied its history, he found there had always been a divide. The names changed: left versus right, anticlerical versus clerical, reformist versus strict Catholic, and back two millennia. A deep division found different vehicles of expression, but its structure persisted.

The huge changes engendered by globalization, whipped up by the financial disaster of 2008, aggravated by the social changes of migration and by policy stumbles, opened the door to old arguments of resentment: As Haimuller and Hopkins write, "Existing work focuses on individuals as the unit of analysis, which leads to a misleading dichotomy *cum* debate between cultural and interest-based explanations of populism. Yet we know that there are strong geographic patterns in the populist backlash, and that political choices are powerfully affected by aggregate (local) socio-economic conditions."[35]

Robert Kuttner argues workers have moved right because the left parties have abandoned them. David Autor, David Dorn, and Gordon Hanson show that American workers most impact by Chinese imports voted more strongly for Trump. Thomas Piketty sees major parties dominated by highly educated elites, intellectuals, and business, which abandon the masses.[36]

The old resentments diminished, but angers and exclusions persisted in the red belts of northern France, while in the labor communities of Scotland and Wales a different sense of national identity provided an alternative vehicle for protest, and in Italy and Germany regional and religious identities reemerge. These identities were available for new political directions when faced with immigration and economic decline. The political game is split open. New arguments for integration are needed to knit the pieces together. Creating larger unities, solidarities, and new pacts of consensus requires leadership able to construct bargains and followers able to accept them. In earlier periods these sorts of bargains were constructed by the leaders of organization whose members accepted a degree of deference to their leaders and were connected by different kinds of incentives.[37] The old bargains of 1950 are not working. The same dilemmas of societal accommodation appear in a new context, with some old resentments and some new ones, in a different framework.

THE SOCIAL DEMOCRATIC ORDER AND THE RISE AND DECAY OF DEMOCRACY IN WESTERN EUROPE

Sheri Berman

Western democracies are facing their greatest crisis in decades. Liberal democracy has faltered in eastern Europe, is threatened by populists in western Europe and the United States, and is challenged by resurgent authoritarianism in Russia, China and elsewhere. Reflecting these trends, scholarship and commentary is consumed by debates about "illiberal democracy," "global authoritarianism," and democratic "deconsolidation."[1] Summing up what has become a widespread view, Viktor Orbán, Hungary's current prime minister, once proclaimed: "The era of liberal democracy is over."[2]

At this point, a massive amount of scholarship and political commentary has been devoted to debating whether, and if so, why the era of liberal democracy is coming to an end. Rather than diving directly into such debates, this chapter argues that in order to fully understand what is happening we need to go back and examine the how liberal democracy consolidated in the first place.

Too easily forgotten is that consolidated liberal democracy is a recent phenomenon not merely in eastern but also in western Europe.[3] During the nineteenth and early twentieth centuries consolidated liberal democracies did not exist in Europe. Instead, these years were characterized by war, economic crises, social and political conflict, and innumerable failed attempts at democracy.[4] Given this history and the conditions on the ground in Europe at the end of the World War II, there was every reason to be pessimistic about the fate of democracy in the years ahead.

It is now hard to fathom how thoroughly devastated Europe was in 1945. Surveying the postwar scene, Winston Churchill, for example, asked, "What is Europe now? A rubble heap, a charnel house, a breeding ground of pestilence and hate." As was often the case, Churchill's description was colorful and accurate. During the war the full force of the modern state was mobilized for the purpose of annihilating entire peoples, and the war's human and material costs were greater than anything the world had ever experienced. Estimates range from fifty to eighty million dead, with at least two-thirds of these civilians.[5] World War II was "a war of occupation, of repression, of exploitation and extermination in which soldiers, storm-troopers, and policemen disposed of the daily lives and very existence of tens of millions of . . . peoples." Unlike the First World War the Second was a near-universal experience.[6] Bombing left cities and regions in ruins and tens of millions homeless; it obliterated road, transportation, communication, and food-supply networks.[7] The suffering continued after the war's end.[8] The Soviet army swept through central and eastern Europe, slaughtering any men they came across, and engaged in an unprecedented campaign of violence against women. In Vienna and Berlin, for example, approximately ninety thousand women were raped within a week or so of the arrival of the Red army and hundreds of thousands of women ultimately suffered this fate.[9] Postwar Europe was also plagued by famine and disease. In 1945 the residents of Budapest subsisted on about 550 calories a day, those in Vienna 800, and even in the Netherlands thousands of people starved.[10] In some countries it became commonplace to see women and even children selling their bodies for scraps of food.[11] Conditions in Germany were particularly dire: the last months of the war were the bloodiest by far, and suffering continued after defeat.[12] During 1945 in Berlin as many a quarter of the children under the age of one died, thousands starved, malnutrition and disease were rampant, and about a quarter of the population was homeless.[13] Alongside unprecedented material destruction and suffering, the war also left much of Europe in a state of almost complete political, social, and economic collapse. Governments, schools, civil society, libraries, post offices, newspapers, and markets simply ceased to exist.

Yet despite these conditions, extremism did not flourish and democracy consolidated in western Europe. There were many reasons for this remarkable transformation.

The old order was discredited by the collapse of the interwar years and the war that followed, and groups that had supported antidemocratic regimes and movements in the past were eliminated by the chaos and destruction of the 1940s. As Mark Mazower noted, "Wartime losses tore gaping holes in the social and physical fabric; they provoked bitter memories and angry emotions, but also new challenges and opportunities."[14] This was particularly true in Germany, where old social hierarchies were shattered by the Nazis and the old conservative and Junker elite were disproportionately killed off in large numbers during the war and then dispossessed by the communist regime in the East after it.[15]

In addition to eliminating many social obstacles to democratic consolidation, the war also helped deal with another long-standing impediment to consolidation in Europe: nationalism. One way in which it did this was through the ethnic cleansing that happened during the war—between them, Stalin and Hitler uprooted, transplanted, expelled, deported, and dispersed some thirty million people in 1939–43.[16] And after the war, ethnic cleansing and population transfer continued, rendering many of the countries of central and eastern Europe in particular more ethnically homogenous than they had ever been. To quote Mazower once again, "War, violence and massive social dislocation had turned Versailles's dream of national homogeneity into realities."[17]

The Postwar Order

Changes that occurred during the postwar period at the international, regional, and domestic levels were critical in promoting democratic consolidation in western Europe. The United States played a crucial role in reconstructing new international economic and security orders. Triggered by fears that western Europe could not alone protect itself from Soviet aggression, President Harry Truman committed the United States to defending western Europe and liberal democracy with the Truman Doctrine, and in 1949 NATO was formed, linking western European countries to each other and the United States, and eventually integrating Germany into the western security bloc. The United States also helped construct international economic institutions, including the Bretton Woods system, General Agreement on Tariffs and Trade (GATT), and the International Monetary Fund (IMF), to jumpstart postwar economic reconstruction, promote growth, and tie together western Europe and the United States.

These new American-led international security and economic arrangements were designed to undergird peace and prosperity. They also, along with the Marshall Plan, which required recipient nations to decide together how aid was to be used, contributed to the formation of the second, regional pillar of the postwar order—European integration. Fundamentally, European integration stemmed from the recognition that successful liberal democracy required overcoming challenges too great be solved by the uncoordinated efforts of individual governments acting alone. In particular, reconciling Germany to Europe and vice versa and ensuring postwar economic reconstruction and growth would necessitate cooperation among European nations. This led to the formation of a series of agreements and institutions, beginning with Council of Europe (1949) and the European Coal and Steel Community (1951), that gradually propelled forward the process of European integration.

But however important changes at the international and regional levels were, without changes at the domestic level, democratic consolidation in postwar western Europe would have been difficult if not impossible.

The tragedies of the interwar years and of World War II produced a new commitment among European elites to making democracy work and a new understanding of what it would take to do so. Successful liberal democracy was now understood to require more than changing political institutions and procedures; it required new social and economic arrangements and relationships as well. In particular, the economic crises, inequality, and social divisions that had generated the socioeconomic conflicts and political extremism that had undermined democracy in the past needed to be avoided.

Although it is easy to forget, before 1945 it was widely believed that democracy could not be reconciled with capitalism. Liberals and conservatives generally believed that giving workers, the poor, and the disadvantaged the vote would lead to mob rule, the end of private property, and other horrors. As the British historian and Whig politician Thomas Macaulay, for example, once wrote in response to demands for universal suffrage, "If you grant that, the country is lost. . . . My firm conviction is that, in our country, universal suffrage is incompatible, not only with this or that form of government, and with everything for the sake of which government exists; that it is incompatible with property and that it is consequently incompatible with civilization."[18] Marx agreed with Macauley and other liberals and conservatives that "democracy and capitalism [were] an inherently unstable" combination, given that the poor would use "democracy to expropriate the rich" and that once they did so capitalists would "subvert democracy" rather than give up their property.[19] (Or as another socialist put it, the bourgeoisie would inevitably "resort to bayonets" rather than allow a democratically elected government to threaten their economic power and privileges.)[20]

The interwar years, and Great Depression in particular, where capitalism's failures produced social chaos, conflict, and political extremism seemed to confirm an inherent tension if not conflict between capitalism and democracy. When World War II ended, political actors on both sides of the Atlantic understood that if democracy were going to succeed in Europe, they needed to confront head-on the socioeconomic conflicts and economic crises that capitalism had generated and that had fed extremism and undermined democracy in the past.[21]

In addition, the war profoundly changed many people's views of the appropriate roles of states and markets. All European governments assumed responsibility for managing the economy during the war, and shared wartime suffering fostered national unity and a broad sense that states could and should provide for citizens' basic needs. And finally, Europe's desperate postwar situation, combined with the commanding position of the Soviet Union after the war and the heroic role played by many communist resistance movements during it, along with the sense that capitalism had failed during the 1930s, led many to fear that communism rather than democratic capitalism was the wave of the future. (Indeed, communist parties in western Europe got off to auspicious starts after 1945, receiving much higher shares of the vote almost everywhere than they had before the war and being included in a number of postwar governments as a result.)[22] These experiences and conditions, combined with a broader sense that Europe could not allow itself to fall back into patterns that had led it to ruin in the past, reinforced the belief that a new socioeconomic order capable of ensuring prosperity and social stability and blunting the siren song of extremism was necessary if the democratic wave of 1945 was not to meet the same fate as its predecessors.

Following John Ruggie many, including authors in this volume, characterize the order that emerged as an "embedded liberal" one.[23] Although this may make sense for the international economic component of the postwar order—which is what Ruggie originally used the term to refer to—it is misleading for its domestic pillar. The point of labels is to identify, clarify, and understand, and how we characterize the various components of the postwar order is therefore of more than semantic import. Calling the reconstructed domestic political economies of western European countries "liberal" implies something about their nature and consequences. Moreover, given how central reconstructed domestic political economies were to the consolidation of democracy in postwar Europe, it is critical that we understand their goals and logic. "Liberal," accordingly, is not merely inaccurate, it also obscures what it took to finally make democracy work in Europe.

As I showed in *The Primacy of Politics*, advocating a shift toward a system where democratic states assumed responsibility for overseeing capitalism and protecting citizens from its negative effects had long been the distinguishing feature of the social democratic left—not of liberalism or, for that matter, of Christian democracy, the dominant political force in many European countries during the immediate postwar period.[24] The postwar order should be referred to as "social democratic," in short, because that label fits most clearly with the view of the relationship between states, markets, and society developed by social democrats during the prewar period.

Before 1945 some liberals and Christian democrats recognized problems with capitalism, but neither developed either an ideological profile or a political platform around the idea that it was both possible and desirable for governments to tame capitalism in order to make it compatible with democracy as well as the health and well-being of society, as social democrats did.

Many liberals, as noted above, were wary of democracy. And historically, of course, liberalism was certainly not associated with the idea that unchecked markets were dangerous and that states had the right to intervene in the economy to protect society from their malign effects. A strand of progressive liberalism that arose in the late nineteenth and early twentieth centuries was sympathetic to democracy as well as more cognizant of capitalism's negative consequences than were other forms of liberalism. But progressive liberals generally favored dealing with these negative consequences after the fact. They did not believe that it was either possible or desirable for governments to intervene in markets to prevent negative outcomes or that it was the job of democratic governments to protect and promote the public interest.[25]

Christian democrats, meanwhile, were also generally unsympathetic to democracy during the prewar period. Moreover, though many recognized that capitalism had negative effects, the Christian democratic understanding of these effects differed greatly from that of social democrats (or progressive liberals). In general, the Christian democratic critique of capitalism focused on its tendency to undermine the foundations of a corporate, illiberal society as well as traditional norms and values, rather than stressing, as social democrats did, how it threatened democracy, individual freedom, or the creation of a more just and equal society.

After 1945 the traditional social democratic view of the correct relationship between states and markets was broadly embraced. Not only did it gradually become the dominant view on the left—in contrast to the interwar period, when it faced formidable Marxist and communist foes—but liberals and Christian democrats moved closer to it as well.

The 1947 program of the German Christian Democrats, for example, declared, "The new structure of the German economy must start from the realization that the period of uncurtailed rule by private capitalism is over." In France, meanwhile, the Catholic Mouvement Républicain Populaire declared in its first manifesto in 1944 that it supported a "revolution" to create a state "liberated from the power of those who possess wealth."[26] Even the United States, least affected by the war and most committed to the restoration of a global free trade order, recognized that democratic stability in Europe would require a significant break with the socioeconomic status quo ante. Reflecting this, in his opening speech to the Bretton Woods conference, US Treasury Secretary

Henry Morgenthau noted, "All of us have seen the great economic tragedy of our time. We saw the worldwide depression of the 1930s. . . . We saw bewilderment and bitterness become the breeders of fascism and finally of war." To prevent a recurrence of this phenomenon, Morgenthau argued, national governments would have to be able to do more to protect people from capitalism's 'malign effects.'"[27]

After 1945, accordingly, western European nations began constructing a new social democratic order at the domestic level.[28] This order represented a decisive break with the past. States would not be limited to ensuring that markets could flourish, nor would economic interests be given the widest possible leeway. Instead, after 1945 the state was to become the guardian of society rather than of the economy, and economic imperatives would sometimes have to take a back seat to social ones.

The two most often noted manifestations of this change were Keynesianism and the welfare state. As Jonathan Kirshner's chapter on John Maynard Keynes makes clear, Keynesianism's significance lay in its rejection of the view that markets operated best when left to themselves and its recognition that state intervention in the economy was sometimes necessary to avoid the economic dislocation and crises that could threaten democracy and capitalism. Having lived through the rise of the Soviet Union and the Great Depression, Keynes understood that unchecked markets could be socially and politically dangerous. As Kirshner, echoing Keynes's biographer Robert Skidelsky, notes, "Keynes was quite conscious in seeking an alternative to dictatorship . . . a program on which to fight back against fascism and communism."[29] It is important to stress that Keynes favored a more active role for the state for political as much as for economic reasons. He understood the appeal of communism's insistence that capitalism could not be rescued from its flaws and fascism's insistence that that only a strong, nonliberal state could deal with challenges like Great Depression. Keynes hoped that by designing a "system that held out the prospect that the state could reconcile the private ownership of the means of production with democratic management of the economy" he could convince people that there was a democratic solution to capitalism's downsides.[30]

Like Keynesianism, the welfare state helped transform the relationship between states and markets during the postwar era in ways that helped promote democratic consolidation. Welfare states did not, of course, develop de novo after the war, but they did change quantitively and qualitatively during the postwar period—expanding in scope as well as taking on clearer decommodifying functions.[31] As C. A. R. Crosland noted, after 1945, "it was increasingly regarded as a proper function and indeed obligation of Government to ward off distress and strain not only among the poor but almost all classes of society."[32]

Postwar western European welfare states were significant not only because they protected individuals from economic distress but also because they gave renewed importance to membership in a national community. Because they both required and fostered a sense of kinship and solidarity among citizens, welfare states could only be sustained if individuals believed that ensuring a basic level of well-being for all citizens was a worthy goal. The postwar welfare state contributed to creating a new understanding of citizenship or a new social contract between governments and citizens, with the former committing to ensuring the economic welfare and security of the latter and latter committing to supporting the welfare state and the larger liberal democratic system of which it was a part.[33] Welfare states thereby marked a significant break with a liberal *gesellschaft*—the anomie, dislocation, and atomization that had proved so politically destabilizing during the nineteenth and early twentieth centuries—and a move toward a more communitarian *gemeinschaft* where governments committed to taking care of their citizens. The postwar expansion of welfare states was thus not merely a reflection of a desire to rectify past mistakes but also a deliberate attempt to undercut the support of extremists on the left and right that had played off anomie, dislocation, and atomization in the past in order to undermine support for liberal democracy.

Of course, Keynesianism and welfare states were not the only ways in which postwar European political economies changed. Each European country developed its own set of policies that used the power of the state to protect societies from capitalism's most destructive effects and promote social stability. In France, for example, the Fourth Republic engaged in nationalization and planning, which were designed to ensure economic growth and that "the main sources of common wealth [were] worked and managed not for the profit of a few individuals, but for the benefit of all."[34]

In Britain, where class distinctions remained immensely important up through the interwar years, the war had a significant leveling effect. Food and other essential items were rationed during the war on the basis of need rather than wealth or social standing and the shared suffering caused by war gave an immense boost to social solidarity. As one broadcaster put it, Britain had been "bombed and burned into democracy."[35] Similarly, observing the wartime social changes occurring in Britain, the American war reporter Edward R. Murrow remarked, "You must understand that a world is dying, that old values, the old prejudices, and the old bases of power and prestige are going."[36] Against this backdrop the Beveridge Report appeared in 1942, spurring a postwar commitment by British governments to ensuring "freedom from want." William Beveridge had earlier been a critic of welfare capitalism, but like many others had been converted by the war to a belief that the governments could and should protect citizens from economic suffering and take responsibility for equitable economic development.

After the war Britain expanded its welfare state, committed to full employment, and nationalized parts of the economy.[37]

In Italy, meanwhile, a large state sector was carried over from the fascist period and viewed as part of a broader strategy for using the state to ensure economic growth and social well-being. The idea that democratic governments were responsible for steering the economy and protecting citizens was enshrined in Italy's postwar constitution, which declared the country a democratic republic "founded on labor" and promised that all "economic and social obstacles" to workers' advancement would be demolished. Recognizing the primacy of certain societal goals and needs, the constitution also refrained from according private property the status of "absolute right . . . instead emphasiz[ing] its social obligations and limitations."[38]

In Germany there was a clearer commitment to economic liberalism than in other parts of Europe because of the extreme statism of the Nazis and the more direct influence of the United States. (On the flipside, the West German state inherited from its Nazi predecessor a history of economic planning, crucial infrastructure investments in communications, transport, and key industries, and a business community used to state intervention or coordination—all of which proved useful during the postwar period.)[39] Nonetheless, postwar West German governments also intervened in the economy in myriad ways and made a firm commitment to social protection and stability. The welfare state grew and a number of innovative policies, including codetermination, that gave workers the ability to oversee and in some cases even help direct business decisions and activity (and were accordingly initially opposed by business), eventually helped workers and management come to view themselves as social partners rather than adversaries, thus breaking a pattern that had contributed to economic, social, and political instability in the past.[40]

The most dramatic transformation in the relationship among state, market, and society came in Scandinavia, particularly Sweden. The Swedish state was tasked with promoting growth and equity and protecting society—goals that were seen as complementary rather than contradictory.[41] As Gunnar Adler-Karlsson, a well-known theorist of the postwar Swedish order, noted, "All the parties of the economic process have realized that the most important economic task is to make the national cake grow bigger and bigger, because then everyone can satisfy his demanding stomach with a greater piece of that common cake. When instead, there is strong fighting between the classes in that society, we believe that the cake will often crumble or be destroyed in the fight, and because of this everyone loses."[42]

To achieve these goals, the Swedish state employed a wide range of tools, including planning, manipulating investment funds and fiscal policy, and encouraging cooperation between labor-market partners. (Interestingly, one tool that the Swedish state did not use much was nationalization, which was viewed as economically unnecessary and politically unwise.) But perhaps the two most distinctive features of Sweden's postwar political economy were the Rehn-Meidner model and a universal welfare state, both of which were distinguished by their focus on promoting economic growth, equity, and social solidarity.

The Rehn-Meidner model featured a centralized system of wage bargaining that set wages at what was seen as a just level (which in practice seems to have meant ensuring equal pay for equal work, consistently rising incomes, and improvements for the worse-off to reduce inequality). Wages would be set "too high" for firms that were inefficient or uncompetitive and "too low" for firms that were highly productive and competitive. Firms in the former category faced the choice of either improving or going out of business, whereas those in the latter would increase their profitability (because the wages they paid would be less than they could otherwise afford). To compensate workers who lost their jobs, the state committed to retraining and relocating them for new ones. The system aimed to promote business efficiency and productivity while generating a more equal wage structure and social solidarity.[43]

The Swedish welfare state provided a range of programs and benefits that dwarfed those of most other welfare states and socialized—i.e., brought into the public sector—services like health care, education, and child care in order to ensure the equitable distribution of resources and the universal nature and high quality of social programs was designed to ensure that the welfare state retained the support of a broad cross-sector of the population.[44]

For these and other reasons, Sweden was long recognized as a social democratic showplace. But though it may have been at one end of the spectrum, the postwar domestic order in western Europe more broadly marked a significant break with the past. Capitalism remained, but it was capitalism of a very different type than had existed before the war—one tempered and limited by liberal democratic states committed to a social contract that promised citizens protection from its downsides. This social democratic order worked remarkably well. Despite fears after the war that it might take decades for Europe to recover economically, by the early 1950s most of Europe had easily surpassed interwar economic figures and the thirty years after 1945 were Europe's fastest period of growth ever.[45]

Perhaps even more impressive than the postwar domestic order's economic effects were its political ones. Social stability and a willingness to compromise— things that liberal democracy requires and that Europe had so often previously lacked—became possible. The restructured political economies of the postwar era offered something to everyone. As Peter Gourevitch notes in this volume with regard to the postwar order more generally, social democratic political economies succeeded because they were built on compromise and consensus. Various groups made trade-offs, holding firm to key fundamental commitments but giving up on others. More specifically, economic growth and growing economic equality facilitated compromises between workers and capitalists and poor and rich, and attenuated the view, so prevalent during the nineteenth and early twentieth centuries, that capitalism was a zero-sum game.[46] As Claus Offe put it,

> What was at issue in class conflicts [after 1945] was no longer the mode of production, but the volume of distribution, not control but growth, and this type of conflict was particularly suited for being processed on the political plan through party competition because it does not involve "either/or" questions, but questions of a "more or less" or "sooner or later" nature. Overarching this limited type of conflict, there was a consensus concerning basic priorities, desirabilities and values of the political economy, namely economic growth and social . . . security.[47]

Accordingly, the left- and right-wing extremism that plagued late nineteenth- and early twentieth-century Europe diminished; good times pushed parties and voters back toward the political center and support for liberal democracy. The war largely discredited the fascist and National Socialist right, but communism was powerful after 1945 in parts of western Europe. Over the postwar period, however, western European communist parties moderated; even where they remained a significant electoral force, as in Italy and France, they gradually committed to playing by the democratic rules of the game, distanced themselves from the Soviet Union, and ceased engaging in violent behavior.[48] With right-wing extremism largely gone and left-wing extremism moderated, during the postwar decades western European party systems became dominated by parties of the center-left and center-right (generally social democratic and Christian democratic, respectively) that appealed to a broad, cross-class constituency and accepted the democratic rules of the game.

In short, by reshaping the relationship between states, markets, and society, the social democratic postwar order helped underpin democratic consolidation in western Europe. It helped mitigate and moderate social divisions and conflict and promote economic growth and equality, thereby dulling the appeal of extremism. It undercut liberal fears that democracy "would lead by necessity to tyranny and expropriation by the poor and uneducated,"[49] Marxist assertions that giving the poor and workers the vote would lead inexorably to the end of bourgeois society, and fascism's and National Socialism's claim that only dictatorships could produce national cohesion. The emergence of the social democratic postwar order, in short, played a crucial role in making liberal democracy the norm rather than the exception in western Europe for the first time since the modern struggle for democracy began in 1789.

The Unraveling of the Postwar Order

As Frank Gavin and other authors in this volume discuss, despite its success the postwar order began unraveling during the 1970s. After decades of economic success, Europe and much of the rest of the West was hit by a noxious mix of inflation, unemployment, and slow growth—stagflation. These economic problems provided an opening for a neoliberal right that had been organizing and thinking about what it saw as the drawbacks of the social democratic aspects of the postwar order and was ready with explanations for the West's problems as well as solutions to them.[50] As Milton Friedman, the intellectual godfather of this movement put it, "Only a crisis—actual or perceived—produces real change. When that crisis occurs, the actions that are taken depend on the ideas that are lying around. That, I believe, is our basic function: to develop alternatives to existing policies, to keep them alive and available until the politically impossible becomes politically inevitable."[51]

The shift toward neoliberalism was helped along by the collapse of communism after 1989. With the communist threat gone, the right was further emboldened to attack the social democratic order that many had previously viewed as the lesser evil. More generally, in a tragic inversion of the postwar pattern where a recognition of the dangers of uncontrolled capitalism was widely accepted, communism's collapse led to a triumphalist belief across the political spectrum in the inherent superiority and stability of capitalist democracy.

This was clearly true in the economics profession, which had largely abandoned Keynes's concern about capitalism's propensity toward disequilibrium and tendency to cause political and social instability. (As Robert Lucas asserted in his presidential address to the American Economic Association in 2003, "The central problem of depression prevention has been solved.")[52] Economists and think tanks helped spread neoliberal views of capitalism and the correct relationship between states, markets, and societies on both sides of the Atlantic.[53]

So pervasive was this process of ideological diffusion that it swept over parties of the left as well the right. Even ostensibly left politicians like Tony Blair and Bill Clinton argued that "the old battles between state and market" had become outdated and that rather than being wary overlords of capitalism, as their social democratic predecessors had understood themselves to be, politicians were now essentially technocrats, managing a system that more or less worked well.[54]

Reflecting this, by the end of twentieth century the Keynesian economists who dominated economic policymaking within most left parties during the postwar period had been replaced by "trans-national finance-oriented economists" and products of neoliberal think tanks who viewed themselves as interpreters of markets and saw their mission in technocratic, efficiency terms—urging the left to embrace globalization, deregulation, welfare-state retrenchment, and other reforms.[55]

The results of these shift were predictable. Western Europe's success after 1945 was predicated on the assertion that the democratic state could temper or even eliminate capitalism's dangerous consequences and promote both growth and equality. But by the end of the twentieth century capitalism was generating the opposite: slow growth and rising inequality.

The unraveling of the postwar social democratic order had negative political consequences as well. Citizens grew resentful of the political elites, parties, and institutions (including the European Union) viewed as responsible for grow-ing economic problems. Hardest hit were social democratic and other center-left parties, because a defense of the social democratic view of the relationship between states, markets, and society in general and a defense of those most negatively impacted by capitalism in particular had been central to their tra-ditional profiles and identities. The watering-down or abandonment of these profiles and identities during the late twentieth and early twenty-first centuries rendered these parties unable to take advantage of the resentment and anger that materialized as the negative economic consequences of neoliberalism became increasingly apparent. The 2008 financial crisis aggravated these trends, sharp-ening popular frustration with neoliberalism and the elites and parties that had embraced it.[56]

With the center-left no longer able to capture growing popular discontent, a golden opportunity arose for an enterprising political force. This force turned out to be populism. When right-wing populist parties began emerging in the 1980s and 1990s, they supported free markets and opposed high taxes and state intervention. But recognizing the space left open by the center-left's abandon-ment of the social democratic view of capitalism, in the early 2000s right-wing populist parties shifted course, criticizing globalization and the loss of state sovereignty, and embracing what is sometimes called "welfare chauvinism" (the idea that the main question regarding the welfare state is less its size than who gets to enjoy its benefits: not immigrants and refugees but "native-born" citizens).

In addition to providing populists with an opportunity to exploit growing economic discontent, as center-left parties converged with their traditional center-right counterparts on economic issues, social and cultural issues were pushed to the forefront of political competition.[57] Many studies have noted that, over recent decades, economic issues have become less salient in almost all European countries."[58] This benefited right-wing populists, who have consistently focused on social and cultural issues, particularly immigration and national identity. These issues tend, moreover, to divide center-left voters while uniting far-right voters. They also touch on questions of morality and identity and have a zero-sum nature, making them less amenable to the compromise and bargaining that lay at the heart of democracy.

Another consequence of the decline of the social democratic postwar order has been a return of the belief that democracy and capitalism are in tension if not inexorable conflict. On the left, academics have published articles and books with titles like "Is Capitalism Compatible with Democracy?"[59] Wolfgang Streeck, for example, perhaps the most forceful of capitalism's contemporary critics, has argued that "disequilibrium and instability" are the "rule rather than the exception" in capitalist societies. There is a "basic underlying tension" between capitalism and democracy; it is a "'utopian' fantasy to assume they can be reconciled."[60] Outside of the academy increasingly vociferous and mobilized far-left movements question the viability and desirability of capitalism as well.[61]

In response to growing attacks on capitalism, few on the right have gone as far as their prewar predecessors in openly calling for an end to democracy, but some have made clear their skepticism of democracy and their sympathy for illiberal authoritarians like Viktor Orbán; others have simply thrown in their lot with populists like Trump.[62] As the *Financial Times*'s Ed Luce put it, some elites "see Trump as a shelter from the populist hurricanes battering at their estates." (When asked how he could justify supporting a politician with clearly illiberal and antidemocratic tendencies, Lloyd Blankfein replied, "At least Trump has been good for the economy.")[63]

It was only during the postwar era that successful liberal democracy became the norm in western Europe. The success of liberal democracy was predicated on the rise of new international, regional, and domestic orders. This chapter has focused on the latter—the transformation of western European political economies along the lines advocated by late nineteenth- and early twentieth-century social democrats after 1945.

These social democratic political economies undergirded western Europe's remarkable recovery from the war; economic growth exploded, inequality diminished, and social mobility increased. Economic progress helped spur a political turnaround. Beginning with the French revolution, innumerable democratic transitions occurred in Europe, but it was only after 1945 that liberal democracy became the norm. By alleviating the socioeconomic conflict and zero-sum politics that fed the rise of extremism and undermined democracy during the pre–World War II period, social democratic political economies facilitated the consolidation of democracy in postwar western Europe.

Alongside recognizing this order's critical economic and political consequences, it is important to remind ourselves of how optimistic, even idealistic, the beliefs underpinning this order were. In contrast to liberals, who believed that rule by the masses would lead to the end of private property, tyranny of the majority, and other horrors, and thus favored limiting the reach of democratic politics, and communists who argued that a better world could only emerge with the destruction of capitalism and bourgeois democracy, social democrats insisted on democracy's immense transformative and progressive power. It could maximize capitalism's upsides, minimize its downsides, and create more prosperous and just societies.

As discussed above, as the order based on these beliefs unraveled during the late twentieth and early twenty-first centuries, many of the problems characterizing European societies and polities during the pre–World War II period, including growing socioeconomic conflict and extremism, returned. Right-wing populism, perhaps the most obvious symptom of democracy's current problems, is in many ways the polar opposite or evil twin of the social democratic consensus of the postwar decades. Right-wing populists peddle a politics of fear—of crime, terrorism, unemployment, economic decline, and the loss of national values and tradition—and assert that other parties are leading their countries to disaster. Populists and their voters are also extremely pessimistic; they believe the past was better than the present and are anxious about the future.[64]

It is important to remember that postwar order was explicitly designed to counteract the negative dynamics that had led to extremism and scuttled democracy in the past by providing the context within which democratic governments could respond to demands of their citizens. Although it is of course true that twenty-first-century Western societies, economies, and polities differ from their mid-twentieth-century counterparts, the social democratic postwar order's basic insight—that without reconfiguring the relationship among states, markets, and society to ensure that citizens were protected from the negative effects of capitalism, political dissatisfaction and extremism would emerge—remains valid. This is not because the only problems European countries must solve are economic—although increasing growth, diminishing economic and geographic inequalities, and improving social mobility are crucial. It is also because economic problems create fertile ground for the exploitation of social and cultural grievance. It is much easier for extremists to whip up antiminority sentiment during times when people fear for their and their children's economic future and worry about access to government and public resources.

In short, if democratic political actors cannot restore the postwar order or create a new one that will enable governments to come up with effective responses to contemporary challenges like economic inequality, slow growth, and disconcerting social and cultural change, extremism and democratic dissatisfaction will continue to rise—just as those who lived through the interwar years and helped reconstruct Europe after World War II would predict.

CALIFORNIA DREAMING

The Crisis and Rebirth of American Power in the
1970s and Its Consequences for World Order

Francis J. Gavin

The American-created and American-led liberal international order appears to
be in a steep, potentially terminal decline. If true, how did this happen to a set of
arrangements that the editors of this volume point out was, despite its blemishes,
"successful to an extent that would have been far beyond the most wildly optimistic hopes of its founders"? At first blush, its demise is a puzzle. Arising from
the horrors of revolution, the Great Depression, and World War II, what John
Ruggie famously called "embedded liberalism" led to the rise of the social welfare
state to ameliorate domestic woes, international arrangements to stabilize global
economic relations, and a rough intellectual consensus about the relationship of
politics to economics, society, and the individual.[1]

It is widely agreed that the pillars of postwar order faced sharp challenges in
the 1970s. As Jonathan Kirshner highlights in his chapter in this volume, both
the foundational "middle way" ideas of John Maynard Keyes and the institutional
arrangements he helped create—the Bretton Woods economic order—were
besieged. Mark Blyth explains the origins and consequences of this attack, emanating from monetarist, University of Chicago–style economics, which helped
push the American-led order toward what he argues was the less promising, neoliberal order that has, to his mind, marked international relations since at least
the early 1980s. Rawi Abdelal has a somewhat more generous view of this shift,
arguing that "the economic malaise of the 1970s led policymakers and politicians to conclude that the Keynesian consensus had its own intolerable risks and

unmanageable consequences." He believes that what emerged in the 1980s and beyond generated both benefits and burdens. Regardless of how one assesses the global economic changes wrought by the tumultuous 1970s, the decade had important domestic consequences. As Sheri Berman points out, the shift to neoliberalism that began in the 1970s helped to undermine the social democratic consensus that she argues was the crucial element for the impressive success of western Europe in the decades after World War II.

My chapter augments this analysis but goes in a different direction. Like others in this volume, I agree that the 1970s were a crucial if often underappreciated period of national and global transformation, with profound consequences for the postwar order that resonate today. Similarly to Ilene Grabel, I recognize both the peril and promise of such economic, political, and social disorder. Although the disruptions and messiness of the 1970s came at some cost, highlighted in several chapters in the book, it also helped inspire innovation from unexpected places and directions.

Unlike other analyses, however, this chapter does not focus on the postwar institutional or even political arrangements that were under pressure. Instead, I argue that American society underwent profound changes during this critical decade, brought on by often amorphous but powerful technological and sociocultural forces that ultimately spread globally. Using 1970s California as both a historical focal point and a metaphor, I suggest that these changes transformed core elements of how human beings lived and understood themselves and their connection to the world around them, in ways that ultimately may have been more consequential than concurrent shifts in political or economic institutions associated with the postwar liberal order's decline. I acknowledge up front that this is a challenging argument to make, as identifying the causes and consequences of changing patterns of mores, identity, and social purpose can be difficult—certainly harder than charting the rise and demise of economic and political bureaucracies and practices. Ultimately, however, I believe these powerful forces may hold a key to better understanding our current, complex moment.

Citizen X

Imagine a Citizen X, born sometime in the 1990s, spending Saturday evening in her high-rise. Although she was born abroad, she is an American citizen and embraces American culture and values. X is multiethnic and lives in Vancouver, or perhaps Singapore—no, it's Helsinki, after some time in Buenos Aires.

It doesn't matter—her identity is more closely attuned to her profession than to her ethnic identity or geographic location, despite the fact that the company she works for is headquartered in Menlo Park, California, and she works from her rented home (and local cafes), flying to the corporate hub and her clients around the world whenever she needs to. Her day was a good one; after writing a bit of code in the morning for an iPhone app she is developing, X took the hot new exercise class at her gym, met up with friends at the trendy Japanese-Mexican fusion gastro pub, and saw a comedy show performed by the cutting-edge lesbian from Lagos whom everyone is talking about. She has opened up some excellent South African wine she purchased online and internally debates the end-of-evening activities. Stream a movie? Use bitcoin or shift other assets around in her stock portfolio? Watch porn? Use Tinder or Grindr to make a connection? Unlike her father or grandfather, Citizen X thinks very little about the International Monetary Fund, military service, geopolitics, industrial-labor relations, nuclear deterrence, or the social welfare state. She is vaguely aware that the United States and China have, to her mind, regrettable disputes over issues ranging from intellectual property theft to different views on human rights. A military confrontation, to say nothing of the kind of fully mobilized war that marked much of human history, would strike Citizen X and her friends as an absurd tragedy.

The world Citizen X inhabits was inconceivable before 1970. Few people worked abroad, and their identity was closely tied to the nation and even the locality they grew up in. As a woman, X's current career would have been unthinkable, and her life likely shaped by an early marriage, children, and homemaking. Her country was also much different. At the start of the 1970s, the United Sates defined power and purpose much like states had for centuries and focused on the health and capacity of the state, its industrial production, and its military might. In the midst of a disastrous war in Vietnam and economic and political troubles at home, the picture generated by those variables was not a bright one. As the decade unfolded, the United States appeared to face steep economic and geopolitical challenges. Domestic consensus about America and its role in the world collapsed in the wake of the Vietnam War and Watergate, and sociocultural tensions exploded in ways that appeared to threaten the republic. These events, combined with geopolitical uncertainty, the seemingly increasing strength of the Soviet Union, a crisis in governance, and the end of the dollar-dominated Bretton Woods system made the future for America's role in the world seem bleaker than at any time in the twentieth century. Stagnation and decline appeared to be the most likely future for the country. The liberal world order that the United States had constructed in the years after World War II was falling apart.

America in the 1970s is an interesting puzzle. Within recent memory, the United States had been economically and geopolitically dominant. And it was to return to economic and geopolitical primacy soon after the decade ended. But the 1970s represented a trough, a low point, a period of pessimism and malaise. It was also, once again, a time of unexpected turbulence in the world order, sandwiched between decades of relative peace, prosperity, and stability—what Peter Katzenstein and Kirshner aptly label an "untidy interregnum." It is also a decade that was long ignored by analysts, only generating greater interest from scholars in recent decades.[2] This interest has pulled in a larger public, perhaps because of what people see as similarities to American domestic and international politics in the 2020s. These issues all make the 1970s in the United States a period well worth reexamining.[3]

I would add another reason for exploring that decade—to better understand where Citizen X and her world came from. In the midst of what seemed to be decline and even chaos in America's domestic and international politics, transformative new forces and factors were emerging. Many of them emerged from the most populous state in the Union, facing the great Pacific Ocean: California. Some of these dynamics were technological and economic, like the rise of Silicon Valley and its dominance in computing, or the emergence of the great California shipping ports, like Los Angeles and Long Beach, on the back of growing trade with Asia and new shipping-container technology. Other examples were more in the realm of how people ate, laughed, and thought about their bodies and human sexuality. Although the causal origins of many of these forces are mysterious and their consequences uncertain, on some of the most basic categories of human potential, expression, and freedom, something important if elusive took place during the 1970s, symbolized by changes emerging from the so-called Golden State. Although these economic, technological, and sociocultural disjunctures were significant in themselves, and well worth further reflection, I tentatively suggest they might also challenge us to rethink how we discuss and evaluate the disconcerting situation that the United States finds itself in today.

This chapter identifies aspects of this new world and ponders its consequences. It was the product of a profound and unusual set of disruptions—some connected, others seemingly not—that began during the 1970s. These changes encompassed technological innovations, shifting norms and practices, and new ways of understanding and actualizing lived human experience, individualism, and identity.

Several caveats. First, though many of these forces emerged from the state of California, others did not; California is both historical locus and metaphor for this change, capturing the spirit and symbolism of such change.[4] Second, though the forces and phenomena captured in the phrase "California Dreaming" are, I argue, consequential, drawing causal arrows—suggesting both what generated these forces and how they affected the health and vitality of the postwar liberal world order—is not always easy. Third, there is tension within these forces, both separately and collectively, making normative judgments about their affects, positive or negative, potentially contentious. What one analyst might see as a story about individual rights and self-realized identity, innovation, wealth generation, and adaptability, another might see as a tale of greed, communal dissolution, environmental disaster, and inequality.[5]

That said, the California Dreaming story matters, for at least four reasons.

First, what happened in California in the 1970s played an outsized role in creating the world we live in today—both in the United States and in large parts of the globe—for better or worse. It is not an exaggeration to say this was a historical shift on par with the changes wrought by the industrial revolution in the late eighteenth through the nineteenth centuries. The means of producing wealth moved from a domestically based, mass, industrialized economy to a more decentralized system focused on just-in-time manufacturing, sensitive and integrated global supply chains, complex finance, and, especially, revolutionary information and communication technology.[6] Personal identity shifted away from fixed characteristics and affiliation with large, inflexible histories and organizations— ethnic origin, political parties, places of worship, unions, corporations, and communities—to curated, flexible, often autonomous conceptions of the self, based on individual preferences and tastes. Demographics were upended; where and how people lived and with whom they cohabited, transformed, as the structure and composition of both family units and communities evolved dramatically. Politics became more microtargeted and focused as much on cultural issues as on the socioeconomic concerns that dominated the first three-quarters of the twentieth century. Everything from markets to culture to identity to politics became fluid, disaggregated, and disintermediated from legacy institutions, shaped by historically unprecedented choice and impermanence.

There were many benefits to this transformation. Enormous amounts of wealth were generated. Tolerance of difference increasingly became the norm. Diversity was celebrated as a positive attribute. Global economic and cultural interaction intensified. Innovation exploded, technology dramatically increased access to vast amounts of knowledge and information, and communication became much easier and cheaper. The choices available to the newly empowered individual, from travel to what she ate or worshiped to how she earned her living to what she laughed at or to whom or even if she married, was unparalleled.

There were also obvious downsides to this world. New wealth was spread unevenly, inequality worsened, and the super wealthy pushed even the middle class out of California's cities. Despite new attention to the environment, the emerging California economy and lifestyle had negative ecological ramifications. Although entertainment and cultural options became more diverse, they did not necessarily become more sophisticated. California foreshadowed the increase in the use of illegal drugs and its crippling consequences. It also witnessed a surge in crime and perhaps more devastatingly, responded with draconian criminal justice policies that disproportionately targeted minority communities. Even the most positive developments—the rise of tolerance and the celebration of diversity—engendered a fierce counterreaction and generated the culture wars frame that has dominated politics ever since. California arguably inaugurated what the scholar Daniel Rodgers labeled the "Age of Fracture," which has left American politics deeply splintered and polarized.[7]

The second reason the California Dreaming story matters is that it highlights the existence of competing histories and the importance of understanding them. Conventional wisdom about the United States during the 1970s concentrates on malaise, chaos, and American decline. It focuses on the failings of traditional economic and political institutions, largely on the Eastern Seaboard of the United States, particularly New York City and Washington DC. The California Dreaming story, noted above, is not uniformly positive. It is, however, a dynamic story of American growth, rebirth, and reimagination. The historical sketch presented here focuses on different actors, processes, causes, time horizons, and outcomes. In this historical retelling, culture and technology matter as much as politics and, over time, intersect with each other. Change, though dramatic, often was hard to recognize in real time, unlike in the more traditional domestic and international economic and political narrative of the 1970s. Time horizons are not measured as much by shifting presidential administrations or foreign wars as by new technologies and popular mass entertainment events. To be clear, these competing narratives can both be true, and are obviously inextricably linked. But by focusing our lens on only the most conventional political and economic history, we may risk missing the profoundly important tectonic forces shaping the world.

This observation brings up the third reason the California Dreaming story is important. When assessing the how political and economic order developed in the postwar world, both domestically and globally, California Dreaming forces us to expand the aperture of what matters. A history that focuses on legacy institutions, be it the US Congress or the World Bank, will not suffice. The history of Apple Computer or the rising influence of Hollywood tells us as much, if not more, about the rise, fall, and rebirth of the postwar order than a microanalysis of any G-7 summit or annual World Bank meeting. California Dreaming should force us to think in more creative ways about the actors and agents that matter, what time horizons shape our current world, how to locate complex historical causality, and perhaps most importantly, how to reimagine how we understand power. Power in international relations has often been understood as fixed, kinetic, and material, built on mass-industrialized economies that could convert its economic assets into the capacity to build armies and navies and conquer territory. But the 1970s inaugurated the world we live in today, which looks nothing like the 1870s. What began to matter is what Peter Katzenstein and his coauthors has labeled protean power:

> It is diffuse in its effects and lacks an identifiable core as it operates from multiple, often uncoordinated sites. Ultimately, this power can enhance political conformity and social stability while also engendering political innovation and social change. Protean power links actors and networks with distinctive discursive structures. It comes into effect through creative individual or collective actions that tap into the distinctive capacities of and relationships among dispersed actors that do not necessarily mirror the apparent distribution of control power or the propensity to use it.[8]

Fourth, revisiting the 1970s through this perspective also allows us to reconsider what we mean by world order. As several of the chapters in this volume make clear, the decade served as an interregnum. On the economic side, Bretton Woods had collapsed, but the so-called neoliberal period of intensified globalization had yet to appear. The same was true for international security. Global politics, vacillating among détente, malaise, and competition, looked like neither the frightening bipolar clash of the 1950s and 1960s nor the unfettered American unipolarity that was to come. Similar to today, the 1970s were a disjuncture, a pivot from one world to another, the seeds of transformation easily clouded by the sense of uncertainty and even decline.[9]

California Dreaming is not only an origin story. It also reminds us that the often unsettling things that we see on in the headlines may not be the historical forces that matter most in shaping the order of the future.

The 1970s Reconsidered

The standard narrative of the United States and world order in the 1970s presents a bleak picture. Geopolitically, the Cold War competition had settled into an uncomfortable stalemate. Although strategic arms control and détente lessened the possibility of great power war, such stability had come at a cost: recognizing the political and moral equivalence of a communist, authoritarian, and often ruthless great power, the Soviet Union. The Helsinki Accords had accepted the postwar boundaries of Europe and implicitly acknowledged a pressing Soviet empire in the once independent states of eastern Europe. Western Europe, mired in its own political and economic frustration, increasingly distrusted the policies of its transatlantic patron, the United States. Although the threat of great power war receded, murderous interstate and intrastate conflict raged on every continent.

The international economic order was in even greater disarray. The Bretton Woods system of fixed exchange rates backed by dollar-gold convertibility was unilaterally suspended by the United States in 1971 and abandoned in 1973. Resource shocks, especially dramatic increases in the price of oil, dragged down growth. Currency volatility, debt crisis, inflation, and stagnation were all worsened by a lack of global coordination, and protectionism and economic nationalism increasingly framed politics. Global institutions intended to manage these crises, such as the International Monetary Fund, the World Bank, and even the United Nations, were sidelined or not up to the task.

The challenges to order were greatest within the anchor and author of the postwar system, the United States. The disastrous US military intervention in Vietnam, undermined the postwar consensus on both America's role in the world and its supposed goodness. Richard Nixon's deep political corruption, most visibly revealed in the Watergate scandal, was less anomalous than representative of national, state, and local politics throughout the country. A crime and drug epidemic was destroying America's largest cities. Racial, ethnic, gender, and class divisions polarized and poisoned America's politics. America's economy suffered the twin plagues of inflation and unemployment as traditional manufacturing collapsed. The technological innovation needed to increase productivity seemed far more likely to come from the booming economies of East Asia, led by Japan, or even western Europe.

To contemporary observers, this grim narrative spelled a slow but inevitable death, both to the postwar liberal order and to the leading role of its architect, the United States. Simultaneously, however, powerful, tectonic forces were at work that would dramatically upend this narrative.

By the end of the 1970s, the outlines of a new and completely unanticipated way of living had begun to take shape. How at least certain people—first in parts of the United States, then, as the decades moved on, in large parts of the world— ate and drank, met partners, communicated, and worked was changing. Certain types of freedom, opportunity, and possibilities to realize human potential expanded enormously. For countless others, this way of living became an aspiration, while for still others, it reflected a disconcerting rupture with a more stable, understandable past. Many of these changes were driven by profound changes in the international system, the global economy, and the technology that shaped it. An equally important and interrelated set of changes, however, came in how people thought about their identity, their individuality, and what it means to be human. These changes were not the result of decisions taken in world capitals, least of all Washington DC. Rather, they emerged in California.[10]

California: Technology, Socioeconomics, and Culture

Perhaps the most consequential shift was the disruptive emergence of Silicon Valley as a hub for profound technological change. This was preceded and accelerated by a less well recognized development: the emergence of California as a defense and aerospace superpower. The 1960s and 1970s saw Southern California, in particular, become the hub for innovative companies and institutions in this field, ranging from the California Institute of Technology and NASA's Jet Propulsion Laboratory to Northrop Grumman. This less noted but crucial development created the hardware engineering culture in places like Pasadena that complimented the north. This not only drew technological talent to California but also highlighted the crucial if often controversial relationship between the national security state and the more libertarian, hippie culture that emerged in companies like Apple (a tension that continues in Silicon Valley tech superpowers like Google to this day).

That said, if the world we live in is defined by the digital revolution, and in profound changes in the way we use computers to navigate life, this change began, expanded, and intensified in an area that is part of the greater San Francisco area, around Santa Clara Valley. It did not simply do things like increase computing power and capabilities, but first through Apple, begin to put these tools in the hands of individuals, rather than at the service of larger, collective organization. It also connected these technologies to increased levels of access to information, unmediated through the state or other collective organizations, providing individual independence and communication. The Silicon Valley experience also transformed how innovation was encouraged and financed, with the rise of venture capital and start-ups. A culture of entrepreneurship, which celebrated risk and tolerated failure, took hold. The consequences for America's power position in the world were undeniable. Many of these technologies were related to and accelerated a revolution in military affairs that emerged in the 1990s and have provided the United States with both strategic and battlefield advantages ever since. It also created both immeasurable wealth and soft power as Silicon Valley's success became a model that cities and nations around the world attempted to emulate.

This is what the historian Margaret O'Mara calls "the American Revolution," which combined "entrepreneurship *and* government, new *and* old economies, far-thinking engineers *and* the many nontechnical thousands who made their innovation possible." As she points out, "few people had heard of 'Silicon Valley'" before a "journalist decided to give it that snappy nickname in early 1971." At that point, "America's centers of manufacturing, of finance, of politics" were three thousand miles away, and "Boston outranked Northern California in money raised, markets ruled, and media attention attracted." Ten years later, the situation had transformed, creating the foundation for the radically different world we live in today. This "only in America" story that disrupted the world was born of a particular "lucky place and time: the West coast of the United States in that remarkable quarter of a century after the end of the Second World War."[11]

A year after the term Silicon Valley was coined, the firm Kleiner Perkins Caufield & Byers opened offices in Menlo Park, becoming the leading entity of a new way of financing emerging technology that avoided traditional and more conservative banks by pooling venture capital. California also hosted the nation's first discount airline, Pacific Coast Airlines, whose cheap fares in the unregulated state market helped inspire the Carter administration's deregulation of the airline industry in 1978, transforming the cost and availability of air travel.

A more mundane but perhaps equally important example is the container-shipping revolution, which emerged in several places but turned the ports of California—and in particular, the adjacent ports of Los Angeles and Long Beach—into global trading powerhouses.[12] Trade as a percentage of American gross national product was low in 1970. But as the restrictions on capital and finance were lifted and global economic interactions exploded, the ports of California—utilizing the new, less labor-intensive technologies of containers and container ships—became the hub in the massively increased economic interaction between the United States and the rising economies of East Asia. These included, first, Japan, then the Pacific Tigers, and then China.

A force that combined economic power and American soft power was the Hollywood film and television industry. Hollywood had always made entertainment for the world. But in the mid-1970s, the American film industry began to produce blockbusters on a new scale with increased global reach. The movies *Jaws* and *Star Wars* began this trend, and the volume of film receipts, nationally but especially globally, has increased ever since.[13] Post-1970s Hollywood powerfully influenced tastes, fashions, and ideas around the world. And despite great efforts, no other national film industry has been able to approach Hollywood's power.

A similar conflation of economic and cultural power fueled the rise of Napa and Sonoma Valleys' wine industry.[14] Wine was first grown in those areas in the eighteenth century, and by the late nineteenth century, a wine industry existed. Georges Latour protégé Andre Tchelistcheff moved to Napa Valley in the late 1930s and introduced new techniques. But throughout most of the twentieth century, Americans were not heavy consumers of wine. Nor were American wines seen as comparable in quality to those made in Europe. In the 1960s and 1970s, a group of innovators led by Robert Mondavi transformed California winemaking. The quality of Golden State wines was demonstrated during a 1976 wine test in Paris—captured in the book and film *Judgement at Paris*—when a group of California whites dominated the top rankings and the gold medal for red wine was awarded to the 1973 Stag's Leap.[15]

These are the obvious manifestations of the energy and innovation emerging from California during the 1970s, which upended American society and eventually large parts of the globe. But they are not the only ones. In 1969, then governor Ronald Reagan signed the nation's first no-fault divorce law, fundamentally altering American family dynamics. California developed some of the first legal protections against discrimination in housing and employment, including an early law (1978) protecting pregnant women from termination. How humor was generated and employed changed in this period. When the popular late-night-show host Johnny Carson moved his show from New York City to Burbank, California, California became the capital for a modern stand-up comedy, which aimed at subjects ranging from gender and race relations to politics to routine observations. Although much of this humor upended polite norms and challenged traditional authority and belief, it became enormously popular.[16] The Comedy Store in Los Angeles trained a generation of comedians whose humor transformed how and at what people laughed.

Human bodies and identities were not immune to these California changes. San Francisco clothing store Levi Strauss went public in 1971, moving from providing blue jeans to cowboys to creating a global brand that became part of a universal uniform. San Francisco also became the global epicenter for a gay culture and lifestyle that was no longer kept hidden. It developed as a nascent political force with gay advocate Harvey Milk's election to the San Francisco Board of

Supervisors (and his tragic assassination). A fine meal in an American restaurant before the 1970s likely consisted of surf and turf. Alice Waters, using fresh ingredients (from places like the Corti Brothers' supermarket in Sacramento), transformed the American palette with her Berkeley restaurant, Chez Panisse.[17] Its success spawned successors everywhere and marked the birth of the modern foodie restaurant. Before 1970, specific exercise regimens were rare, and exercise in public was even rarer. Professional athletes were warned off weightlifting for fear it would damage their health. Gold's Gym and the muscle pen of Venice Beach became the models for the ubiquitous health clubs now seen throughout the world.[18] The San Fernando Valley became the capital of a booming global trade in pornography, films and photos showing human sexuality in ways that were unthinkable before 1970, a phenomenon captured in the Paul Thomas Anderson's 1997 film *Boogie Nights*.

As part of a nation of immigrants, California's role in welcoming and resisting people from around the globe was crucial. The Latino influence throughout California preceded but accelerated in the 1970s. Less recognized was the dramatic increase in immigration from East and Southeast Asia. California became home to the largest diaspora of ethnic Chinese, Filipinos, and, after the end of the war in Vietnam, refugees from Southeast Asia. California, more than any part of the country, reflected the profound changes in the ethnic composition of the nation first made possible by President Lyndon B. Johnson's 1965 immigration reform. California also became, from the 1970s onward, ground zero for intense political fights over immigration policy.

Immigration was not the only way in which California foreshadowed divided national politics. California met the rise in crime with draconian policies that fell disproportionately on minority communities and saw a massive build-up in prisons that was soon emulated by the rest of the country. Resistance to the increasing size and scope of government and the so-called taxpayer revolts, which have shaped local and national politics for the last four decades, began in California. By the late 1970s, the proportion of Californians employed by state and local governments was almost 15 percent, twice the percentage from two decades earlier. The percentage of income paid in taxes was far higher than in other states. This had allowed for, among other things, a revolution in higher education. Built on the 1960 California Master Plan, the state's universities and colleges—the University of California flagships, the Cal State institutions, and the community colleges—had by the 1970s become world leaders in research as well as providing low-cost education to all Californians. The system was expensive. The 1978 Proposition 13, which froze property-tax rates, symbolized the unwillingness of many Californians to increase their contributions to state-driven efforts. It also foreshadowed the rise of a national conservative movement best reflected by the elevation of Reagan to the White House in his landslide presidential election in 1980.

What Matters: Rethinking Order

But what do these economic, demographic, and sociocultural changes have to do with American power and purpose in the world? Did these changes shape, first, American power and foreign policy, and second, the international system and world order? I suspect that they did.

The 1970s have long been understood more as an in-between time, following the upheaval of the 1960s and preceding the end of the Cold War. They have been characterized by an unappealing mixture of malaise, stability, and decline, hardly the qualities of positive transformation. Profound changes, however, were afoot in governance, economics, and international politics, sometimes explicitly, other times beneath the surface. These crucial shifts may have been a root cause of the rebirth of American power in the international system in the 1980s and beyond. Perhaps more controversially than the idea of an American rebirth, I believe that the changes emerging from California in the 1970s began to transform the structure and incentives within the international system itself in ways that shape international relations today.

The changes wrought by this history concentrated on individuals rather than the collective, movement rather than stasis, tolerance and inclusivity instead of definition by type or background. Disruption and fluidity were their essential characteristics. They focused on values such as opportunity, difference, and individual expression. These values have come to dominate our culture, economics, and politics in ways that we scarcely notice, and in time, I believe, have affected international relations. The story is obviously mixed—positives qualities such as increased interdependence, prosperity, tolerance, and individual freedom balance against worrying outcomes such as inequality, environmental degradation, and decreased social cohesion. These changes have sparked backlash in many circles, both within the United States and globally.[19] Troubling signs of chaos and disorder both emanate from these changes and challenge some of their benefits.

What do the history and consequences of the California Dreaming story mean for the fate of the liberal world order created during and after the World War II? It is important to recall that this order, broadly defined, was very successful even as it frayed. Great power war was avoided, and conflict and violence. Imperialism was discredited, and though often messy, a system of sovereign states replaced empire. Arms control and deterrence—based on treaties and alliances—reined in the worst fears of a nuclearized world. Though growth was often uneven and unequal, the world economy expanded, and sharp economic crises were largely avoided. The postwar order also allowed the West to prevail in the Cold War struggle with the Soviet Union, and just as important and often unrecognized, allowed it to guide a peaceful, stable, prosperous transition to the post–Cold War world. Although there have been ups and downs, human rights and tolerance have become powerful global norms, and governments are increasingly expected to be responsive to the needs of their citizens.[20]

There is, however, an irony in the California Dreaming story. The changes it wrought would have been unlikely without the success of the postwar liberal order. That order, however, was on life support during the 1970s, and would have likely continued to fracture and dissipate without the rebirth in American power and purpose initiated in the 1970s. And the challenges brought on by California Dreaming that we see in the early 2020s make it clear that the post-1945 order is no longer able to help the United States and the world navigate the promises and perils of our new age. Even the rise of China must be understood, at least in part, through a California Dreaming lens. Beginning in the United States in the 1960s, accelerating in the 1970s, and spreading and intensifying thereafter, how the global system operates has been completely upended. The upending is, to a great extent, the reason for China's rise. The consequences of this revolution are impossible to overstate and hard to fully accommodate under current global economic and political arrangements.

Much of the transformation has to do with the digital revolution and the profound expansion of access to information, unmediated by traditional institutions. Part of the makeover is a reinvention of how, where, and at what cost things were manufactured, with world trade and prosperity built on a complex and deeply integrated global supply chain. Some of it has to do with a financial revolution even larger and more profound than that which launched early modern Europe. Part of it has to do with a rights revolution that completely overturned traditional categories of gender, race, ethnicity, and sexual orientation, with a focus on individual autonomy and tolerance of difference. Much of this change has to do with a complete reshaping of identity and how people live and relate to each other—as individuals, families, and communities—that upends historical relationships between personal autonomy and collective belonging.

These shifts in core demographics, identity, finance and trade, technology, socioeconomics, and the relationship of the individual to institutions have generated both profound opportunities and worrying challenges. They have also created a dizzying puzzle, where things seem at once both wonderful and terrible.

In material terms, statistics reveal a world that has witnessed remarkable improvements in recent decades.[21] Poverty has fallen dramatically, as has infant mortality. Many diseases have been eliminated, starvation is rare, and life expectancy has increased. The COVID-19 pandemic, and the world's inept and uncoordinated response, has exposed many of the deep dangers and profound weaknesses of our current global order. Even here, however, the COVID-19 crisis is the exception that proves the rule, as plagues and pandemics were once a normal and unremarked on part of life. Education has spread, resources have become more abundant, and violence of all types—between states, within states, between communities, and within families—has fallen dramatically around the world. There has been a profound if largely unrecognized and uneven embrace of tolerance and human rights. Extraordinary amounts of wealth have been created, although obviously not always distributed fairly. Military expenditures have fallen as a percentage of gross domestic product, and new technologies have vastly increased access to information and knowledge. Even legacy institutions, such as central banks, have adapted to new realities and innovated in important ways in the face of looming disaster.[22]

Despite these accomplishments, however, there is an overriding sense of anxiety, dread, worry and concern—a sense that world order is trending in the wrong direction.[23] The fraying of alliances, the dramatic increases in inequality, the rise of disinformation, the return of political populism, the new energy behind authoritarianism, and in particular, the election of a polarizing and incompetent American president, Donald Trump, has led many to see both national and world politics as in irreversible decline. The catastrophic consequences of the COVID-19 crisis, as well as the inadequate national and global response, dramatically heighten these fears. This public health crisis may be a vision of things to come, as other transnational crises—climate change, financial volatility, the militarization of new cyber, machine learning/artificial intelligence, and biotech capabilities, terrorism and state collapse, and refugee flows—may overwhelm what remains of the postwar order. Given the profound changes wrought by the California Dreaming story, however, it is not clear that a nostalgic effort to return to embedded liberalism is either wise or possible.

Over a century ago, the economist John Maynard Keynes described a Mr. X who, like Citizen X above, inhabited a world of great technological prowess—only in 1913. "The inhabitant of London could order by telephone, sipping his morning tea in bed, the various products of the whole Earth, in such quantity as he might see fit, and reasonably expect their early delivery on his doorstep." Extraordinary increases in wealth, as well as unimaginable advances in communications and transportation, meant that Mr. X truly was a global citizen. This connection to the world made Mr. X—like Citizen X after him—believe that continued progress was inevitable. "But most important of all, he regarded this state of affairs as normal, certain and permanent—except in the direction of further improvement."[24] Under such circumstances, war and strife seemed distant, impossible, and unlikely to affect his circumstances. Needless to say, Mr. X did not anticipate the decades of devastating world war, revolution, and economic volatility that would shape his life and the lives of everyone around the globe.

What is the future for Citizen X and her colleagues? Will it be as dark as the world that Keynes's Mr. X eventually found?

The answer is not clear. The headlines of the *New York Times* and the *Washington Post* are often poor indicators of what historians will identify decades later as the core forces shaping what matters over the long term. Unforeseen, quiet, tectonic forces, similar to those of the 1970s, may be at work shaping underlying conditions that will shape the future of world order in important ways. The disruptive California Dreaming story generated both great benefit and large amounts of harm; the balance of good and bad is open to debate. What is not open to argument is that this history has produced the world we are struggling with now, and that it has exposed the vulnerabilities and even irrelevance of much of the postwar liberal international order.

The elements of the postwar order that were helpful in the second half of the twentieth century may not be relevant to the issues we face today. Although they could return, great power wars of imperial conquest—the great scourge of human history through the twentieth century—no longer appear to be the most looming threat. Nuclear deterrence combined with demographics make a return to the bloodiness of the past hard to imagine. Aging populations, especially those who have indulged in decades of California Dreaming–style material and cultural indulgence, seem unlikely to risk their comfort through great power war. Land and territory are no longer the most important source of power and wealth, and in some cases, they are actually a burden. Hong Kong, which embraced much of the California Dreaming ethos, is valuable (and at the same time, threatening) to China, not because of its land features or natural resources, but because it is a center of financial and technological innovation and one of three places in the world possessing deep capital markets. As China moves to suppress the territory's liberties and freedoms, one must watch and appreciate how Citizen X and her colleagues respond. She will not be eager to live, work, innovate, and generate wealth in a city threatened by the People's Liberation Army. She may not vote or hold strong opinions on political institutions, but she finds violence repugnant and will resist any effort to control her cultural identity or her access to exercise, new cuisine, or digital technology. Much of the future in East Asia, to say nothing of world order, will be shaped by the question of whether China will succeed in harvesting the economic benefits created by Citizen X's world while controlling the political consequences. Economies and societies are deeply integrated, and any move away from such interdependence would come at great cost to the welfare of many.

How should we think about new global arrangements that deal with the challenges to our current and future order? As we think about order-building for the future, we should be motivated by the same questions that successfully animated postwar liberal order builders over seven decades ago. What do we want to see happen? What do we want to avoid?

For a start, any future world order needs to better account for what counts as power in this current and future world, and what that power is used for. In 1890, 1950, and even 1970, the answer to these questions was clear. A state's power consisted of favorable geography, a large population, abundant natural resources, an industrial economy focused on coal, steel, and electricity, and a centralized governance structure that could mobilize these resources into war-making capabilities to conquer rivals. Does anyone think that is the recipe for success in the 2020s and beyond? It is not clear how nuclear weapons or tanks will confront climate change, disinformation, epidemics, or financial collapse. Our order-building should reflect the recognition that we live in a much different world than the one faced by Keynes and his colleagues.

The challenges that we faced in the past were based on scarcity. Wealth, resources, information, security, and health were all in limited supply. With populations increasing by leaps and bounds in the nineteenth century and first part of the twentieth, intense competition for these scarce resources was bound to be violent. The postwar liberal order was built with those challenges in mind.

The problems generated by California Dreaming—the explosion of information and disinformation, unthinkably massive global financial flows, vast movement of people, climate change generated largely by worldwide economic success, anxiety and uncertainty stemming in part from the dizzying increase in individual freedoms—these might be called the problems of plenty. In a world of nuclear deterrence, integration, and flattening demographics, where the costs of occupation are high and conquest unappealing, military security is far more abundant than we recognize. The postwar institutional order of embedded liberalism is less relevant to these issues the United States and the world face today and in the future.

Neither our intellectual tools nor our governing institutions were constructed to make sense of and solve the problems of plenty. The postwar, state-based international order was built to handle great power war and old-timey economic crises like currency depreciations. It is completely overwhelmed by California Dreaming and often responds to new problems with old solutions (such as a focus on kinetic military capabilities or outdated tariff policies). Likewise, our scholarly models, whether in international relations or economics, are based on a presumption of scarcity and don't always do well dealing with the problems of plenty. The types of insecurity that we face look nothing like those that worried order builders in the middle of the twentieth century. This has generated a legitimacy crisis for governance, both nationally and internationally.

Why? We know how to prevent World War III. As 2008 and the 2021 economic recovery from the pandemic revealed, we have a decent sense of how to prevent the worst from happening when the global economy faces steep crisis and avoid a Great Depression. We don't, however, have effective policy answers to deal with many of the consequences of California Dreaming.

We face two issues when dealing with these new challenges from the California Dreaming world. The first is to think that the solutions will come from the institutions and best practices of the past. The second is to recognize and remember that these changes, though destabilizing and occasionally frightening, have often proved profoundly positive. The remarkable global revolution of the past few decades has generated wealth and massively reduced poverty, helped eliminate disease, increased individual tolerance and freedom, provided access to unimaginable levels of communication and information, and diminished the dark cloud of war and violence. The challenge for any future order-building is to recognize, capture, and build on these great accomplishments while generating novel, effective institutional and normative responses to deal with the troubling, upsetting, disorienting, and dangerous aspects of these changes.

How we do this is unclear. A start, however, would be to acknowledge, assess, and understand the profound consequences of the history of California Dreaming. While doing so, it is important to remember that California is as much a metaphor as it is a history—one we've seen before. Chronicling the great Gold Rush of 1848–49, the historian Daniel Walker Howe explained, "California was the first state to be settled by peoples from all over the world," setting the foundation for it to become, in the twenty-first century, "the most ethnically cosmopolitan society in existence today." The similarities to the 1970s are striking: "The Gold Rush of 1848–49 represented an unprecedented worldwide concentration of human purpose and mobilization of human effort. To those who lived through it, the well-named "Rush" seemed a dramatic example of the individualism, instability, rapid change, eager pursuit of wealth, and preoccupation with speed characteristic of America in their lifetime." In the mid-nineteenth century and the 1970s, these characteristics generated both profoundly positive and deeply negative historical consequences in the years and decades that followed. Civil war, racism, and environmental degradation emerged with new wealth and unbounded opportunity. What could not be doubted was its the Rush's influence. As Howe pointed out, however, the primary legacy of the Gold Rush—like that of California Dreaming—was not its material repercussions but a set of powerful ideals and beliefs that drove historical change: "It also testified to the power of hope, and hope built the United States."[25]

OF LEARNING AND FORGETTING

Centrism, Populism, and the Legitimacy
Crisis of Globalization

Rawi Abdelal

**And so it is with our own past. It is a labor in vain to attempt to
recapture it: all the efforts of our intellect must prove futile.**

—Marcel Proust, *Swann's Way*

A newly liberal, deregulating international order was built to underpin a second
great era of globalization during the 1980s and 1990s. The new order undermined the post-1945 social bargain: the compromise of embedded liberalism.
The "resurgent ethos of liberal capitalism," John Ruggie explained at the beginning of this process, threatened the compromise that had created a stable, prosperous West.[1]

In this chapter, I argue that the politics of creating our current era of globalization were composed of transformations of both the left and the right in the
developed world; their convergence created the new system. The new system
delivered financial instability as well as an uneven distribution of income and
dignity within the United States and much of Europe. The international order—
more transatlantic than American—thus created the beginnings of its own end.
The convergence of center-left and center-right parties, furthermore, made possible the particular forms of the populist revolt of the 2010s and 2020s by leaving
unattended the politics of economic anxiety and nationalism.

Thus continues a recurring cycle of learning and forgetting. During the late
nineteenth and early twentieth centuries European leaders learned that an open
world economy facilitated growth and dynamism. They believed that the free
flow of goods, services, and capital—combined with a system of fixed exchange
rates—would create an era of prosperity with tolerable risks and manageable consequences. The financial chaos, income inequality, populist backlash of the 1920s
and 1930s, and two devastating wars ruptured the policy consensus of that first

age of globalization. The compromise of embedded liberalism represented the social learning from that unstable era. Just a few decades later, the economic malaise of the 1970s led policymakers and politicians to conclude that the Keynesian consensus had its own intolerable risks and unmanageable consequences; they had, they believed, learned something new about the desirability and usefulness of deregulating, integrating markets.

First came a change in practices created by a reactionary right: transformations associated with Margaret Thatcher, Ronald Reagan, and Augusto Pinochet, among others. This reactionary edifice was buttressed by a language of learning. We now know, the argument went, that the old ways do not work, that they stifle and suffocate putatively natural sentiments of market participants. Critics on the intellectual left blamed the right for this "neoliberalism," a word no neoliberal ever used to describe the shift. The intellectual scaffolding of learning created by political elites supplemented economic elites' more venal appetite for release from sovereign borders, national regulation, and social obligations. The result was that capital flowed more freely across borders. Barriers to the movement of goods and services declined. The US financial sector internationalized. The US government promoted globalization, for which it was a prominent cheerleader. This neoliberalism came to be seen as part of a US-centric international system in which the ideas of the right triumphed. The right moved toward the center by prioritizing the globalization of markets over the insularity of nationalism.

The transformation of the left—particularly the European left—was, however, more important for the emergence of this era of globalization.[2] The most significant turning point in the emergence of what would eventually be called the Third Way and the New Left was the famous *tournant* of François Mitterrand's government in 1983. Later Tony Blair, Bill Clinton, Gerhard Schröder, Wim Kok, and Massimo d'Alema, to name a few, helped to bring their left parties toward the center as well.[3] The international compromise of embedded liberalism was domestically, as Sheri Berman argues, a social democratic order designed to make democracy compatible with capitalism and social stability. The decline of the left's commitment to social democracy thereby made the ongoing process of taming capitalism a subsidiary goal of national politics.[4]

The left's narrative was also one of learning; the old left was anachronistic, naive, too obsessed with high taxes and regulations that did not work. The policy elite of this neoliberal center-left was technocratic and far removed from the traditional critiques of capitalism.[5] Thus right and left moved toward the center almost simultaneously during the late 1980s and early 1990s. This convergence created the possibility for both political and policy consensus. Without the acquiescence of the left, neither the political elites of the right nor the economic elites could have possibly succeeded in their agenda to escape the trade-offs of the first postwar order.

The consensus of center-right and center-left created our era of globalization and the post–Cold War order. It was a technocratic consensus: economistic, scientific, and market-oriented. The achievements of this policy convergence were profound. Newly liberalizing practices were memorialized in national legislation and international rules. Capital was liberalized by national governments and then, increasingly, in the European Union (EU), the Organization for Economic Cooperation and Development (OECD), and, very nearly, in the International Monetary Fund (IMF). A proliferation of regional trade agreements and the historic creation of the World Trade Organization supported the movement of goods and services across sovereign borders.[6]

The left-right convergence was, in a way, a reassuring achievement of modern politics. Gone were the wild policy swings of the past. The extreme left and right were, as Peter Gourevitch argues, "contained."[7] Patterns of economic policymaking varied only marginally based on who held public office. Firms could rely on a business environment that progressively allowed the free movement of the factors of production. Supply chains became globally dispersed. "Where Ricardo and Marx were as one," Karl Polanyi once observed, "the nineteenth century knew not doubt."[8] Seemingly doubtless, too, was the late twentieth century.

Thus, learning the lessons of the 1970s required a forgetting of the lessons seemingly learned from the experiences of the 1920s and 1930s.[9] The certainty of the left-right convergence of the 1980s recreated the trade-offs of the 1910s and 1920s, trade-offs that, once upon a time, we had discovered were difficult to manage. Every order contains trade-offs that are difficult to manage. The only questions are which set of trade-offs we choose and for how long we try to live with them.

Then doubt began to return precisely as a consequence of the properties of the system that the left-right convergence produced. Unshackled, globalized financial markets were more prone to crisis.[10] The social purpose of the corporation shifted from one that recognized firms as social entities embedded in national societies to one that saw them as entities with responsibilities only to shareholders—mere pieces of property.[11]

The new orthodoxy of capital mobility was first undermined by a wave of financial crises that struck emerging markets during the 1990s.[12] The global crisis of 2007 and 2008 introduced further doubt within the developed world, a process that ushered in an era not of orthodoxy but, as Ilene Grabel describes it, of "productive incoherence."[13] That crisis unraveled the intellectual and ideational underpinnings of the international order.[14] During the 2010s the intellectual incoherence of policy practice became increasingly unproductive, even destructive.[15] As Mark Blyth argues, the contemporary international order serves no well-understood, consensual purpose.[16] Without such a purpose, it is impossible to derive the principles that might inform the efforts to save it from itself.

The internationalization of production also led, in part, to rising income inequality and a crisis of dignity for the working class in much of the developed world. A backlash against globalization emerged. Indeed, the backlash against the system was perhaps most profound in the United States, the country at the center of the international order. The biggest threat to the so-called American order became American doubt.

The particular political manifestations of the backlash also resulted from the convergence of center-left and center-right.[17] Critics of the technocratic, neoliberal consensus became entrepreneurial. The populist left found that the traditional concerns for the working class had been left unattended by the center-left, which had ceased to be the vehicle of economic resentment.[18] The populist right made use of the fact that the center-right had left unattended traditional concerns for nationalism and nativism. Some populist politicians on the right were even more creative, combining the antiglobalization rhetoric of the old left and the nationalism of the old right. Donald Trump and Marine Le Pen, for example, offered this new combination. The populist left and populist right argued against global capitalism, political systems that offered no meaningful choices, technocracy, expertise, and borderlessness.[19] The "governance deficit" of corporate and financial globalization also generated polarization.[20] The resulting backlash is hastening the end of this era of globalization.

In the rest of this chapter I describe how the cycles of liberation and regulation of global finance follow a pattern of learning and forgetting. Then I explore the process by which the left moved toward the center and thereby made possible a consensus in favor of liberalization and globalization. I argue that liberalization and globalization created the instability and inequality that began to undermine the system from within. Finally, I explore the new modes of populist politics and their creative attacks on the norms and rules of the international order.

Capital Mobility, Embedded Liberalism, and the Emergent International Order

The compromise of embedded liberalism required the political management of capital mobility in two ways.[21] First, policymakers during the 1940s and 1950s regarded restrictions on the movement of capital across sovereign borders as a means to insulate national economies from quickly spreading financial crises. They saw this as an obvious lesson of the financial chaos of the 1920s and 1930s. Second, and more important, capital mobility might undermine the ability of national governments to manage one of the most difficult trade-offs in macroeconomic policymaking: whether to prioritize domestic goals over the demands or requirements of international financial markets.

Both of these elements reflected the underlying principle, if not always an explicit practice, of embedded liberalism.[22] Global capitalism—much like any capitalist system—must be regarded as legitimate in the eyes of national societies. No organization of economic activity that lacks the endorsement of the majority of the public can last for long.

I present these arguments not as conjecture, but as a composite of the widely held views of the 1940s and 1950s.[23] These lessons of an era of instability were understood then as obvious and self-evident. This consensus was memorialized in the institutional architecture of the post-1945 system. The rules of the IMF explicitly carved out for member states the right to regulate capital movements as they saw fit. The Treaty of Rome in 1957 enshrined fundamental freedoms that would create the contours of the European Community (EC), but again the rules treated short-term capital movements as a dangerous, potentially destabilizing force. The OECD's 1961 Code of Liberalization of Capital Movements endorsed long-term, "productive" capital, but, bearing the influence of the consensus, left the regulation of hot money as a prerogative of member states.

Insofar as the compromise of embedded liberalism required restrictions on capital mobility, it was remarkably short-lived. Although it was not until 1986 that the bargain truly unraveled, the process began during the 1960s and 1970s. The eurocurrency markets created fissures in the edifice. The unilateral liberalizations of the United States and the United Kingdom during the late 1970s made multilateral management of hot money increasingly untenable.

An additional set of disappointments emerged during the economic malaise of the 1970s. In addition to the American abandonment of a more or less universal set of fixed exchange rates in 1971, the combination of high unemployment and high inflation undermined the technocratic belief that governments could systematically manage the trade-offs implied by the Phillips curve. Sluggish output growth seemed to invite a rethinking of the postwar bargains.

Then, as financial globalization unfolded, unmanaged, European policymakers began to try to master the process in a new way: by writing its rules.

The Paris Consensus: The European Left and the Rules of Global Finance

Capital mobility had long been a contentious matter within the European project. Germany had always been in the minority in supporting capital mobility. Almost all other EU member states opposed it, and France, the most skeptical, was always in the way. Neither the right in general nor the center-right in particular could have created an institutional architecture that supported the liberalization of capital and the eventual disembedding of liberalism. For that, the left needed convincing.

The first decisive moment arrived early in the spring of 1983, when the Socialist government of François Mitterrand tried and failed to pursue its reflationary policy priorities as capital flowed out of the country. Mitterrand and his advisers changed course and recommitted to the European project—including exchange-rate stability—despite its domestic costs.

The Mitterrand team, which included Jacques Delors, Pascal Lamy, Michel Camdessus, and Henri Chavranski, recognized the difficult trade-offs the nation faced. Thus, this crucial collection of European political elites learned that they could no longer live within the first postwar order. Three criteria were paramount.

These French Socialists and policy elites had become disillusioned with the practice of capital controls. They found that only the middle and upper-middle classes were constrained by their regulations. The wealthy made their way around the capital controls with relative ease. Thus, the government's efforts were, at best, regressive. A group of modernizing, highly educated French elites in the Socialist Party saw France's thoroughly regulated financial system as a burden for the working and middle classes, which also endured, they believed, higher interest rates as a result. So part of their agenda was to remake domestic finance.[24]

Delors and his team also saw the opportunity for a new European bargain with Germany, one in which France would agree to capital liberalization in exchange for a commitment to progress toward a European currency union. German policymakers had unwaveringly favored freedom for capital movements for Europe as early as the 1950s and ever since then. The Franco-German bargain, then, put into place a collection of rules that reflected German understandings of the discipline and market-proved stability that would emerge from a system of capital mobility amid fixed exchange rates in Europe. German policymakers, particularly Hans Tietmeyer and Karl Otto Pöhl, insisted that capital movements be liberalized *erga omnes*—that is, with all countries, not only EU member states.[25]

Most importantly, the French left believed increasingly that an international-izing financial system should be governed by rules. Neither the United States nor the United Kingdom seemed remotely interested in such a rules-based international financial system. This was, then, an opportunity for France—and Europe more generally—to exercise decisive leadership in rewriting the rules of global finance. The Paris Consensus, more than the Washington Consensus, was responsible for the international order that we eventually called American.[26] The results may have appeared to be the result of neoliberals' efforts, but other logics were at work in the minds of those who created the new order. Neoliberal-ism was not the creation of neoliberals.[27]

So Delors, by then president of the European Commission, helped to broker a historic agreement. A 1988 directive by the ministerial Council of the European Union, Europe's main decision-making body, obliged EC members to remove all restrictions on the movement of capital among member states, as well as between members and nonmembers. Europe thereby created the most liberal obligations in the history of the modern capitalist system.[28]

In 1989 the OECD's Code of Liberalization of Capital Movements, which had previously excluded short-term capital flows, was amended to oblige members to liberalize virtually all capital movements. As had been true for the EC in 1988, the amendment became possible only when the French government dropped its opposition. Another member of the Delors team, Chavranski, played a decisive role in the process of rule-making.[29]

One final, nearly universal rule remained: the IMF's Articles of Agreement, which have no authority over the financial account transactions of member states. Camdessus, a member of the Delors team, was then managing director of the IMF. Under his guidance and leadership, the IMF began to debate an amend-ment to its constitution to deliver to the organization authority over the financial account of members and the legal right to oblige liberalization. The United States was largely indifferent to this process.[30]

Ultimately the effort to rewrite fully the rules of the international financial architecture failed. The struggle was doomed by the Asian financial crisis of 1997 and 1998. That crisis sowed seeds of doubt. By the spring of 1999 it was clear that the IMF's Articles would not be thus amended. This was the beginning of the end of the process of codifying the norm of capital mobility.

So a cadre of French Socialists from the original Mitterrand team helped to rewrite the rules of the international financial architecture. Although their lead-ership was essential and often decisive, many other policymakers played impor-tant roles. Within Europe and the OECD, the Franco-German partnership was, as is always the case in Europe, integral to decision-making and rule writing. The Germans were, after all, finally getting what they wanted—what they had long been certain Europe needed. Institution-builders in Europe, the OECD, and the IMF also saw in these new liberalizing rules opportunities to enhance the influence of the international organizations of which they were a part. Without the transformation of the French left, its *Réalisme de Gauche*, however, none of this would have been possible.

The French were not the only policymakers of the left who had turned toward liberalization. By the late 1990s almost all of the European left had become center-left.[31] The United Kingdom's Labour Party became New Labour.[32] The German Social Democratic Party became the New Middle.[33] Sweden's Social Democratic Party chose their Third Road. In the Netherlands, the Labor Party created the Dutch Purple Coalition. The virtue of profit, the value of the market, the primacy of social virtue over political economy, and the embrace of the supply side, according to Peter Hall, characterized this new configuration of center-left.[34] Thus this new center was, to use Anthony Giddens's exhortation and description, "beyond left and right."[35] The left moved further toward the center than did the right, such that "a new political center emerged."[36]

The new center-left went beyond the liberalization of capital. Its leaders would not have seen it that way at the time, but they were disembedding liberalism out of a sense of having learned that embedded liberalism and social democracy created trade-offs that they could no longer manage. The center-right would never have dared to undertake such a through transformation. Central banking practices evolved away from discretion and toward more rigid rules. Domestic financial systems were deregulated. Cross-border movements of capital were liberalized.

The United States was, of course, at the center of the new international order. Europe's "open regionalism" was, however, essential to its creation.[37] The international system was built and maintained by transatlanticism. It is as much a European creation as it is an American one.

Achievements and Disappointments of Globalization

Then we tried to live in this transformed world. The macroeconomic environment seemed, for a time, benign. We had evidently transcended the Phillips curve. Unemployment declined, inflation was stable, and interest rates remained low. Capital flowed increasingly freely around the world, as did goods and services. Market forces triumphed.

The achievements of this era of globalization are many. Within the developed world, market efficiencies created the possibilities for extraordinary technological progress, and goods and services from around the world flowed freely to be purchased at relatively low prices. For developing countries, the open markets of globalization represented an opportunity for growth and development. Chinese output grew at an annualized rate of nearly ten percent for thirty years, all while household consumption as a share of output shrank every year. Thus, the Chinese economy flourished precisely because of its access to world—and especially American and European—markets. After 1991 India was for services what China was for goods: the most successful exporter among emerging markets. Scores of developing countries flourished as a result of globalization. Some 800 million people around the world were thereby lifted out of poverty.

But every system creates trade-offs: risks, consequences, and vulnerabilities. And every system has its enemies and creates particular resentments. Worrying developments belied the calm façade. Sovereigns, firms, and households borrowed ever more at low interest rates. The US government and US households borrowed to maintain a standard of living well beyond what production and income could support. Massive US current account deficits were financed by emerging-market sovereigns and societies. As real wages stagnated in the United States, access to credit replaced income.

A number of trends created a legitimacy crisis for this system. That legitimacy crisis was most profound within the developed world—in the United States and Europe. The primary threat to the sustainability of this era of globalization exists at the very center of its system.

A world of mobile capital is more prone to crisis through a variety of mechanisms: overborrowing, overlending, cross-border contagion, and panic. The pattern was well described by the economist Hyman Minsky, who regarded moments of financial crisis as endogenous to periods of stability.[38]

The emerging-market financial crises of the late 1990s led to the crisis of legitimacy for the new orthodoxy of capital mobility. The peak of our era of global finance was, intellectually, the autumn of 1998.[39] A series of crises culminated, finally, in the global crisis of 2007 and 2008. That great crisis delegitimized both global and domestic financial deregulation.[40]

Another feature of our era of globalization was increasing income inequality across much of both the developed and developing world. The globalization of finance and production were not the only reasons for the dispersion of wages—automation and increasing returns to talent and education also played their part. National societies overemphasized the role of globalization in the rise of inequality because it seemed both knowable and potentially manageable. The US data are striking comparatively and historically. By the end of the 2010s the United States was approximately as unequal as it was in 1929.

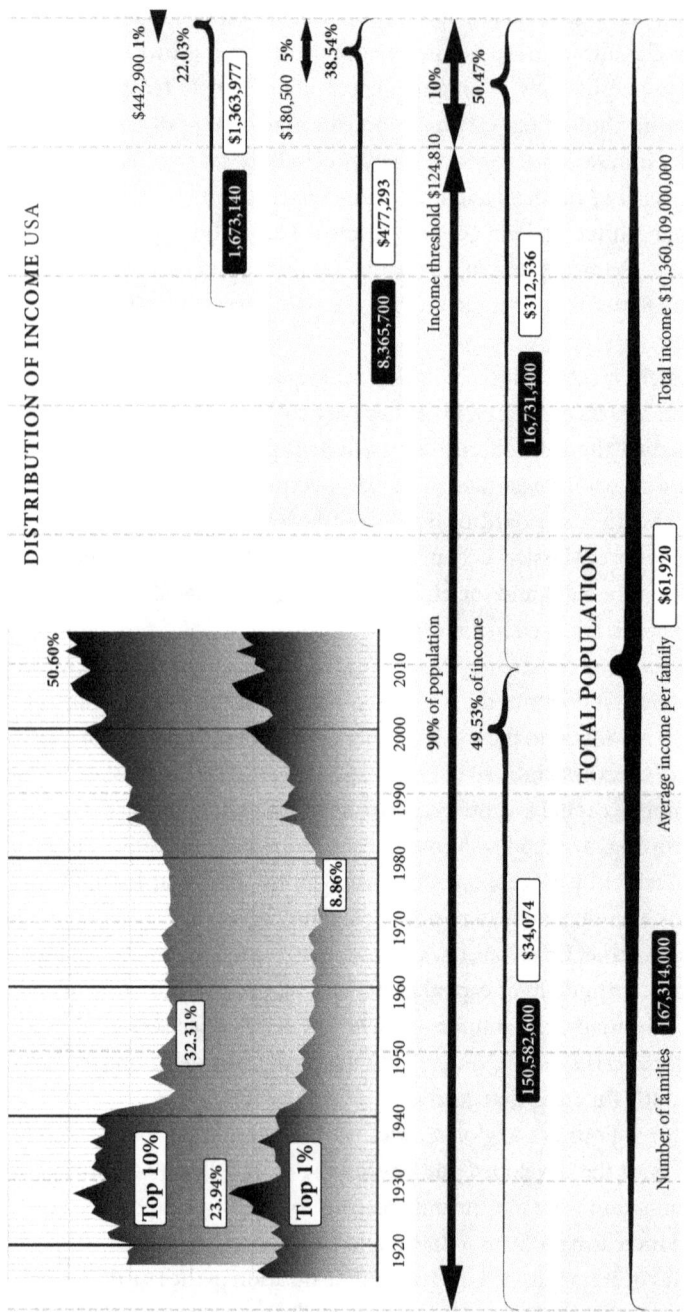

DISTRIBUTION OF INCOME USA

Top 10% — 50.60%
32.31%
23.94%
Top 1% — 8.86%

90% of population
49.53% of income

$442,900 1%
22.03%
$1,363,977
1,673,140
$180,500 5%
38.54%
$477,293
8,365,700
Income threshold $124,810
10%
50.47%
$312,536
16,731,400

TOTAL POPULATION

Total income $10,360,109,000,000

	Number of families	Average income per family
	167,314,000	$61,920
	150,582,600	$34,074

FIGURE 1. Distribution of income, United States

Note: Data is for 2015. Income is defined as pre-tax cash market income, including capital gains and excluding government transfers. Fractiles, defined by total income, also include capital gains.

Source: Based on data from table 0, table A3, and table A6 in the data file for Thomas Piketty and Emmanuel Saez, "Income Inequality in the United States, 1913–1998," *Quarterly Journal of Economics* 118, no. 1 (2003): 1–39, updated to 2015, available at https://eml.berkeley.edu/~saez/TabFig2015prel.xls. Chart by Sogomon Tarontsi for © Rawi Abdelal.

I suggest that it was not merely the material fact of inequality that created a legitimacy crisis for the system. Data from the United States, France, and a number of other countries are suggestive. First, in the United States, as in some other parts of Europe, generational expectations were declining.[41] The percent of Americans who earn—and expect to be able to earn—more income than their parents has declined for the last forty or so years.

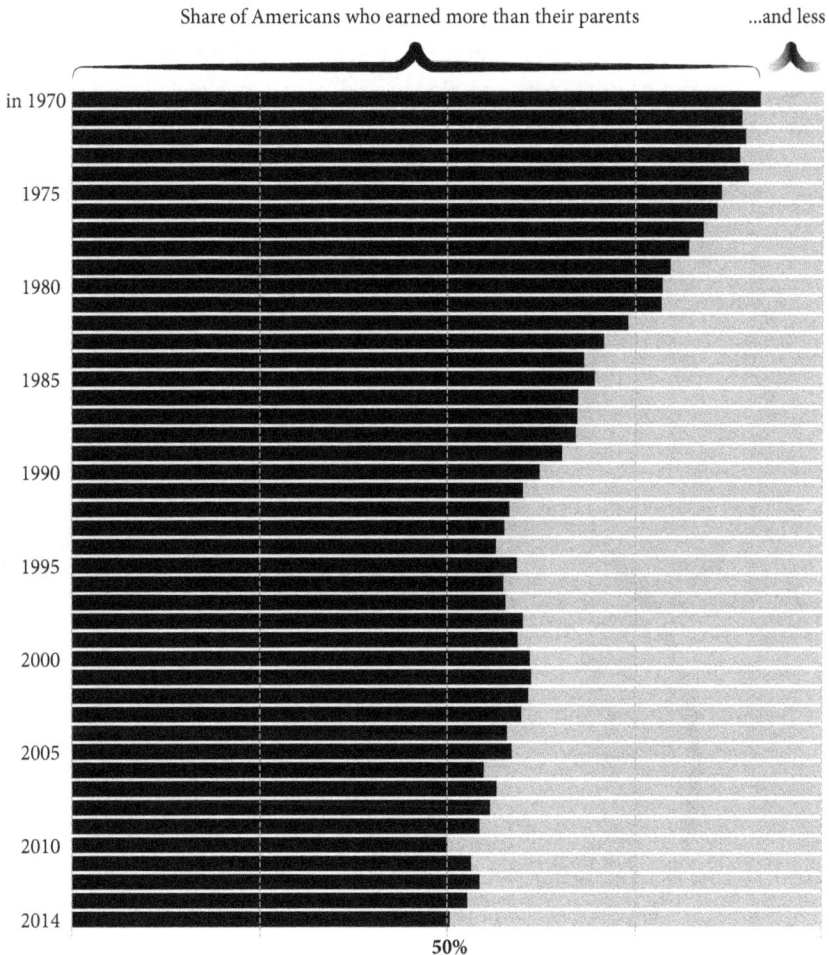

FIGURE 2.   Income mobility, United States, 1940–2014

Note: The chart presents the mean of all parent income percentile estimates. For each child birth cohort from 1940 to 1984, the authors estimated whether children earned more than their parents at the age of thirty, by parent income percentile.

Source: Based on "Online Data Table 1: Baseline Estimates of Absolute Mobility by Parent Income Percentile and Child Birth Cohort," data set for Raj Chetty et al., "The Fading American Dream: Trends in Absolute Income Mobility since 1940," *Science* 356, no. 6336 (2017): 398–406, http://www.equality-of-opportunity.org/data/index.html#absolute. Chart by Sogomon Tarontsi for © Rawi Abdelal.

Second, intergenerational economic mobility—what we might have once called class mobility—was declining.[42] Thus in the United States, among a number of other developed countries, an era of stagnating real wages, rising inequality, and declining generational expectations was combined with the accident of birth into either a poor or rich household to determine one's economic fate. Societies came to feel—correctly—that the distribution of income no longer reflected individual merit. Rather, fate—in the form of unequal access to education, family investment, and elite networks—trumped hope. Unfairness as a social fact—rather than distribution as a material fact—contributed to delegitimizing the system. A sense of unfairness had also pervaded previous eras. Every order is composed of a series of bargains that leave out some.[43] In the first decades of the new century that sense of unfairness was felt increasingly by white Americans and nonimmigrant Europeans. People of color had always been left out of these political bargains.

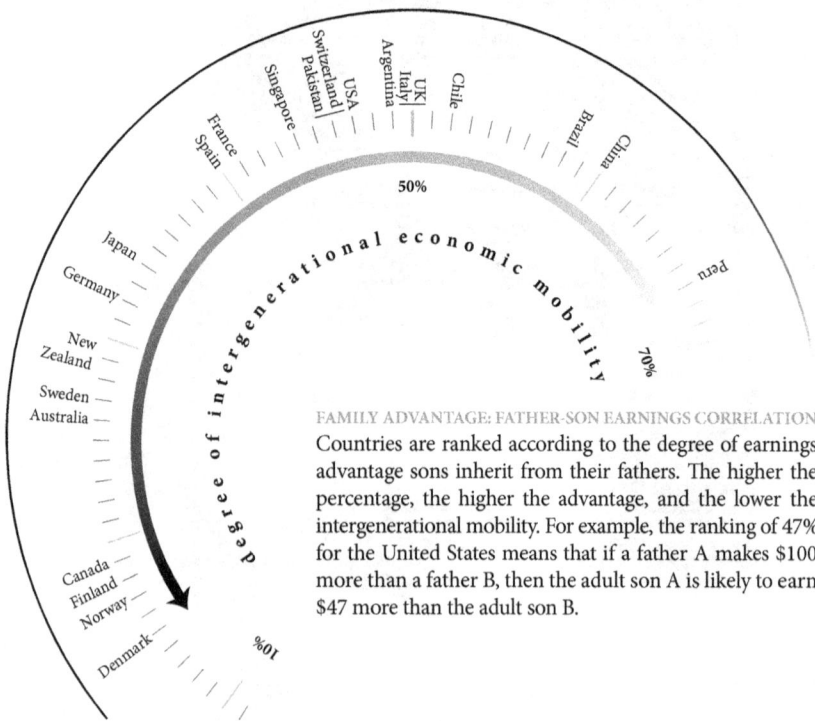

FAMILY ADVANTAGE: FATHER-SON EARNINGS CORRELATION
Countries are ranked according to the degree of earnings advantage sons inherit from their fathers. The higher the percentage, the higher the advantage, and the lower the intergenerational mobility. For example, the ranking of 47% for the United States means that if a father A makes $100 more than a father B, then the adult son A is likely to earn $47 more than the adult son B.

FIGURE 3. Income mobility around the world

Source: Based on data from Miles Corak, "Inequality from Generation to Generation: The United States in Comparison," Discussion Paper no. 9929, Bonn, Germany (Institute for the Study of Labor, May 2016). Chart by Sogomon Tarontsi for © Rawi Abdelal.

Third, this era of globalization was also, like the last, accompanied by extraordinarily large movements of people across the borders of sovereign states. Some of those people were in motion in search of a better life in Europe and the United States. Others, migrants and refugees, were fleeing violence and institutional upheaval. Thus, this era of globalization was coincident with a wave of mass migration at a scale that the world has not witnessed for a century. European societies struggled in various ways to manage the challenges of assimilation, integration, and multiculturalism at precisely the same moment that their frustrations with the economy reached their peak. Much the same was true in the United States. And so race, nationality, religion, and migration became bound up with national debates about identity, dignity, and worth.

Finally, the French experiment with redistribution suggests that concerns beyond money itself shape societies' anger and frustration. The French government has remained committed to the social democratic project of income equality for the past thirty years. Indeed, France's after-tax, after-transfer Gini

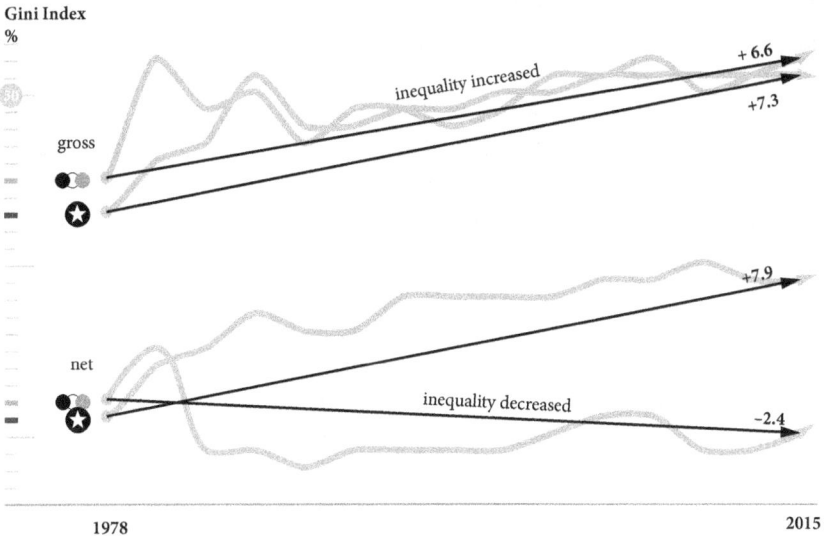

Gini Index
%

gross

inequality increased   + 6.6
+7.3

net
+7.9

inequality decreased   -2.4

1978   2015

FIGURE 4.   Distribution of income, France and United States

Note: At 0 percent, the Gini coefficient indicates equally distributed income; the greater numbers express increasing inequality, culminating at 100 percent in a theoretical case of all income accruing to one person or household. The Gini coefficient here is measured at two stages, before and after income redistribution by the social welfare systems of France and the United States. "Gross" represents market income, before taxes and transfers. The effect of the tax system and grants is drawn in the category "net."

Source: Calculated based on data from OECD.Stat, http://stats.oecd.org, and Luxembourg Income Study Database microdata, cited in Max Roser and Esteban Ortiz-Ospina, "Income Inequality," *Our World in Data*, 2016, https://ourworldindata.org/income-inequality. Chart by Sogomon Tarontsi for © Rawi Abdelal.

coefficient is lower than it was several decades ago. The pressures for wage dispersion in France manifested themselves in higher unemployment, particularly youth unemployment. France's unemployed are, however, relatively well compensated. Yet they—among *Les exclus*, the excluded—are unable to participate fully in a society that values the status of particular forms of labor and the dignity that thereby accrues to individuals. Money alone cannot buy status or dignity, and this sense of indignity has turned to outrage.[44]

This suggests that the central promise of the New Left—that it could be liberalizing and manage the social and distributional consequences after the fact—cannot prevent the backlash against the international order. The fragilities of this system in national economies and polities run deeper than money. Those fragilities have been exploited by varieties of populisms throughout Europe and the United States.

The Entrepreneurship of Contemporary Populisms

Populism is a mode of politics, a series of tropes, and a rhetorical style. The politics of populism contrast the people with the elites and the establishment. Populism is, as Rogers Brubaker suggested, "a discursive and stylistic repertoire."[45] Populist politics prioritize recognition and dignity more than material gains or losses.[46] The repertoire, according to Brubaker, includes "antagonistic re-politicization," "majoritarianism," "anti-institutionalism," and "protectionism" of various kinds.[47]

The convergence of traditional left and right parties toward the center of the political spectrum across the developed world thus created the economic conditions for the backlash that is undermining the international order, as well as a range of domestic political and economic orders. That center-left and center-right consensus opened political possibilities that entrepreneurial populist politicians and movements have pursued. The opportunities were there for the traditional left and right parties to take, but mostly they did not until they had been overrun by the extremes. In some developed countries, near-majorities of citizens felt angry and aggrieved. Elections seemed not to matter, given that the center-left and center-right had become status quo parties. For many voters, it seemed that real choice had, for better and for worse, dissipated. "Social-democratic parties," wrote Brubaker, "did not seize the political opportunity created by these major economic shifts." These center-left parties turned away from a vast swathe of space on the political spectrum.[48] Their "neoliberal turn in recent decades left the field open to other parties, on the right as well as the left, to advance populist economic claims."[49] Sheri Berman and Maria Snegovaya similarly highlighted the crisis of the social democratic left and blamed "the Left's shift to the center on economic issues, and in particular its acceptance of 'neoliberal' reforms such as privatization of parts of the public sector, cuts to taxes and the welfare state, and deregulation of the business and financial sectors."[50]

The insecurities of economic change had been, for most of the twentieth century, the political purview of the left in the United States and Europe. The New Left had, however, either committed to managing distributional politics after the fact—as in France—or not at all—as in the United States. So the politics of economic insecurity were left unattended by the left.

Concerns with national and racial identities had been, during that same era, a political focus of the right. The neoliberal center-right flirted with nationalism and racism, of course, but economic priorities were paramount. Explicit nationalist and racist language had been, by the early years of the twenty-first century, largely excluded from the more polite discourse of the center. So the politics of national and racial identities were left insufficiently attended by the right, other than an increasing reliance on racist and nationalist subtleties and dog whistles.

Clever populist politicians—and their advisers—recognized the political opportunities, or "representation gaps," that were thereby created.[51] The most creative among them did not merely reproduce the egalitarianism and resentment of the erstwhile left or the nationalist fears of the right. With so many political issues left unattended, a new breed of populists felt license to mix and match. Indeed, the left-right axis has become decreasingly useful as way to characterize these new moments of populism.[52]

The UK Independence Party (UKIP) succeeded in turning the 2016 referendum on EU membership into a referendum on globalization and the status quo. A populist right movement combined some of the traditional concerns of the far right—nationalism, nativism, immigration, and identity—and those of the traditional left—economic insecurity and the ravages of global markets. Thus, Brexit was metaphor. Although the text of the referendum invited UK citizens to choose or unchoose their EU membership, data from exit polls suggest that they were expressing preferences about a range of other issues. Those who voted for the Brexit clearly expressed a preference to leave the EU, but they also expressed antipathy for multiculturalism, social liberalism, feminism, the Green movement, globalization, and immigration. This was a novel combination of the politics of the traditional left and right.

Similarly, President Trump creatively, cleverly combined a fear of borderlessness and national grievances against the global order with the concerns of white Americans, and in particular the white working class. Senator Bernie Sanders also tapped into concerns about the implications of globalization for the working class, and the 2016 US presidential election was nearly a struggle between the

Remain

Leave

Share of survey participants who both supported remaining in the European Union and felt positive about a number of concepts

Share of survey participants who supported both leaving the European Union and felt negative about a number of concepts

	Remain (50%)		Leave (50%)
Multiculturalism	71		81
Social liberalism	68		80
Feminism	60		74
The Green movement	62		78
Globalization	62		69
Internet	51		71
Capitalism	49		51
Immigration	79		80

FIGURE 5. Brexit: Fault lines of globalization

Source: Based on data from Michael Ashcroft, "How the United Kingdom Voted on Thursday . . . and Why," *Lord Ashcroft Polls*, June 24, 2016, https://lordashcroftpolls.com/2016/06/how-the-united-kingdom-voted-and-why/. Chart by Sogomon Tarontsi for © Rawi Abdelal.

competing populist visions of Sanders and Trump. In the end, however, Secretary of State Hillary Clinton presented an ideal contest for an antisystemic, anti–status quo candidate like Trump. Clinton could hardly embody more fully the American establishment and the economic and political status quo. Thus, the left ran its center-left candidate against a candidate of the populist right who also claimed, however improbably, to speak on behalf of the Americans who felt left behind by the declining status of whiteness and of the distributional consequences of globalization.

In France, Marine Le Pen's Front National also borrowed from far right and far left to create a potent, motivating combination. Like the campaigns for Brexit and President Trump, Le Pen endorsed cultural conservatism, nationalism, protectionism, and antipathy toward the EU (itself, like Brexit, a metaphor for supranationalism, borderlessness, and globalization). President Emmanuel Macron may have saved us temporarily from the tumult of a French populist victory, but we should remember that Macron ran for office from neither the center-left nor the center-right party. Had Le Pen faced one of the candidates from either of those parties in the second round of the French presidential contest, she may well have emerged victorious. Data from surveys conducted by the Center for Political Research at Paris-based Sciences Po reveal that supporters of Marine Le Pen's populist bid for the French presidency are far less likely than others to believe that "society is structured so that people get what they deserve." Le Pen's supporters are also far less likely to believe that the state "should take from the rich to give to the poor." They conclude, in other words, that the system is unfair, but they do not want the state's post hoc management of that unfairness.[53]

Italy's simultaneous turn to the hard right—with the rise of Lega Nord (the Northern League)—and the hard left—in the form of the Five-Star Movement (M5S) demonstrated how much political space had been ceded by the centrist consensus. Prime Minister Matteo Renzi's center-left coalition, which had enjoyed so much success only five years earlier, was decimated in the 2018 parliamentary elections. Although neither the League nor M5S won a majority of seats in parliament, their combined total was approximately 60 percent. Both the League and M5S were vehemently antiestablishment, antielite, anti-EU, antiimmigrant, and antiglobalization. The League, representing primarily the industrialized north, favored a business-friendly taxation regime, whereas M5S focused more on a universal basic income for Italians. Their improbable, short-lived coalition reflected the country's collective appetite to combine right and left into a mix that would have been inconceivable a decade ago in European politics.[54]

Common to all of these episodes was another account of putative learning. In these cases, the populists had informed us that the old orthodoxies were no longer a useful guide. The so-called experts could be disregarded as we found our way forward—and away from the centrist consensus. The examples are many, but perhaps the sentiment was best expressed by British Conservative politician Michael Gove, who insisted, "I think the people in this country have had enough

Distribution of seats in the lower house of the parliament of Italy by political parties

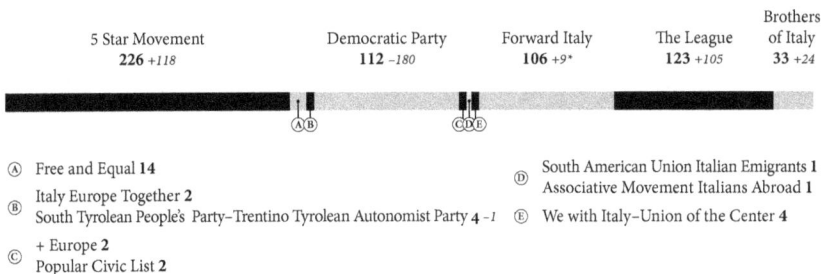

5 Star Movement	Democratic Party	Forward Italy	The League	Brothers of Italy
226 *+118*	**112** *–180*	**106** *+9**	**123** *+105*	**33** *+24*

Ⓐ Free and Equal **14**

Ⓑ Italy Europe Together **2**
    South Tyrolean People's Party–Trentino Tyrolean Autonomist Party **4** *-1*

Ⓒ + Europe **2**
    Popular Civic List **2**

Ⓓ South American Union Italian Emigrants **1**
    Associative Movement Italians Abroad **1**

Ⓔ We with Italy–Union of the Center **4**

FIGURE 6   Italy's electoral tsunami

Note: The seat-distribution figures combine gains through proportional representation and gains through single-member districts immediately after the elections in March 2018. Parliamentary groups tend to change slightly over time. Gains and losses are in relation to the elections of 2013. The gains of Forward Italy (Forza Italia) are compared to the 2013 achievement of Berlusconi's The People of Freedom (Il Popolo della Libertà). The results of the elections to the Senate are nearly identical.

Source: Based on data from Ministry of the Interior of Italy. Chart by Sogomon Tarontsi for © Rawi Abdelal.

of experts, with organizations from acronyms."[55] The populists are defeating the technocrats of the center-left and the center-right. We no longer know who might know, but increasingly we think that we know who does not know: those who told us that they did.

Finally, these episodes coincide with a rupture of one of the essential foundations of the international order: transatlanticism. Across a wide variety of issues, including political economy, defense, and the management of threats emanating from Iran and Russia, the United States and Europe have grown ever further apart. Although this process of disatlanticism began before the Brexit referendum and the election of President Trump, those phenomena accelerated it.[56]

Reflections on Learning and Forgetting

As this era of globalization either winds down or collapses, we will learn some valuable lessons about national economies and the international order. The next generation of policymakers and scholars will, after a time, put them into place as the world discovers—again—that a disintegrating, fragmenting world economy makes for slower growth, more inefficiency, higher prices, and constrained opportunities for economic development. The world will most likely learn—again—that populist politicians are unable to deliver on their promises of economic revival. We will learn once more that nationalist resentments breed interstate conflict of various kinds.

As the coming generation begins to rebuild a system that promotes international trade, its leaders will, I hope, implement the lessons that we will have learned from the crisis of this era of globalization.

Some lessons implicate the international system. The liberalization of movements of goods and services—freer trade—can promote both growth and international stability. The liberalization of capital can as well, as long as finance primarily serves the real economy. The full liberalization of capital movements—including hot money—can be dangerous and destabilizing. Such an international order is more manageable with multilateral negotiating and decision-making. An era of globalization in which markets determine almost all outcomes delivers more unequal societies.

Still other lessons focus on domestic politics and economics. Economic systems that do not benefit majorities of citizens cannot last. Dignity and respect are as important as income. The social fact of unfairness is more important than the material fact of income and wealth distribution. And the social fact of unfairness, particularly when combined with the challenge of mass migration, creates domestic political systems prone to upheaval. When mainstream political parties converge on a technocratic, liberalizing consensus, such convergence creates opportunities for new forms of populist discourse to emerge. Clever populist politicians will try to exploit these political and economic weaknesses.

With these lessons in mind, perhaps the coming generation will build a more stable international order. Still, it is difficult not to be disappointed that we had to learn these lessons again, for they are identical to those that we were forced to learn from the years between the two great wars. Unfortunately, we forgot.

POST-AMERICAN MOMENTS IN CONTEMPORARY GLOBAL FINANCIAL GOVERNANCE

Ilene Grabel

The American-led international economic order that emerged from World War II featured the dominance of embedded liberal ideas and practices.[1] This first American-led order involved, inter alia, a unipolar global financial governance architecture organized around the dollar and the Bretton Woods institutions (BWIs) and wide consensus around Keynesian principles of economic management. The order featured domestic and international economic arrangements designed to promote growth, along with mechanisms to protect domestic policy objectives (and the domestic economy itself) from external pressures and volatility—especially those emanating from the financial sector.[2] The ambitions and compromises at the heart of this order reflected the widely held view, cemented during World War II, that economic nationalism was untenable and dangerous. The way forward required cooperation and multilateralism as cornerstones of economic restoration and international peace.[3] The multilateralism was permissive, providing space for cross-national domestic policy heterogeneity. Indeed, the agreement to disagree on matters of domestic policy was hardwired into the system through Article IV of the newly created International Monetary Fund (IMF).

The second American-led international order was characterized by the displacement of Keynesian sensibilities by the neoliberal doctrine of Milton Friedman and Friedrich Hayek. The order reified markets and diminished the role of the state as an economic actor and protector while installing a restrictive multilateralism that promoted convergence to US policy and institutional norms.

The neoliberal order placed a straightjacket on national policy autonomy. The emergent neoliberalism reinforced existing US-led financial unipolarity in ways that amplified the role and power of the BWIs and US-based financial actors and interests. With notable exceptions, this order promoted the primacy of the hyper-liberalized American financial model as the global ideal. It dismantled embedded liberalism where its foundations were weakest and put it on the defensive elsewhere.

A series of financial crises exposed internal contradictions in the neoliberal order. Unlike the demise of the first order, the crises of the 1990s and the global crisis of 2008 (hereafter "global crisis") threatened not just the predominant economic model but also the centripetal force of the global financial governance architecture. The global crisis generated contradictory effects on the global financial governance architecture and on neoliberalism, deepening fissures in the US-led regime while also reinforcing the central role of the United States.

But where does this leave us? The best that can be said is that we are in an interregnum in which there is no consensus among economists and policymakers, no coherent, singular "ism" to guide policy formation, nor even a set of contending coherent systems of economic arrangements. Instead, we confront the simultaneous proliferation of a range of regimes that include kleptocratic capitalism, state capitalism, social democratic multilateralism, neoliberal nationalism, neonationalism, and what I call below "embedded populism."[4] An expanded set of diverse actors and institutions has joined the conversation in global economic governance, pushing forward with ambitious new institutions and initiatives. Many are encouraging; others certainly are not. Some of the initiatives threaten existing arrangements, while others mimic practices pioneered by established actors and institutions. Still others are establishing new networks beyond the direct control of established institutions.

Interregnums are not welcomed by social scientists (and especially by economists), trained as we are to value analytical fastidiousness, certainty, and coherence.[5] I call that longing for coherence "ism-ism," reflecting the professional imperative to capture the proliferation of discordant tendencies in a neat analytical package, some ism or other, so that we can impose analytical order. That new ism is proving to be elusive. Instead, we confront the 2020s anxious about the shape of what is emerging and what is to come. The current conjuncture provides few indications of a new ism. A post–embedded liberal, post-neoliberal American order may yet emerge, but it is difficult to see just where the seeds of such an order lie.[6] I maintain that the unease helps to explain the continuing appeal of what I term the "continuity" view—the view that in the absence of a new, well-defined ism, nothing of consequence has changed. Continuitists argue that we remain locked in the coherent (and coherently damaging) neoliberal order.[7]

Academics and other observers are drawn to coherence, tidiness, and the orderliness of orders. Sustaining continuity requires making the case—again and again—that the United States is still top dog.[8] Proving this is taken as the rejoinder to the naivete of those (like me) who hold less certain and messier views of the present and near future. To head off confusion, let me say that there is no doubt that the United States has powerful legacy advantages and that the US Federal Reserve (the Fed) and the dollar still matter. But that concession does not undermine the point that the world—well before the COVID-19 crisis—bore little resemblance to the world of the second American order. Features of an order can persist long after their order-giving capacities have evaporated.

I view the current state of affairs as at loose ends. If this period of aperture has one dominant feature, it is that it is incoherent.[9] By incoherence I mean dissensus in the domain of ideas and inconsistency in the domain of policy. Incoherence is particularly acute in international economic governance, especially as concerns finance, where we find evidence of fragmentation, conflict, experimentation, and unevenness at the same time that we see the resilience of legacy practices. We do not see any ism, unless incoherence-ism counts (I think it does not). Instead, there is a proliferation of conflicting norms, ideals, and strategies, and a profound and disturbing nostalgia for the tidiness of the embedded liberal and neoliberal eras, even among their critics. After all, the playbook was clear. Advocates knew what they were pushing for, and critics knew exactly what they were up against. Nostalgia perhaps stems from the fact that the first order looks awfully good from where we now stand. In contrast, many fewer are mourning the eclipse of the second order, given the ravages associated with neoliberal convergence. Writing during a previous interregnum, Antonio Gramsci spoke of the "morbid symptoms" readily apparent as "the old is dying and the new cannot be born."[10] This is an apt description of the current conjuncture.[11] Our current morbidity includes a popular rejection of expertise, especially economics, a profession that certainly shares responsibility for the contemporary crisis.[12]

It is difficult to find much to celebrate about the current conjuncture. Incoherence entails risks, some of which are deeply threatening. The list of contemporary maladies is a long one. It includes bourgeoning household, corporate, and public debt burdens that have created pervasive financial fragilities; the assault on postwar multilateral traditions and institutions; the exhaustion of central bank arsenals; and a trade war between the United States and China that is recruiting them into currency wars not of their choosing. In addition, the world's central bank, the Fed, faces a hostile Republican party that was mobilized by President Donald Trump. Domestic and international politics have turned inward, nasty, and conflictual in many contexts as a Polanyian double movement plays out.[13] The countermovement has many roots, but among the most important are the real and perceived damages associated with the creation of a coherent, internationally integrated system under the banner of US-led neoliberalism and elite-led cosmopolitanism. The same cocktail of resentments toward neoliberalism and cosmopolitanism fuels a variety of authoritarianisms and illiberalisms. Progressive and retrograde deglobalization impulses have undermined the prospects of regional and international cooperation, especially as concerns the provision of public goods and protection of the global commons. These developments jeopardize essential international projects, such as the pursuit of the United Nations' Sustainable Development Goals and the prospects of a new New Deal, while substantially weakening collective responses to challenges in the global commons, such as the refugee, environmental, and COVID-19 crises.[14] The world economy is experiencing a deficient and uneven recovery from the COVID-19 crisis, which is worsening already vast national and cross-national inequalities in human development, while exposing and intensifying the effects of racism and other forms of structural violence. The prospects for global coordination in response to imminent financial crises are dim.

All of this is deeply worrisome. But today's incoherence also includes productive and even transformative moments. In other work I have used the deliberately provocative term "productive incoherence" to capture this idea.[15] The concept of productive incoherence is deeply indebted to Albert Hirschman's epistemic and theoretical commitments.[16] Hirschman's embrace of possibilism and his epistemic commitment to uncertainty and humility led him to reject entirely the social scientist's penchant for narrating the future. Hirschman also emphasized the vital role of experimentation, the importance of pragmatic problem solving in response to unforeseen or underestimated challenges, the centrality of learning by doing and from others, and the virtues of messiness over real and contrived coherence and parsimony. Hirschman urged us to look at small scale innovations, and to interrogate grand narratives and the tendency to valorize epochal visions of institutional and ideational change.[17] These are key features of what I have elsewhere termed a "Hirschmanian mindset."[18] This mindset informs the claims I advance in this chapter.[19]

Incoherence in global financial governance should be understood as productive in several respects. Incoherence creates and widens alternative spaces in which some of the values, practices, tools, objectives, and goals associated with embedded liberalism can be rearticulated in a world in which there is no order, American-led or otherwise. The silver lining of incoherence is that it makes room for experimentation and innovation unconstrained by an overarching ism. Incoherence opens what we might think of as exits or leakages from a noxious national and global policy environment, rendering it less poisonous than it would be in the absence of ideational aperture and competing policies, institutions, networks, and poles of power. The abdication by the United States of its traditional role, as exerted under the first and second American orders, offers opportunities for more permissive and varied reembededdness and diverse structures of economic integration. Agile, pragmatic, ideationally elastic, networked actors and those that enjoy high levels of policy autonomy are in the best position to thrive in an environment of incoherence.[20] China is the exemplar in this connection. The evolving and reinvented BWIs, and even many entirely new players in the financial landscape, are stepping forward with strategies that defy theoretical encapsulation.

To be clear, my intervention here does not derive from an optimistic disposition driving us to see just the upside of the current conjuncture—a point to which I return later. But I do seek to push back against what Hirschman identified as "futilism"—the common social scientific temptation to pronounce on the inadequacies in emerging experiments in economic arrangements. Hirschman pointed out that such narratives have performative force, undermining initiatives that might otherwise flourish. My goal is to explore spaces where aperture and agency are emerging as sites of possibility. The crumbling of the American financial order is providing many such spaces, even while it creates serious risks. An unscripted world provides opportunities for actors to carve out new roles— for better or worse.

In this chapter I examine the contradictory implications of this era of incoherence for rearticulations of embedded liberalisms in the context of global governance that is more heterogeneous, pluripolar, resilient, and permissive. I focus only on global financial governance, encompassing institutions, policies, and practices, because this is where my interests and expertise lie and because, for several reasons, it is particularly germane to discussions of embedded liberalisms. Global financial governance was a crucial supporting pillar for both embedded liberalism and neoliberalism. Transformations and conflict in the arena of global finance were central to the unraveling of postwar embedded liberalism and to the emergence and ultimate fracturing of neoliberalism. But I argue that incoherence in global financial governance is also creating opportunities for reconstituted embedded liberalisms. This is the case even though financial incoherence also incorporates retrograde or destructive impulses. The emerging regime reflects neither your grandmother's embeddedness nor her liberalism— but it may achieve some of the results of her embedded liberalism nonetheless.[21]

I do not want to be misunderstood as suggesting that the two American-led international economic orders were internally consistent, unified, or comprehensive, whereas the current moment is uniquely marked by incoherence. To a large degree, order is something we impose on regimes ex post through our analytical schema—order is not an objective, simple, or obvious feature of social arrangements.[22] Moreover, when making comparisons between the present and prior eras we should remember that much scholarship has amply demonstrated that the emergence of embedded liberalism and neoliberalism involved contestation, contradiction, and exclusion that were never overcome. These regimes unfolded unevenly over long periods, and they coexisted with other isms in a heterogeneous global landscape.[23] Coherence is always a matter of degree; it is not a matter of present-absent. In my view, these earlier eras were coherent only in comparison to the present period. Expert understandings, policy practice, and institutional design were significantly guided by an overarching ism that established a logic of appropriateness and structured choices, even if the logic was widely violated in practice. Coherence is typically more of an aspiration than an accomplishment. Social scientists and social engineers tend toward visions that are analytically neat and clean. These visions exceed in parsimony, tidiness, and purity the degree to which these attributes are achieved in practice. "Is there a coherent political project?" is just as important a question as "Is there a coherent regime in practice?"

The Crises of Neoliberalism and the Beginning of the End of the Second American Order

The crises that swept through countries of the Global South and East (hereafter developing economies) in the 1990s had paradoxical effects on neoliberalism, global financial governance, and the second US-led international economic order. Most importantly, the financial crises of the 1990s, especially the East Asian crisis (hereafter the Asian crisis), laid the groundwork for the ideational, policy, and institutional transformations that deepened significantly during the global crisis of 2008. One critical effect was the opening of space for the rearticulation of central pillars of embedded liberalism.[24]

At first, the Asian crisis solidified neoliberalism. The Stand-By Arrangements (SBAs) of the crisis dismantled key attributes of the developmental-state model.[25] But the crisis also induced cracks in the neoliberal consensus. Prior to the Asian crisis, the IMF was poised to enshrine capital flow liberalization in its Articles of Agreement. The Asian crisis put paid to that effort. Moreover, and despite the neoliberal tenor of the times, some countries stubbornly maintained capital controls, with notable success.[26] Partly in response, the Asian crisis precipitated the beginning of a begrudging, uneven reevaluation of capital flow liberalization.[27]

The Asian crisis had contradictory effects on the BWIs, especially the IMF.[28] The crisis was ultimately costly to the IMF insofar as its response led developing economies to implement strategies to escape its orbit through self-insurance pro-grams. The combination of a curtailed geographic reach and widespread con-demnation of institutional performance undermined the IMF's legitimacy and reduced the material resources at its disposal.

The Asian crisis also renewed interest by developing-economy policymakers in the creation of institutions that could supplement and even substitute for the BWIs. The Asian Monetary Fund, proposed in the summer of 1997, failed to materialize. Nevertheless, it had powerful effects in the region and across devel-oping economies more broadly. Indeed, as I argue below, the roots of today's more pluripolar global financial architecture lie in the Asian crisis.

The crises of the 1990s also induced policymakers to create informal financial governance networks. This informal architecture of networked financial gover-nance evolved and broadened during the global crisis.[29]

The brief history sketched above suggests a degree of openness that was not in evidence over the past several decades. The 2008 crisis deepened and wid-ened that aperture in numerous respects. I draw attention here to those aspects of global financial governance in the present period that bear most directly on the fate of embedded liberalisms. These include the eclipse of the US-centric neoliberal financial model; an expanded central bank toolkit; the resurrection of capital controls; the hollowing out of the BWIs in a more crowded landscape; and trends pointing in the direction of deglobalization, reglobalization, new multilateralisms, and "networked bilateralisms." These trends do not all line up—instead, they can and do sometimes compete and conflict.[30] My chief argument is that the evolving, incoherent nature of global financial governance can support the financial pillars of rearticulated, heterogeneous embedded liberalisms, along with other, less appealing isms.[31] The diverse policy responses to the COVID-19 crisis provide a window into the operation of the incoherent "order," revealing both its productive and destructive potential.

The Eclipse of the US Order and the Rise of Hybridized Financial Models

The global crisis tarnished claims for the superiority and universality of the lib-eralized, liquid US financial model. The crisis validated the views of critics of the model in the United States, China, and elsewhere who had long identified the failings of light-touch financial regulation.[32]

The hegemony of the neoliberal financial model was threatened by the sharp divergence between the performance of the United States and Europe during the global crisis and that of many developing economies, and by the United States' crucial retreats in financial governance. A large set of developing economies navigated the challenges of rapid growth, inflation, and the currency appreciation and asset bubbles caused by large capital inflows. Many developing economies facing these favorable conditions had messy, hybridized financial systems. These systems combined financial openness with stringent regulation, including capital controls. Policymakers were attuned to and had the ability to adjust financial regulations and close channels of evasion. Robust mechanisms influenced credit allocation through networks of public and private institutions.

Emboldened by their superior performance, developing-economy policymakers exploited the global crisis to call for alternatives to a US-based financial order. The most widely publicized salvo was the 2009 essay by Xiaochuan Zhou, governor of the People's Bank of China. The Chinese also downgraded US government debt in 2011 and 2013, something that would have been unthinkable just a few years prior, and took steps to internationalize the renminbi. Since 2015 China has promoted development of the CIPS (Cross Border International Payments System) as an alternative to SWIFT (Society for Worldwide Interbank Financial Telecommunication), the West's dominant international financial messaging system, used widely for cross-border payments.[33] China's monetary and financial internationalization have had far less impact to date than some predicted. Moreover, and paradoxically, some Chinese initiatives have confirmed the pivotal role of the dollar in international finance. (In point of fact, the dollar has outperformed most predictions regarding its role as an international currency since the global crisis.) But this is to be expected given both the legacy advantages that the dollar and US institutions enjoy and the cautious approach that marks China's policy strategy.

Chinese policymakers in general have taken an experimental, uneven, incoherent, impulsive, and quasi-Keynesian approach to finance.[34] For instance, the government has used offshore markets as sites of experimentation, while also conducting experiments in national and local markets on the mainland.[35] We can understand Chinese policy as being both backward and forward looking. A number of initiatives involve practices and instruments associated with neoliberalism and financialization, such as securitized lending and shadow banking.[36] In 2018, for instance, the government announced an ambitious three- to-five-year plan to liberalize financial services, including international capital flows. This was surprising given the fragilities that such practices necessarily induce, especially in an economy already overstretched by domestic and foreign overlending. Nonetheless, these measures were consistent with the overall messiness of China's approach. The government typically introduces new controls even as it liberalizes, especially during moments of financial and political volatility. The start-stop of renminbi liberalization in late 2015–early 2016 is one example. Unlike the United States' ideological commitment to financial openness, China's initiatives are best viewed as pragmatic, ad hoc, and inconsistent innovations in financial governance in a state that is increasingly challenged by competing demands and pressures. The political crackdown on Hong Kong in 2020 exemplifies the internal tension between pressures for change and the commitment to maintain control. Repression off the mainland (coupled with early efforts to hide the spread of the coronavirus) has seriously undermined trust in China, domestically and internationally.

China's Belt and Road Initiative (BRI) and numerous other cross-border investment and aid initiatives are outgrowths of China's muscular state-capitalist model. The model reflects embedded liberal–adjacent aims on the one hand, and realpolitik on the other. The former is seen in prioritization of commitments to financial and broader economic stability, high levels of policy autonomy, real-sector and employment growth, and maintenance of export markets. Realpolitik involves securing control over natural resources through an ambitious vision of reglobalization that places the country at the center of a hub and spoke model of global integration, cultivating political allies, crushing dissent in Hong Kong, using the COVID-19 crisis as an excuse to increase surveillance, and stepping into the void created by the withdrawal of the United States from its traditional global role. Chinese policymakers do not share the US presumption that its model should be universalized, though there is ample evidence of significant ambition and rivalry with the US model and the dollar.[37]

The trade and currency wars unleashed by the Donald Trump administration provided additional momentum to the case against US economic leadership, especially as these conflicts unfolded in 2019 and early 2020.[38] The erratic nationalism of the Trump administration widened the void in global economic governance opened by the Barack Obama administration's refusal to accept China's invitation to join the Asian Infrastructure Investment Bank (AIIB) as a founding member in 2015. Moreover, the failed, chaotic, and inward-looking response by the United States to the COVID-19 crisis moves it even further away from any semblance of global leadership.

The Trump administration's weaponization of finance and trade relations (e.g., through its use and abuse of sanctions) led US foes and allies to develop a range of early stage innovations and enter into blue sky discussions aimed at gradually reducing dependence on the dollar.[39] Among US allies, former Bank of England governor Mark Carney proposed far-reaching adjustments that would demote the role of the dollar.[40] He argued that the world's reliance on the dollar "won't hold" and that the IMF should manage a multipolar system of currencies.[41]

The fractured hegemony of the US model has created space for a pluriculture of financial models, features of which are consistent with embedded liberalism. China's model is the most notable of these alternatives, but we should keep an eye on other inchoate initiatives in South Korean, Indian, Malaysian, and Islamic finance that represent alternative modes of organizing finance.[42] We should also keep in mind that even in the case of China, the term "model" should be treated cautiously as it suggests a degree of orderliness and consistency that is apparent mostly in hindsight.

Empowered Central Banks, Revived Capital Controls, and the Hollowing Out of the BWIs

Central banks scrambled to respond to the uncertain dimensions and geography of the global crisis by drawing on a broad range of tools to stabilize markets, support financial and nonfinancial firms, and inject liquidity into the financial system. What became known as "unconventional monetary policies" became a norm for central banks in many advanced economies during the global crisis. During the global and the COVID-19 crises, central banks in advanced economies ceased making inflation targeting their primary objective. This is less indicative of a change in priorities or ideas than it is of the deflationary environment that prevailed during much of the COVID-19 crisis.[43] At the same time, central banks in developing economies and other national contexts began to target financial stability and asset bubbles and the reduction of systemic risk through macroprudential policies.[44] It also became more acceptable for central banks in advanced economies and developing economies to target the exchange rate to protect exports and employment from currency appreciations fueled by foreign capital inflows. Central banks created large, broad, ad hoc international liquidity networks through vast swap lines. Swap agreements were driven by a variety of concerns, including financial stability but also domestic bank exposure, geopolitical considerations, national interest, and export-market protection.

The new normal for central banks involves unconventional monetary policies in an environment marked by low and even negative interest rates, interbank conflict reminiscent of the 1930s, disruptions in international trade, and contagious crises. Indeed the 2019 Jackson Hole central banker conference focused on the strange new environment.[45] In addition, populists have attacked the credibility and independence of central banks as part of broader attacks on expertise.

Central banks in advanced economies responded to the COVID-19 crisis with multipronged, aggressive and, in many cases, innovative policies that made them the lender of last resort for the financial and real sectors. The banks bought unlimited amounts of US Treasury bonds; signed swap agreements; created temporary liquidity facilities for central banks not party to swap agreements; supported the credit needs of small, medium, and especially large firms; and backstopped banks, municipal and corporate bond markets, commercial paper, and repurchase markets. As during the global crisis, central banks pivoted in the direction of embedded central banking, deploying new tools and attacking new targets, including real-sector conditions and financial instability.

I should note as an aside that beyond the policy imperatives driven by the global and COVID-19 crises, central bank officials, such as those at the Fed and the European Central Bank (ECB) are increasingly emphasizing the importance of developing new tools to "green" monetary policy. They seek to use monetary policy to support a transition to a low-carbon economy and to build climate risk assessments into lending decisions.[46] IMF managing director Kristalina Georgieva made similar calls for the IMF to place climate risk at the centerpiece of its work.[47] Central bankers in 2020 and 2021 have also begun to speak openly about racism and inequality and speculated in public forums about whether and how to use the tools at their disposal to respond to these inequities.[48]

Capital controls were a defining feature of the first American-led order. Capital controls were legitimized by then dominant Keynesianism. They fell out of favor in the 1970s and remained so during the long neoliberal era. But ideas and practices began to evolve during the crises of the 1990s. As the global crisis emerged, capital controls were quickly relegitimized.[49]

A wide range of developing economies used diverse capital controls to slow the tide and dampen the negative spillover effects of large capital inflows. Examples of countries that used controls for this reason include Brazil, China, India, Indonesia, South Korea, Thailand, and Uruguay. Other countries, including Argentina, Cyprus, Greece, Iceland, Indonesia, and Ukraine, used capital controls to mitigate the effects of crisis-induced capital outflows. Formerly denigrated as a policy tool favored by the weak and misguided, capital controls were normalized as a legitimate tool of prudential financial management. Particularly notable in this context is the behavior of the IMF. It prescribed capital controls to both borrowing and nonborrowing economies during the global crisis, and the resulting initiatives were validated by the credit rating agencies. The deeply conservative neoclassical heart of the economics profession followed the lead of those IMF researchers, who domesticated the idea of capital controls by referring to them as a "legitimate part of the policy toolkit."[50]

The restoration of capital controls has by no means been consistent, as experiences in Argentina (2018–19), Ecuador (2019), and Lebanon (2019) underscore. As with most rebranding exercises, there is also uncertainty about whether the new framing will stick, especially in the context of tensions and countervailing impulses at the IMF and elsewhere. The emergence of illiberal governments that pander to capital owners, along with a resilient bias against state management of economic flows among many economists who were trained and cut their professional teeth during the neoliberal era, also threaten the endurance of controls. But it is most unlikely that we will see a return to the reification of capital flow liberalization, given the widespread, productive use of capital controls during the global crisis. IMF chief economist Gita Goinpath discussed controls used in "normal times" as prudential measures in what she termed an "Integrated Policy Framework."[51] Those of us who remember the IMF effort to banish capital controls for good as recently as the early 2000s can't help but take note of the sea change in thinking that this statement reveals.

The rethinking of capital controls marks a decisive shift back toward the vision of BWI architects John Maynard Keynes and Harry Dexter White. The implications for the emergence of embedded liberalisms are profound.[52] Most immediately, the restoration of capital controls provides a degree of policy autonomy as developing economies shoulder the effects of currency depreciations, capital flight, financial crisis, and severe economic and social dislocation associated with the COVID-19 crisis. Indeed, in 2020 IMF staff highlighted the role that capital controls can play in this context.[53] This is in keeping with the insulating and supportive role that capital controls played in the embedded liberal era. Beyond the serious challenges associated with the COVID-19 crisis, capital controls are an important component of a global Green New Deal in conjunction with the 2030 Sustainable Development Goals agenda.[54]

President Trump's Treasury Department team and his appointments to the IMF and the World Bank displayed the administration's deep hostility to multilateral organizations and its hope to weaken the institutions from within. In a 2017 speech at the Council on Foreign Relations, then Treasury Department official David Malpass asserted, "Now is an opportune time to discuss . . . the rapid increase in globalism . . . multilateralism has gone substantially too far."[55] In 2018 Malpass urged the Inter-American Development Bank not to hold its annual meeting in China in 2019. He made clear that the administration was increasingly discomforted by China's growing influence at the multilateral development banks. The Inter-American Development Bank again became a flashpoint in the Trump campaign to ring fence China in 2020. The administration appointed a hardline China critic, Mauricio Claver-Carone, to serve as president the institution. In 2020 Malpass, by then president of the World Bank, skipped the annual World Economic Forum. This was widely seen to reflect the Trump administration's go-it-alone approach. So was Malpass's veto of the word "multilateralism" in the collective statement issued at the G7 2019 summit.[56] Like his predecessor at the World Bank (former president Dr. Jim Yong Kim), Malpass also appeared to be hostile to large-scale cross-border infrastructure projects that involved cofinancing with China.

The Trump administration's attack on multilateralism was also reflected in a 2019 decision to block an IMF quota increase and redistribution of voting rights. Observers speculated that the administration's move to block quota reform sought to prevent China from garnering more voting power.[57] The US Treasury Department blocked efforts to increase the capacity of the IMF during the COVID-19 crisis by allocating a large new tranche of special drawing rights (SDRs) to members.[58] (A scaled up version of this proposal involving release of US$650 billion in SDRs was reintroduced in 2021 with the support of the Biden administration. It was approved by the IMF's Board of Governors in August 2021.[59]) The Trump administration's decision to halt funding to the World Health Organization (WHO) during the COVID-19 crisis reflected the strength of its antiglobalist impulses and its commitment to punish a multilateral institution for both a real and an exaggerated tilt toward China.[60]

To sum up, the present conjuncture is a time of uncertainty for the BWIs and for their roles in economic governance. There are ample signs of evolution in ideology and strategies, as we see most clearly in the case of capital controls. The new stance toward prudential financial management is a necessary though insufficient condition for the reconstruction and sustenance of embedded liberal strategies. In addition, a new and as yet underdeveloped open-minded approach to industrial policy might ultimately prove to be just as consequential (see the notes to this chapter), as could consideration of a global Green New Deal. The BWIs might become more relevant in the COVID-19 crisis, especially as they are called on and have begun to respond tepidly to the needs of low-income countries. Nonetheless, the BWIs and other multilateral institutions face hostility from many political leaders in the United States, their primary sponsor over the long post–World War II period. The Trump attack was intended to hollow out the BWIs, in part to deny China and other developing-economy competitors a foothold to extend their role in global economic affairs. But the inconsistent, volatile Trumpian approach was short-sighted. It incentivized friend and foe alike to create new institutions and linkages that circumvented and constrained US influence over financial flows and financial governance. Moreover, Trump's timing could not have been be worse. The uncertainty around the BWIs provided possibilities for more permissive and varied multilateralisms at a time when at least some developing economies had the resources and backbone to withstand Washington's threats. We see clear signs that the shape of multilateralism is being contested and rethought. Since the global crisis a new, more densely populated ecosystem of financial governance has emerged. It was already threatening the privileged place of the United States even before Trump's election.[61]

A More Heterogeneous Institutional Landscape

Reserves accumulated after the Asian crisis and robust developing-economy performance during the global crisis provided the means to support innovations in financial governance architectures. For institutions whose existence pre-dates the global crisis there was expansion in the scale of activity, geographic reach, and the introduction of novel mechanisms. New developing-economy institutions were also created during the crisis, a few focusing on countercyclical support, others on development finance, and a handful doing both. Many of the institutions signed cooperation agreements with one another. A subset of these institutions hews to the Bretton Woods model in various respects while others even link their decisions (formally and informally) to IMF surveillance programs. Others deploy entirely different models, disbursement criteria, and approaches to surveillance, and extend loans in local currencies. In contrast to its opposition to the Asian Monetary Fund proposal, the IMF has encouraged the expansion of and connections among these institutions and between them and itself. This engagement surely stems from several factors—including institutional self-preservation in a world of hollowed-out and contested multilateralism and recognition that the IMF's resources are inadequate in the face of a turbulent financial horizon.[62]

The new arrangements do not coalesce around a singular, grand new global architecture that might replace the foundering BWIs. Indeed, they are explicitly not intended to do so. Nor do they yet amount to a potent challenge to the financial power of the United States and other leading advanced economies. But displacement is the wrong standard against which to measure their significance. Instead, we are observing productive incoherence in the expansion of disparate, overlapping, and interconnected institutions that complement the BWIs. Taken together, they are diversifying the financial landscape and introducing the possibility of a transition to a more complex, decentralized, multitiered, pluripolar global financial and monetary system. The initiatives are complicating the terrain on which the BWIs operate—and that's a good thing. A more densely populated, pluripolar global financial governance architecture is more likely to be tolerant or supportive of experimentation and a diversity of economic models and to enable a variety of embedded liberalisms. That kind of tolerance is typically absent under an architectural monoculture that exerts a gravitational pull toward a single idealized model. Today, new players hold diverse ideas about policy autonomy, the role of the state in the economy, and the importance of financial stability. Is this inconsistency disconcerting? I propose instead that we assess the emerging incoherence with Hirschmanian sensibilities, or via Elinor Ostrom's complimentary arguments for polycentrism.[63] We should also keep in view related arguments in complexity theory concerning the benefits of heterogeneous, adaptive systems and the dangers of monocultures and centripetal systems.[64]

During the first and second American-led orders, lending by the BWIs amplified and transmitted economic policy norms and reinforced the role of the United States in global financial governance. Today, China's international aid, investment, and lending magnify the country's role in reshaping the landscape of global development finance. The stock of outstanding loans made by the China Development Bank alone was US$1.6 trillion in 2017, much larger than loans by the World Bank. Outstanding loans by China grew from approximately zero in 2000 to more than US$700 billion in 2019; China is the world's largest official creditor, more than twice as big as the World Bank and IMF combined.[65] And there is evidence that even these figures understate China's international lending.[66] Many observers have compared the BRI to the Marshall Plan. But it is important to note that 90 percent of Marshall Plan funding involved foreign aid, not loans.[67] The BRI funding comes from a variety of sources, including profit-seeking private entities.[68] The Marshall Plan gave liberal markets a decisive role, whereas the BRI does not.[69]

During the global crisis the Chinese government positioned itself as a savior of multilateralism. The government was alone among the BRICS group (composed of Brazil, Russia, India, China, and South Africa) in its decision to provide finance to the European Financial Stability Facility during the Eurozone crisis. The government also signaled its commitment to multilateralism and Chinese-led reglobalization during the crisis by launching the AIIB, the BRI, other loan and aid programs, the CIPS, and playing a leading role in the financial structures developed by the BRICS. Chinese president Xi Jinping launched a robust defense of globalization and multilateralism at the World Economic Forum in Davos in 2017.[70] Since then Chinese officials have seized the stage on many occasions to defend multilateralism (which in practice often takes the form of networked bilateralism), a rules-based international order, and the benefits of global integration.[71] BRICS representatives have also defended multilateralism while arguing that its traditional institutional supports need significant modernization.

China sought to rebrand its role in the COVID-19 crisis after several months of mismanagement and misinformation. The country stepped into the void created by the US abdication from multilateralism, not least by announcing new funding for the WHO following Trump's decision to halt it. China also donated and sold medical supplies on several continents and sent medical personal abroad.

Many observers worry about the kind of reglobalization and economic integration that is emerging as China steps into the void created by the fracturing of postwar traditions of multilateralism and deepening illiberal nationalisms. For example, Barry Eichengreen raises concerns about a reglobalization that features illiberal politics and where the rules of a new world order are shaped to fit Chinese preferences.[72] Others worry about forum-shopping opportunities, while still others raise concerns about the construction of a parallel system at a time of US retreat and expanding global demand for project finance.[73] To be sure, China's lending raises numerous concerns, particularly its implications for financial fragility, China's power over borrowers and control of natural resources, and the loans' carbon footprint. The COVID-19 crisis also highlights the obvious fragilities associated with a global supply chain organized around one country.

But China is not the only actor seeking to recast the international system. There is substantial support for an unspecified but presumably modernized, heterogeneous, and permissive liberal multilateralism. French, Canadian, and German heads of state and IMF leadership (starting with former managing director Christine Lagarde) have promoted multilateralism. In addition, the Democracy 10 (D10) involves senior officials from a group of leading democracies. The group has been meeting once or twice per year for the past four years to discuss how to coordinate strategies to advance the liberal world order.[74]

The chief inference to be drawn at this point is that economic integration is being contested and reshaped. The most likely outcome in the near and medium terms involves deglobalization, reglobalization, and a variety of new forms of economic integration, against a backdrop of illiberal nationalisms. The latter have been given new life by the exigencies of the COVID-19 crisis, which has been a gift to illiberal politicians and propagandists the world over. Trump is an exception among illiberal peers insofar as he suffered electoral defeat for mishandling the COVID-19 and related economic crises.

The developments discussed above don't resurrect twentieth century embedded liberalism, as it was theorized then and now, and they do not guarantee any particular outcome concerning the role of the state in promoting economic and social welfare. But they do open the door to a rearticulation of central features of embedded liberalism—especially forms of social protection for actors whose well-being has been imperiled by the long neoliberal experiment and by the COVID-19 crisis. We might expect a proliferation of diverse embedded liberalisms that take root at multiple levels via a wide range of instruments. For example, the social protections we associate with embedded liberalism might be pursued through decidedly nonliberal political means. Indeed, we might posit a continuum of approaches to the achievement of social protection. At one pole are forms we might easily recognize as embedded liberalism, with universal protections via democratic, participatory engagement that is universal in scope but that benefits those most vulnerable to the shocks of international economic openness. At the other pole we might find something very different—partial rather than universal protections, directed at particular constituencies that are tied to nationality, race, and other identities and that have experienced the damage of neoliberal engagement as an erosion of rights by the incursion of others who are seen to threaten their claims. I refer to this pole of social protection—particular and exclusionary—as "embedded populism." But the present conjuncture of productive incoherence does not dictate any particular form of social protection. We should indeed expect to see, and indeed are seeing, the proliferation of diverse and contending forms of social protection across the liberal-illiberal continuum—even within individual nations.

The US case is particularly illustrative of the many risks associated with incoherence. These include the inability to manage innocent but damaging spillovers (such as those associated with the return of ultra-accommodative monetary policies), beggar-thy-neighbor policies, systemic risk, currency and trade conflicts, and the absence of a federal response to the COVID-19 crisis.[75] Indeed, all manner of destructive incoherence becomes more apparent daily in the United States as the COVID-19 crisis unfolds. Destructive incoherence is also on full display in the failure to develop a coordinated global or even an EU-wide response to the crisis. That said, many important European states are continuing to hold down features of the embedded liberalism pole—though even here there are important exceptions, such as the Emmanuel Macron administration, which liberalized the economy and especially labor markets while becoming Europe's most powerful champion of multilateralism. However, even Macron changed course as the COVID-19 crisis developed. As in most European contexts, French policies supported furloughed workers in ways that were inconceivable in the United States. And even Germany moved away from its deficit obsession early in the COVID-19 crisis. Thus, which countries support the tent poles of embedded liberalism and how they do so is fluid and evolving.[76] We can also situate countries like China, India, and other developmental states—and even states with more liberal politics, like Chile—at various points along the continuum, reflecting their apparently contradictory mix of liberal and illiberal strategies that, inter alia, promote social protection.

Dismal as this account might seem, it presents opportunities that begin to restore protections of the most vulnerable. The changes in global financial governance surveyed above provide far more extensive policy space than was

available during the neoliberal era, and this space can be exploited for progressive purposes. Policy space can of course also be exploited for regressive ends.
But Hirschman was able to look out on unpromising development terrains and
yet hold to his "bias for hope," represented so strongly in his commitment to
possibilism.[77] Hirschman's possibilism provides a basis for considering the current incoherence as productive. Incoherence is agnostic and permissive, opening
up opportunities for progress and experimentation even as it induces the risk of
regress. Incoherence also provides the opportunity to shatter shibboleths, such
as the neoliberal claim that budget deficits are necessarily damaging, that government direction of economic affairs is necessarily harmful, or that democratic
socialism is just one stop on the road to serfdom. Moreover, Hirschman urged
us to push past easy pessimism, because yielding to pessimism could blind us to
chances to achieve meaningful reform. Our rhetoric, Hirschman reminded us,
affects not just what we see but also how we intervene, and so has consequential
effects in the world.[78] Best, then, to err on the side of possibility.[79]

What have we found? The possibilities for embedded liberalism are returning
even if the mid-twentieth century form has largely passed us by. Nostalgia is
not warranted. After all, the American orders were far from benign. Indeed, the
bloody history, harms, and exclusion that indelibly mark the first and second
liberal orders are too often underplayed or even overlooked by their champions.[80]
The particular form of twentieth-century embedded liberalism depended on a
unipolar system of global financial governance that was biased in terms of its
benefits and costs in favor of the Global North, large firms, and other privileged
actors. The new forms of social protection that can arise amid productive incoherence might be more heterogeneous in forms and effects, but also better suited
to the institutional configurations and needs of diverse countries and diverse
social groups. Not all forms promise to be benign—indeed the nationalist, illiberal impulses in play suggest that social protections will be sought via beggar-thy-
neighbor strategies, cronyism, racism, misogyny, xenophobia, propaganda, and
other means that offload risk onto weaker parties at home and abroad. These
strategies in fact test the limits of what we mean by liberalism—they may be better characterized as embedded populisms.

Examples of embedded populism include the Trump administration putting American farmers on welfare; cutting taxes (with disproportionate benefits for the rich) without cutting spending; vilifying China; browbeating US
corporations into investment decisions that favored domestic job creation;
defending steel tariffs that contravened the market in order to give at least the
illusion of protection to Trump's base; and putting pressure on the Fed to pursue expansionary monetary policy at a time of relatively strong growth prior to

the COVID-19 crisis. Similarly, we should take note of the Trump administration's decision during the COVID-19 crisis to bail out large firms while starving state and local governments and hospitals of much-needed funds while stirring anti-Asian nativism, and its exploiting of historical racism against Blacks and Black Americans. Other recent examples of embedded populism include attacks on central bank independence by Presidents Trump and Recep Tayyip Erdoğan; and the use of economic sanctions against Iran. These strategies have nothing to do with neoliberalism, and I therefore reject what has become the common characterization of the Trump (and other backward-looking populists) as neoliberal nationalists.[81]

From Karl Polanyi's perspective, Trump and embedded populism can be understood as a reaction against the social damage wrought by the pursuit of neoliberal coherence. The neoliberalism and elite-led globalization of the second American-led order bred resentment among its victims and primed them for illiberal leaders peddling contrived analyses and solutions. I nonetheless hold that the present incoherence creates space that was unavailable under neoliberalism. It provides opportunities for varied forms of reembeddednesses along with permissive and diverse forms of economic integration. Incoherent systems create space for experimentation, heterogeneity, and complexity, despite the fact that incoherence also creates space for discord, nationalism, racism, and authoritarianism. Polanyi above all others understood the simultaneity of risks and opportunities. Wisely, he provided us with no reassuring guarantees.

The original embedded liberalism of the postwar era was based on rules with universal aspirations and formal multilateral institutions seen as necessary to protect an open international economic order with the United States at its unquestioned center. Perhaps in light of the uneven changes highlighted in the discussion above—and the rise of informal governance networks, networks emerging among developing-economy financial institutions and officials, and networks between them and the IMF—we should think more about how to nurture informal and varied networked, cross-cutting, messy embedded liberalisms coexisting in a world marked by many isms. The present period has one thing in common with the embedded liberal era. Both provide space for national heterogeneity. Today's permissiveness is not driven by expert consensus on the importance of heterogeneity or the presence of a framework of multilateralism that supports it.[82] Rather, in the uncertainty that marks interregnums, openings emerge for policy autonomy.

Making space for alternative embedded liberalisms necessitates a degree of permissiveness in the international order—what Dani Rodrik referred to as "thin versions of globalization."[83] Thin globalization accepts a collection of diverse national strategies (such as capital controls) whose interactions are regulated by a set of simple, transparent, and common-sense rules set by a range of actors and institutions, which are themselves representative and inclusive. My claim is that this reconstruction can enable but by no means assures a restoration of embedded liberal principles. It may well be that thin globalization is all that is possible or even desirable, given the pending conclusion of the era of US hegemony. In this morbid interregnum there is no singular ism or alternative order, a fact that I do not mourn.

CORPORATE GLOBALIZATION AND THE LIBERAL ORDER

Disembedding and Reembedding
Governing Norms

John Gerard Ruggie

> **You can't go back and change the beginning, but you can start where you are and change the end.**
>
> —Attributed to C. S. Lewis

The international political economy of the post–World War II West was shaped by normative understandings and institutional arrangements that I have elsewhere described as embedded liberalism.[1] It coupled governments' commitments to progressively liberalize trade as well as establish free and stable exchange rates with maintaining adequate domestic policy space, including capital controls, to provide social investments and safety nets, and to buffer economically and socially dislocating effects of liberalization. Unlike the economic nationalism and bilateralism of the 1930s, this regime would be multilateral in character; but unlike the liberalism of the pre–World War I gold standard and free trade, its multilateralism would be predicated on domestic intervention.

Although largely an Anglo-American design, this regime captured enough core interests and concerns of European social democracies and social market economies to constitute the basis of the General Agreement on Tariffs and Trade (GATT) and the Articles of Agreement of the International Monetary Fund (IMF). The World Bank was established, initially to provide postwar reconstruction aid, but it soon turned to long-term assistance to developing countries. No new rules or institutions were established to govern foreign direct investment (FDI). In the West, this grand bargain led to what the French called *les trente glorieuse*—one of the longest and most equitable periods of economic expansion on record. In Mark Blyth's chapter in this volume, this era is depicted as "the first American order" (1945–80).

When I wrote the embedded liberalism article, the threat of a "new protectionism" was all the rage among American political economists: "The emergence of the new protectionism in the Western world reflects the victory of the interventionist, or welfare, economy over the market economy."[2] But my article concluded on a very different note: "The foremost force for discontinuity at present is not 'new protectionism' in money and trade but the resurgent ethos of liberal capitalism."[3] This ethos was soon dubbed "neoliberalism." In Blyth's rendering, its emergence marked the beginning of the second American-led international order.

Despite near-universal usage of the term, the precise meaning, scope, and provenance of neoliberalism remains contested.[4] Nevertheless, in the context of the transformation of Anglo-American capitalism beginning around 1980 it is generally meant to include weakening regulatory, redistributive, and antitrust policies, as well as labor unions; outsourcing government functions to private contractors; offshoring the production of manufactured products and some services to countries where labor costs were cheaper and regulations weak or nonexistent; establishing full capital mobility; and the ascendance of finance together with the financialization of the real economy. These changes were accompanied by a radical shift in the prevailing conception of the publicly listed corporation—from a "social entity" to a "private property" conception, in the words of William Allen, former chancellor of the Delaware Court of Chancery.[5] Maximizing shareholder value, or shareholder primacy, was soon considered to be the overriding if not sole purpose of the corporation by business leaders, investors, and ultimately by regulatory authorities. Apart from the United States and United Kingdom, relatively few countries embraced all these features outright, but they spread internationally through bilateral investment treaties; bilateral/regional free trade agreements; conditionalities imposed by the global financial institutions and World Trade Organization (WTO) rules; and by the new and powerful global market forces these developments unleashed.

The chapters in this volume by Jonathan Kirshner, Mark Blyth, Peter Gourevitch, Rawi Abdelal, and Ilene Grable untangle elements of this complex web of factors and identify why and how they ultimately triggered the political polarization and the rise of populism that characterize large swaths of the industrialized world. To the extent that one can speak of a "third order," Blyth considers it to be "purposeless," though still reliant on the US dollar for international transactions. Grabel considers it an "incoherent order," but one with some "productive and even transformative moments." This chapter places the multinational enterprise within these developments.[6] The chapter spans three forms of liberalism in the political economy sense of the term: embedded liberalism, neoliberalism, and a new form of liberalism that has begun to view the public corporation as more of a social entity, no now longer limited to the national realm nor the exclusive "property" of shareholders. Unlike the first two, this third construct is not the product of America's role as the world's leading power; it emerged as a result of transnational civic reactions against the unregulated social and environmental externalities generated by multinationals in the neoliberal era.

In brief, here is the story. The same policy measures that unraveled embedded liberalism and gave us neoliberalism also enabled the ascendance of corporate globalization. In turn, corporate globalization became the most transformative geo-economic and geopolitical development of the past half century, and shareholder primacy its force multiplier. Their combination brought enormous benefits to people and countries well positioned to seize the new opportunities. But their unfettered expansion would also disrupt and even tear social fabrics as well as overtax natural capital. This was not only predictable; it was predicted. At the January 1999 Davos meeting, then United Nations (UN) secretary general Kofi Annan delivered what turned out to be a highly consequential keynote address. He warned that unless corporate globalization developed stronger social and environmental pillars it would remain "vulnerable to backlash from all the 'isms' of our post-cold-war world: protectionism; populism; nationalism; ethnic chauvinism; fanaticism; and terrorism."[7]

Now turn to August 2019. In the heartland of neoliberal capitalism, the US Business Roundtable (BR) issued a new mission statement on "the purpose of the corporation." The BR comprises the chief executive officers (CEOs) of some two hundred of America's largest corporations. For more than a quarter-century, its corporate governance guidelines had endorsed maximizing shareholder value. In contrast, the new mission statement committed signatory CEOs "to lead their companies for the benefit of all stakeholders—customers, employees, suppliers, communities and shareholders."[8] Later that year, the World Economic Forum announced that "stakeholder capitalism" would be the theme of its upcoming annual Davos confab. Larry Fink, CEO of BlackRock, the world's largest asset manager, addressed his annual letter to CEOs to the same theme: "The importance of serving stakeholders and embracing purpose is becoming increasingly central to the way that companies understand their role in society."[9] BlackRock, he added, would begin to consider sustainability risks in its portfolio offerings, initially focused largely on climate issues.

Not surprisingly, these moves were widely met with both criticism and skepticism. The *Wall Street Journal* savaged the BR statement in an editorial for, among other misdeeds, "undermining the morality of free markets and the moral and fiduciary duty" of corporate leaders.[10] Two Harvard corporate law experts argued that "stakeholderism," if acted on, would leave both stakeholders and shareholders worse off.[11] Anand Giridharadas, author of *Winners Take All: The Elite Charade of Changing the World*, reflected the views of many in seeing in the BR statement "well-meaning activities that are virtuous side hustles . . . while key activities of their business are relatively undisturbed."[12]

Even as I share some of the skepticism, I argue that the current corporate repurposing discussion is an indicator of directional change, although not yet of a final destination. I do so on three grounds. First, given how consequential corporate globalization and shareholder primacy have been to weakening the provision of public goods, social cohesion, and broadly shared prosperity that were the aim of the embedded part of the postwar compromise, any discussion by corporate leaders of a possible shift toward a different conception of corporate purpose deserves scrutiny, whatever immediate rationales might be in play. Second, behind the BR statement, the Davos declarations, and perhaps an opportunistic asset manager there is a history; for more than two decades, social actors including civil society, workers' organizations, elements of the United Nations, some governments, corporate intrapreneurs as well as socially responsible investors have constructed transnational ecosystems of norms and practices regarding corporate conduct and purpose. Examining those ecosystems, as well as why and how they developed, provides context for the current corporate repurposing debate. It helps us to differentiate between pure virtue-signaling and meaningful moves beyond the constricted corporate construct and the hyperglobalization dominant for the past generation. Third, to the extent there is some "there" there, all stakeholders concerned with the challenges facing people and the planet need to understand the opportunities these developments offer, but also the limits of what they can achieve if left to their own devices.

The discussion is organized in six parts. To anchor it, the first identifies several key features of corporate globalization. The second notes the paradox that at the height of the most recent globalization boom in the 1990s and early 2000s, multinationals discovered that their legal license to operate, provided by the state, did not in itself translate into a social license, granted by communities. Firms responded to this pressure by developing enterprise-wide corporate social responsibility (CSR) as a management tool. Although quite superficial in its early iterations, in retrospect CSR marked the first step toward systematically engaging external stakeholders, if only in the attempt to placate them. The following three sections use the lens of three UN initiatives that identified opportunities to build on and expand the opportunities created by this initial step, and to promote moves in the direction of conceiving the firm as more of a social entity. The conclusion returns to the current corporate repurposing debate and reflects on what it may mean for the questions addressed in this volume, written amid global crises.

Corporate Globalization

Raymond Vernon, a pioneer in the study of multinationals since the 1970s, published a book in 1998 entitled *In the Hurricane's Eye: The Troubled Prospects of Multinational Enterprises*. His decision to write it, he stated in the preface "grew out of a sense that the world was slipping into a period in which the inescapable clashes between multinational enterprises and nation-states might be growing in frequency and intensity, evoking responses from the public and the private sectors that would substantial[ly] impair their performance."[13]

Yet multinationals became and remain a standard mode of organizing economic activities across countries. Of course, there exist different national variants of multinational firms, as well as different types of ownership and governance structures. But the convergence around the multinational as an international institutional form is virtually universal.

What Is It?

Some form of globalization has existed throughout the ages; as the historian of the *longue durée*, Fernand Braudel, said of earlier centuries: "Capital laughed at frontiers."[14] The most recent form of corporate globalization, however, had unique characteristics. During the 1990s, 94 percent of all national legislation addressed to the subject of FDI, worldwide, liberalized rules to encourage it.[15] Whereas there were some seven thousand multinationals in 1970, by 2008 they numbered eighty-two thousand.[16] Many operated in more countries and territories than there are UN member states. As a result of complex value chains, by the early 2010s roughly 80 percent of global trade (in terms of gross exports) was linked to multinationals' production networks;[17] trade in intermediate products was greater than all other non-oil traded goods combined.[18] Furthermore, one out of seven jobs in the world was estimated to be global-value-chain related, not counting "informal" and "non-standard" forms of work, to which tasks are often subcontracted, and which may involve home-based, child, or even slave labor.[19] In short, through offshoring, lead firms in effect had decoupled themselves from large parts of their workforce and communities at both ends of their global value chains.

Multinationals based in emerging-market countries have risen to significant numbers in the Global Fortune 500, with China in the lead. The rapid expansion of multinationals has declined more recently because of investment uncertainties following the 2008 financial crisis; trade wars coupled with growing national security restrictions on FDI aimed at China in particular; and some erosion of competitive advantage vis-à-vis national firms. But to date attempts to reverse global value chains and broadly "re-shore" production to the home country as a general proposition have proven to be both costly and largely ineffective.[20] Even before the COVID-19 outbreak in China, Western firms had begun to diversify their supplier bases to other Asian countries with lower labor costs.

The keystone of the multinational institutional form is that it is not derivative of state sovereignty, unlike, say, the United Nations or the WTO—or, for that matter, the East India Company of yesteryear. Its foundation lies in a specific structure of property rights, accepted by states in order to participate in and benefit from the international economic system.[21] The integrated economic organization of the multinational acts through one legal self (often called the corporate parent), which creates the other legal selves that make up the multinational group. The law considers each of these entities to have separate legal personality and limited liability, even if it is wholly owned by the parent. Subsidiaries can have subsidiaries of their own and enter into joint ventures, subject to the same rules. There is no global regulator to govern the multinational as a whole. And national law generally has jurisdiction only over whatever specific entity of the group is incorporated within that jurisdiction.[22]

When powerful multinationals negotiate the terms of a project with a powerful state, they bargain as relative equals, with both sides trading concessions. For example, Disney went through a lengthy negotiation with China for the rights to build the multibillion-dollar Shanghai Disney Resort, with neither side getting everything they wanted. When they were done, Disney's then CEO, Robert Iger, described the result as "authentically Disney, and distinctly Chinese."[23] In asymmetrical situations, multinationals typically have locational options they can invoke as well as superior resources and institutional capacities.

Multinationals also enjoy special legal protection under bilateral investment treaties (BITs). As noted earlier, no rules governing FDI were instituted as part of the postwar international economic regimes. Subsequent efforts to establish a multilateral agreement, whether to regulate multinationals or to protect their interests, failed. As a result, the industrialized countries turned to BITs. After an exponential increase in the 1990s, their number reached three thousand. BITs require the state receiving foreign investment (host state) to provide enforceable guarantees to foreign investors. Expropriation without adequate compensation was the original concern, but treaty terms became increasingly elastic over time to include so-called regulatory takings and ultimately any domestic policy, including environmental, health, and labor standards, that a three-person arbitration panel might construe as being "tantamount to expropriation," with the rules drawn from commercial arbitration even if conducted under the auspices of a World Bank affiliate.[24] There is no appellate process.

The deeper social purpose of BITs—so different from that of embedded liberalism—was explained by José Alvarez, a US BIT negotiator in the Ronald Reagan administration and a distinguished professor of international law. BITs were intended "to entrench the underlying private law regime necessary to support market transactions—and enable international law to become a force to dismantle [host country] public law regulations inimical to the market."[25] BITs generally are in force for fifteen years and then are renegotiated or dropped. Catherine Titi shows that the most recent generation of BITs provides greater policy space to host governments, no doubt because OECD countries, including the United States, have ended up on the respondent side of BIT claims with greater frequency.[26]

In sum, the inescapable clashes between multinationals and states that Vernon feared have not materialized. The prominence of multinationals may stem from their providing access to investments and markets more efficiently than alternatives. But that the convergence occurred so rapidly and so thoroughly suggests that mimetic and even normative factors also might have been in play—in the sense that this, not that, is the appropriate way to conduct international business.

Principals and Agents

Just as multinationals were expanding into virtually every jurisdiction across the globe, the construct of the corporation underwent a fundamental change in the United States. From around the time of the New Deal, what Justice William Allen called the "social entity" conception of the firm had been the dominant form. Nicholas Lemann has gone further, suggesting that the large US corporation in the postwar era "was the American welfare state" for its millions of employees and their families by providing well-paying lifetime jobs, health insurance, and retirement and other such benefits.[27] By the 1980s, however, the private property model resurged.[28] Already in 1970, Milton Friedman published a widely read article in the *New York Times Magazine*, "The Social Responsibility of Business Is to Increase Its Profits."[29] For Friedman the idea that corporations should have a role in addressing larger social issues represented a sure step on the road to socialism. Corporate directors and executives, he maintained, are agents intended to serve the interests of their principals, shareholders, whom he (mistakenly) considered to be the owners of the listed corporation.[30] If agents wished to spend money on worthy causes, they were free to do so using their own. In this scheme, dealing with externalities was the job of governments, while business influence over regulatory policy remained moot.

Friedman's popular writings were intended to promote an ideological agenda. Not so for finance theorists Michael Jensen and William Meckling.[31] In a technical academic article that has some 100,000 citations, they took up in formal terms what became known as the "agency problem." Drawing on the theory of property rights, among other sources, they addressed the means by which principals could most effectively minimize "agency costs"—literally the monitoring costs and incentives to agents that principals incur, and in some situations the bonding costs of agents to principals. In the corporate context, their solution was to structure contracts in such a way that agents were led to behave more like principals by bearing the financial risks of their own decisions. Maximizing shareholder value emerged from this mix. It achieved near epistemic closure in business schools and academic corporate law programs, becoming a social norm in the business world well before it was memorialized in securities regulations and standards. By 2001 it was proclaimed as "The End of History for Corporate Law."[32]

But what accounts for its ultimate dominance, not in theory but practice? Serious stagflation in the 1970s and growing competition stemming from globalization provide contextual explanations. Lynn Stout, a vocal legal critic of shareholder primacy, also suggests several more specific factors. It gave the public and the media easy-to-understand soundbites to account for numerous corporate scandals in the 1980s (framed as out-of-control corporate executives); it was employed to justify the junk bond–fueled takeover frenzy at that time; it provided companies and reformers with a simple metric of corporate performance; it prescribed a solution that fit well with the broader ascendance of the Chicago School of economics and the conservative Law and Economics movement; and, not least, it appealed to self-interest.[33] One of the main means the doctrine's proponents advocated reducing agency costs was linking CEO compensation to stock performance—which in practice often came to mean short-term performance. But earnings reports can be easily manipulated. Buying back shares can boost their price. So too can cost-cutting. In turn, that can be achieved by reducing research and development expenditures and capital investments, and offshoring jobs into remote and opaque supply chains. In these ways, shareholder primacy contributed to soaring executive compensation at a time when income stagnation of workers in the home country began to set in, and with short-termism possibly endangering the long-term health of the firm itself.

BEPS

Corporate globalization has also been boosted by a different conception of property rights: the right of states to commercialize their sovereignty.[34] This has to do with tax havens, which result in what the OECD inelegantly calls BEPS: base erosion and profit shifting.[35] Gabriel Zucman estimates that in the immediate postwar years there was a mere handful of tax havens, led by Switzerland and

Luxembourg.[36] A study published in 2010 reported fifty, with more on the way.[37] Initial increments came from the British Channel Islands and later various remnants of the British Empire, led by the Cayman Islands. Many remained closely tied to the City in London, contributing to its heft as a global financial center. Pacific microstates have since also entered the game.

Tax havens offer low to zero taxation to nonresidents, they provide strict secrecy, and they have minimal requirements for incorporation. Indeed, most are merely booking centers. That is, actual transactions take place elsewhere but are then registered in these jurisdictions, where the parties typically have no physical presence beyond a name plate on the door of a local law firm. According to Ronen Palan, Richard Murphy, and Christian Chavagneux, "About 50% of all international bank lending and 30% of the world's stock of Foreign Direct Investment are registered in these jurisdictions."[38] Tax havens greatly augment the ability of multinationals to engage in intrafirm and related-party transfer pricing, whether of goods, services, or loans. The ownership of intellectual property frequently is registered in such facilities, its value priced by the multinational itself. So too are foreign profits generated by, say, a US company, which would have to pay taxes if the profits were repatriated. Zucman estimates that more than half of US-based companies' foreign profits, which account for a third of their total profits, are "earned" in six low- or zero-tax countries.[39]

The consequences of tax havens coupled with overall corporate tax competition among states are substantial. Former US treasury secretary Lawrence Summers, a leading architect of the recent era of globalization, subsequently concluded: "It is a significant problem for the revenue capacity of states and an immense problem for their capacity to maintain progressive taxation."[40] In short, tax havens have facilitated and augmented the scale, scope, and legal optimization of multinationals. They thereby also drain states' revenue bases and impose heavier tax burdens on smaller businesses, individuals, and families. As a result, domestic safety nets and other public expenditures suffer, contributing to economic inequality and social resentment. Intergovernmental negotiations to fix this problem have been going on for decades; an international agreement on at least a common minimum corporate tax rate may lie within reach.

No country or company is known to have set out with this model of corporate globalization as its long-term vision or strategic plan. The enabling environment for it was constructed over time by governments following a neoliberal playbook. Well-positioned corporations advocated or simply took advantage of successive steps. The cumulative effects of governments' policies helped create the functional and juridical space for the ascendance of corporate globalization. There is no going back to change the beginning. No silver bullet can reverse such a deep and wide systemic transformation. The only way to try to change the end is by identifying strategic points of intervention in what exists and build on what seems to work. At the height of the corporate globalization boom, one such strategic leverage point began to crystalize.

Starting Where You Are

Corporate globalization invigorated already-existing moves by civil society and workers' organizations into the transnational sphere, such as the divestment campaign against apartheid in South Africa; the highly successful Access to Essential Medicines campaign during the devastation wrought by HIV/AIDS in developing countries, particularly sub-Saharan Africa; and campaigns targeting countries' human rights and environmental practices.[41] In the mid-1990s massive antiglobalization demonstrations met the annual meetings of the IMF and World Bank in whatever country they were held. And in November 1999 the so-called Battle of Seattle shut down a GATT ministerial meeting. Targeting multinationals was a subset of this broader transnational civic pressure.

Trouble in the Offshore

Nike was among the first US brands to shift its entire production overseas. Nike was also among the first to trigger a multimedia, multicountry, multiyear campaign in the 1990s protesting worker abuses in its Southeast Asian contractor factories. Local unions in Indonesia began the protests; ultimately, they also involved US unions, college students sporting the Nike swoosh, and the media in the United States, Canada, and Europe. The campaign proved so effective that Phil Knight, founder and CEO, confessed in a tearful 1998 speech at the National Press Club: "The Nike product has become synonymous with slave wages, forced overtime and arbitrary abuse. I truly believe that the American consumer does not want to buy products made in abusive conditions."[42] Nike went on to become a leader in developing CSR practices as a management tool.[43]

At roughly the same time, in the Ogoni territory of Nigeria, massive community demonstrations were held against oil giant Shell, triggered by the company's environmental practices degrading the air, farmland and fish-rich streams, coupled with Shell's alleged complicity with Nigeria's military dictatorship, which routinely used excessive force against the protesters. The government arrested nine Ogoni leaders, charging them with inciting violence. International protests and pleas for clemency poured in from civil society organizations and governments, including leaders of other African countries. But after a sham trial before a military tribunal, the Nigerian government executed the nine. Shell stood meekly by, stating: "A commercial enterprise like Shell cannot and must never interfere with the legal process of any sovereign state."[44] Sir Mark Moody-Stuart, a Shell executive who had advocated for a more robust position at the time and went on to become the firm's chairman, reflected in his memoirs on Shell's "*annus horribilis*,"[45] reporting that as a result Shell adopted new "business principles" and, like Nike, new CSR practices.[46]

In short, Nike and Shell discovered that having a legal license to operate in a country, granted by the government, was insufficient to ensure their social license to operate: "Tacit consent on the part of society toward the activities of the business."[47] This legitimation challenge was local and global at the same time. Elsewhere, I have depicted the routinization and aggregation of these dynamics as creating a "global public domain," an institutionalized arena of discourse, contestation, and action: "It is constituted by interactions among non-state actors as well as states. It permits the direct expression and pursuit of a variety of human interests, not merely those mediated (filtered, interpreted, promoted) by states. It 'exists' in transnational non-territorial spatial formations and is anchored in norms and expectations as well as institutional networks and circuits within, across, and beyond states."[48]

This public domain does not by itself necessarily determine outcomes any more than a domestic civic domain does. But one of its first achievements in relation to multinationals was to lead them to adopt CSR as a new management tool.

CSR

Advocacy groups historically have tended to favor binding global regulations of multinationals. But that would require a widely supported international treaty. At the height of neoliberalism, with President Bill Clinton urging, "We must embrace the inexorable logic of globalization" and proclaiming, "The era of big government is over," the creation of more government at the international level to regulate multinationals seemed highly unlikely. For their part, developing countries were competing for foreign investment, offering increasingly attractive packages through export-processing zones and other such means. What multinationals were willing to do, and what governments encouraged them to do, is what Nike and Shell had already done: adopt CSR policies and practices.

CSR experienced a "phenomenal rise to prominence in the 1990s and 2000s . . . almost unique in the pantheon of ideas in the management literature," along with a similarly impressive ascent in practice.[49] A form of business self-regulation, CSR was neoliberalism's answer to the social and environmental externalities it enabled. During its rise to prominence, global CSR practices exhibited several common features.[50] They originated in western Europe and North America.

Initially, they were most likely to be adopted by brand-sensitive or community-facing businesses like Nike and Shell, although mimetic dynamics soon emerged. The standards they set were largely self-defined and often reflected perceived preferences of home markets or even market segments. For example, premium brands like Nike adopted more robust commitments on workplace standards in supplier factories as well as greater transparency in reporting than did value brands like Walmart. And within firms, CSR typically was siloed off as a cost center, not integrated into core business functions. Despite these weaknesses, however, a social norm was being established: the expectation that firms, particularly Western multinationals operating in developing countries, should have a set of policies and practices that addressed concerns of stakeholders other than shareholders.

Norm Consolidation

The fact that individual firms pursued their own versions of CSR meant that none was authoritative, what each reported was discretionary, and firms based in developing countries were included under these schemes only if they were subject to a Western multinational's supplier code. For UN secretary general Kofi Annan, these gaps presented an opportunity to increase the scale and scope of the CSR norm, while anchoring it to UN aspirational values and legal principles. Thus, in his January 1999 Davos speech, cited earlier, he challenged the assembled business leaders to join him in "a global compact of shared values and principles." Globalization is fragile, he observed. "The spread of markets outpaces the ability of societies and their political systems to adjust to them, let alone to guide the course they take. History teaches us that such an imbalance between the economic, social and political realms can never be sustained for very long." You do not need to wait for every government in the world to act, he continued. "You can uphold human rights and decent labor and environmental standards directly, by your own conduct of your own business."

The proposition Annan put to business leaders was two-fold. First, that they should align their CSR policies and practices behind what ethicists describe as hypernorms: norms that are sufficiently fundamental and universally acknowledged that they can serve as a basis for establishing, guiding, and evaluating lower-order norms.[51] Ethicists have argued forever about what the origins of such norms might be, or whether they even exist. In the UN context there is no mystery. Although the term itself would never be used, hypernorms are high-level norms that governments have agreed to in treaties, declarations, and other formal expressions of universal or near-universal consent. Specifically, Annan was asking businesses to frame their CSR policies and practices in alignment with ten principles drawn from the Universal Declaration of Human Rights, the International Labor Organization's Declaration on Fundamental Rights at Work, the Rio Earth Summit Declaration, and the UN Convention against Corruption. As he put it, "You can use these universal values as the cement binding your global operations, since they are values people all over the world will recognize as their own."

In return, Annan offered the full cooperation of UN agencies in assisting businesses to translate these hypernorms into lower-level norms, operational practices, and partnership projects appropriate for different types of businesses and operating contexts. He also established ongoing learning forums for CSR experts from companies and other stakeholder groups. These forums greatly facilitated information sharing as well as identifying and promoting best practices; they also had the effect of recruiting additional intrapreneurs for the cause within firms and in communities of practice among them. To ensure that the very top of firms was engaged, entry into the Global Compact (GC) club requires a commitment letter from CEOs to the secretary general; a periodic leaders' summit brings CEOs together with the secretary general.

The GC went live in June 2000. It has become the largest international corporate engagement platform, with nearly 14,000 business participants from 160 countries, including every major emerging-market economy (despite delisting 4,000 over the years for not submitting annual progress reports). The GC has also generated self-sustaining national networks in some 60 countries; not surprisingly a Nordic Network was the first, but India and Brazil were not far behind. Early on, the GC signed a memorandum of understanding with the then fledgling Global Reporting Initiative (GRI), an independent multistakeholder entity based in Amsterdam, encouraging GC participants to fulfill their reporting requirement through the GRI. In turn, the GRI became a leading sustainability-reporting organization.

There is a substantial academic literature on the GC. But much of it is based on the premise that it was intended as a regulatory instrument. It was not.[52] Therefore scholars have largely misconstrued the nature of the enterprise. The GC had no intergovernmental mandate, which a regulatory instrument would have required, and initially it had no resources apart from Annan's "charismatic authority," in Weberian terms—or, as US-UN ambassador Richard Holbrooke described him, "the rock star of international diplomacy." In contrast, high-level public understanding and recognition of the GC was swift and impressive. Shortly after the GC's launch in 2000, the *Christian Science Monitor* editorialized that it was "the UN's most creative reinvention to be seen yet."[53] A year later the Nobel Peace Prize was awarded jointly to

Annan and the UN as a whole for, among other achievements, their role in "international mobilization aimed at meeting the world's economic, social and environmental challenges," and to Annan in addition for "bringing new life to the organization."[54]

There is little systematic evidence of why firms chose to be early participants; constructing a sufficiently large data set to perform serious statistical analyses would be a herculean undertaking. My own observations as an architect of and participant in the GC are that Western firms concerned about social license issues sought some authoritative framework within which to frame their CSR policies—but not one that involved direct regulation. Some, like Nike and Shell, also may have perceived first-mover advantages. Two considerations appear to have been key drivers for emerging economy–based firms. The first was signaling to global markets that they were CSR-safe as suppliers or joint-venture partners. The other was helping induce greater dynamism in the typically highly bureaucratized business-government nexus in their own countries. China encouraged even some state-owned enterprises to participate; the CEO of Sinopec served a term as vice-chair of the GC board (which the secretary general chairs). Infosys was the first Indian company to sign up. Its website states: "In our journey of over 37 years, we have catalyzed some of the major changes that have led to India's emergence as the global destination for software services talent." Consultancies were quick to join, sensing business opportunities.

Similarly, little systematic data exists measuring the GC's impact on company practice. But for the GC's fifteenth anniversary, a Norwegian consultancy, DNV-GL, conducted a survey of business participants. One question asked was in which areas the GC had played an important role for them. Sixty percent of respondents agreed or strongly agreed with "motivating our company to advance broader UN goals and issues (e.g., poverty, health, education)"; 65 percent agreed with "guiding our corporate sustainability reporting"; 66 percent agreed with "driving our implementation of sustainability policies and practices"; and 48 percent agreed with "shaping our company's vision."[55] One never knows how accurately such surveys reflect reality, but these responses do suggest movement, at least among participants, toward a broader social-entity conception of the firm.

The term CSR is little used anymore, including by the GC (it now describes itself as a "corporate sustainability" initiative). Moreover, this field of play has become far more diverse, and each niche is densely populated and increasingly professionalized. For leading companies, the concept of responsibility has expanded to include setting carbon emission targets in line with the Paris Accord and using third-party reporting tools. Large consumer-product companies are investing heavily to create substitutes for plastics and to reduce water stress. Others are engaged in joint projects with civil society groups and/or UN agencies to improve agricultural practices, public health, and education. Several have committed to paying fair living wages in their supply chain. And some have changed their legal status to become B-Corps (Benefit Corporations), or *enterprises à mission* in France, in order to expand the scope of their fiduciary duty.[56] Supply-chain codes and monitoring are common, although systematically reaching beyond first-tier suppliers into the deeper layers of subcontracting remains challenging for many.

As the *doyen* in this space, the GC retains considerable convening power. But it now serves primarily as a knowledge aggregator and curator, having published more than seven thousand reports. It also promotes business support for the seventeen Sustainable Development Goals adopted by the UN in 2015. As an overall assessment of the GC in relation to businesses, Andreas Rasche has it just about right. He described the GC as "a necessary supplement."[57] It is necessary because without the norm consolidation it promoted and the communities of practice it helped create and expand, the shared vernacular and practices of CSR might not have formed and evolved in such a coherent manner in support of international "public goods." It is a supplement in that it crystallized and amplified the efforts of countless other stakeholder groups and intrapreneurs whose efforts and pressure put and kept these issues on the agenda.

Market Incentives

The GC also used its UN perch to catalyze corresponding change in the investment realm. A socially responsible investing (SRI) industry in the United States has existed at least since the 1970s, when the first socially screened mutual funds were established.[58] SRI initially focused on the exclusion of certain stocks from portfolios (for example, weapons, tobacco, gambling, or alcohol), and on lobbying companies involved in their production. In the 1980s major pension funds and university endowments took part in the divestment campaign against South Africa's apartheid regime as an expression of their social responsibility. In the 1990s the first research firm was established to market social and environmental data on companies to the investment community. Rating agencies using such data soon followed.

ESG investing—taking a company's environmental, social, and governance performance into account in portfolio construction—morphed out of this context. The concept of ESG itself was introduced in a 2004 Global Compact report, "Who Cares Wins: Connecting Financial Markets to a Changing World," prepared for a GC workshop with some twenty financial institutions from Europe, the United States, Latin America, and Singapore, and co-organized with the International Finance Corporation and the finance initiative of the UN Environment Program.[59] The report spelled out the rationale for integrating ESG criteria into investment analysis and portfolio selection, and it made a series of recommendations to the financial industry. Kofi Annan then convened a larger group of institutional investors at the New York Stock Exchange, launching the Principles for Responsible Investing (PRI). The PRI became an independent nonprofit to promote ESG investing, and by 2020 its signatories included some three thousand asset owners, managers, and analysts, with a combined total of $100 trillion in assets under management.

By the end of 2018, ESG investing accounted for one-quarter of all assets under management globally; it rose to one-third by 2021. Australia, Canada, Europe, and New Zealand remain in the lead, with the United States catching up. For years the increase was incremental. But it turned up like a hockey stick after the 2008 financial crisis, suggesting declining faith in mainstream investing. In the United States, it increased 38 percent from 2016 to 2018, in what *Barron's*, the business magazine, called the "Trump Bump," possibly anticipating that the new administration was not likely to be ESG-friendly.[60] The 2019 net inflow almost quadrupled over the over the prior year.[61] By early 2020, shares in companies with the highest ESG ratings were trading at a 30 percent premium over the lowest performers.[62] In June 2020, Morningstar UK, a financial data provider, published a study of 4,900 European funds that found that ESG funds had higher average returns and greater survivorship rates over the previous ten years than traditional funds.[63] ESG funds also have been more resilient in the face of unprecedented market volatility caused by the outbreak and spread of COVID-19.[64] To date, ESG investing has been driven mostly by large asset-management firms and institutional investors, such as pension funds.[65] A retail boost is expected from millennials (born 1981–96), who are reported to be on track to receive a $30 trillion wealth transfer from their baby boomer parents and who, according to consultancy surveys, have strong preferences for ESG investing.[66] And there is now a powerful push from investors and many governments for common ESG standards.[67]

The remarkable rise in ESG investing and the debate on repurposing the public corporation are closely related. Both express the view that the large public corporation should consider its impacts on stakeholders beyond shareholders. ESG investing introduces a market-incentive mechanism into this normative evolution. In sum, through the lens of the GC we can track the trajectory of both real-economy firms and investors moving toward a more social-entity conception of the firm.

Soft Law and Beyond

In June 2020, the *American Journal of International Law* posted an online symposium on soft and hard law in the area of business and human rights. In his introduction, Steven Ratner, the Bruno Simma Professor of Law at the University of Michigan, stated:

> For the many stakeholders concerned about the impact of business activity on human rights, the last decade has been a whirlwind of norm-making. . . . More important, [it] produced nothing less than a wave of lawmaking and standard setting at the national, international, and corporate level—in particular to elaborate for business the scope of their responsibilities under Pillar II [of the UN Guiding Principles on Business and Human Rights (UNGPs)]: the corporate responsibility to respect human rights. Domestic laws included statutory requirements to implement the UNGPs' promotion of due diligence by companies as a way of determining their exposure to and involvement with human rights violations.[68]

Stepping back for a moment, in 2011 the UN Human Rights Council adopted the UNGPs unanimously—thirty-one principles, each accompanied by commentary elaborating their meaning and implications.[69] I developed the UNGPs over the course of a six-year mandate as special representative of the secretary general for business and human rights. The Council's endorsement marked the first time that the UN had issued any authoritative guidance for states and business enterprises on their respective obligations regarding business and human rights; it also marked the first time it endorsed a normative text on any subject that governments did not negotiate themselves. The endorsement elevated the UNGPs beyond pure voluntarism into the domain of soft law.[70]

Karin Buhmann attributed the UNGPs' success in part to the process legitimacy of how they were developed.[71] She is correct that extensive research reports produced by and for the mandate: some fifty international consultations, building transnational coalitions within and across various stakeholder groups; pilot projects; and posting all documentation as well as criticisms on the independent London-based Business and Human Rights Resource Centre's website, made it difficult for anyone to criticize the process whereby the UNGPs were developed. But let me briefly highlight five substantive features of the UNGPs that relate to the theme of this chapter.[72]

First, the UNGPs clearly delineate the respective roles and responsibilities of states and businesses. By virtue of the human rights obligations that states undertake when adopting international human rights treaties, they have a legal duty to protect against abuses by third parties, which include business. To protect means to have in place effective policies, regulation, legislation, and enforcement. As for business, prior efforts to develop an international regulatory framework simply sought to transpose the full range of state obligations onto enterprises, within their respective spheres of influence: "To promote, secure the fulfillment of, respect, ensure respect of and protect human rights."[73] This was opposed by states and business alike, as it would have created an endless muddle of blame shifting regarding who was responsible for what. In contrast, the UNGPs define the scope of corporate obligations by their own conduct and impact. The foundational principle is that enterprises should respect human rights; that is, they should avoid harming people's human rights through their activities or business relationships and should address harms that do occur. This holds independently of what states do or do not do. It is an independent enterprise responsibility. And it holds throughout global value chains.

Second, for firms to respect human rights they must have systems in place whereby they can know and show that they do. A policy commitment is necessary but insufficient. It also requires companies to conduct human rights due diligence in order to identify, prevent, mitigate, and account for the way they address their human rights risks and impacts. The Guiding Principles lay out a human rights due-diligence process and elaborate its components. This was welcomed by companies, including corporate counsel whose remit includes standard forms of due diligence and risk management. A Harvard Business School case quotes Sybil Veenman, general counsel of the largest global gold-mining company at the time, who explained: "The GPs were the first thing companies had to tell them *how* to respond to these issues. . . . The issues you face are unpredictable, and it's hard to know how to tackle them. The GPs were a starting point and gave our efforts some legitimacy."[74]

Third, the UNGPs avoided long-standing and paralyzing doctrinal debates over whether business enterprises can be duty bearers under international human rights law.[75] The UNGPs sidestepped that issue by stating that businesses should look to the core set of international human rights instruments as an authoritative enumeration, not of international laws that they might violate, but of human rights that they could impact adversely. This framing also made it possible for countries that had not ratified key international human rights conventions, including China and the United States, to endorse the UNGPs and to reference them in their own national policies and guidance to companies.[76] Further clarity was provided regarding what an enterprise may be held liable for, in a nonlegal sense. Under the UNGPs, this depends on whether it caused an adverse impact, contributed to the adverse impact even though the impact was caused by another, or whether the adverse impact was caused by a third party with which the enterprise has an ongoing business relationship, even though the enterprise neither caused nor contributed to the harm at issue. The remedial actions expected of a company are calibrated based on these distinctions. Adding to available sources of remedy, the UNGPs provide extensive guidance on effectiveness and legitimacy criteria of nonjudicial dispute resolution processes, including operational-level grievance mechanisms.

Fourth, from the start we engaged with standard-setting bodies beyond the UN: individual governments (national regulation), the OECD (*Guidelines for Multinational Enterprises*, corporate governance principles), International Finance Corporation (provider of project finance); the United Nations Commission on International Trade Law (sets investor/state arbitration rules); the European Commission (establishes norms and legal directives for corporate conduct); the International Organization of Standardization (sets international technical standards); as well as professional organizations (the International Bar Association, for example). Each has its own mission. But all were closely enough related to the UNGPs to provide insight and, within their remit, to become part of distributed networks for implementation.[77]

For the fifth point, I return to Ratner. The UNGPs, he states, "produced nothing less than a wave of lawmaking and standard setting at the national, international, and corporate level—in particular to elaborate for business the scope of their responsibilities."[78] The uptake by leading companies was impressive; uptake by FIFA, the Fédération Internationale de Football Association, was unexpected; FIFA was persuaded to endorse the UNGPs and include human rights criteria in its bidding requirements for the 2026 men's World Cup.[79] But what was quite new was governments drawing on the UNGPs due-diligence provisions to formulate new national legislation; for the most part, previously they had limited their own role to endorsing or promoting purely voluntary initiatives. The new laws include the *loi de vigilance* (France); modern-day slavery acts (California, the United Kingdom, Australia); child labor laws (the Netherlands); a mandatory human rights due-diligence law (Germany); European Union (EU) nonfinancial reporting requirements; and an EU-level mandatory human rights and environmental due-diligence directive promised for autumn of 2021, which is expected to apply to entire value chains and to include a civil liability provision.[80] It does not escape me that this set of legal moves remains mostly European so far. But Europe is the second-largest home base of all multinationals. Moreover, the EU mandatory due-diligence directive will apply to foreign firms above a certain size that operate within the EU's internal market.

What is taking place in the business and human rights space is yet another instance of a shift produced by strategic interventions on the part of a multitude of social actors. And it also marks the recognition by some legislative bodies that their political operating context vis-à-vis business has changed significantly, considering how far some businesses themselves have come. This should give greater courage to all governments to do what governments are intended to do: to govern, and to govern in the public interest.

In a moment of great insight (or possibly self-congratulation) Milton Friedman wrote this in the preface to the 1982 edition of *Capitalism and Freedom*, which was first published in 1962 and has sold more than a half-million copies: "There is enormous inertia—a tyranny of the status quo—in private and especially governmental arrangements. Only a crisis—actual or perceived—produces real change. When that crisis occurs, the actions that are taken depend on the ideas that are lying around. That, I believe, is our basic function: to develop alternatives to existing policies, to keep them alive and available until the politically impossible becomes politically inevitable."[81]

As I write this, we are amid three crises, each actual: the worst pandemic in more than a century, the widest socioeconomic inequality gaps since the Gilded Age, and climate threats that have no precedent in human history. I cannot say how these will ultimately unfold. But this chapter has tracked "ideas that are lying around" addressed to corporate purpose and identity, which are essential elements for dealing with all three crises. Indeed, the case studies show that some of these ideas have already moved into the realm of corporate and governmental action, energized by the need to leave behind the epistemic and institutional cage that Friedman helped create.

Peter Katzenstein in this volume writes of liberalisms' ends and beginnings. This chapter has addressed several forms of liberalism in the political economy sense: embedded liberalism, which sought to balance international economic openness with domestic stability; neoliberalism, the primary aim of which was to create deep private economic integration at the global level and transform national public regulatory systems in support of that aim; and a new form of liberalism that sees the public corporation as a social entity, not merely the private property of security holders.

In concluding, I also want to address briefly two other forms of liberalism. The first is liberalism as the political philosophy that embraces the inherent dignity and equal, inalienable rights of all, under the rule of law. That this form of liberalism remains an animating force perhaps was nowhere better demonstrated than by the tens of millions of people of every skin color, sex, gender identification, and age marching through cities in more than fifty countries after the brutal murder of George Floyd in 2020, to insist that Black lives matter, and to proclaim that without social justice, including in their own countries, there can be no social peace. Those political leaders who assert that this form of liberalism has become obsolete, or who fancy themselves as illiberal democrats, witnessed what this foundational form means, although none rules a country in which the people are currently permitted fully to enjoy those rights.

Finally, a form of liberalism that is indeed coming to an end is what John Ikenberry described as the "Liberal Leviathan"—the American international political order.[82] An ongoing rebalancing of power among states is the enduring story told in every international relations undergraduate class. Indeed, the neoliberal economic policies discussed earlier in this chapter significantly advanced the rise of China, which is a main external source of current power rebalancing. But what makes the ongoing decline of the liberal leviathan highly unusual is its acceleration since the United States claimed supremacy once the Soviet empire collapsed. Historians in the future no doubt will stress that the origins of this decline go back almost to the beginning of the postwar era. But its rapid acceleration has resulted from self-inflicted wounds in the twenty-first century: an unnecessary war based on lies, and in which the laws prohibiting torture were redefined to permit "enhanced interrogation"; the implosion of the US financial system, fueled by instruments that had little social value but that made those who constructed them out of thin air very wealthy while leaving taxpayers footing the bill and foreclosed homeowners out of luck; and the utter disarray of the Trump administration's response to COVID-19, in which this country ended up leading the industrialized world in infections and deaths—coupled with President Trump's refusal to accept his 2020 electoral loss. The first of these significantly drew down America's moral capital. The second raised fundamental doubts about America's competence to manage the global financial system that it had created. Lastly, America's divisions over COVID-19 added ridicule and pity, while proponents of the "big steal" view of the 2020 presidential election have astonished allies and gratified adversaries. No liberal leviathan can long survive such a combination of body blows.

LIBERALISM'S ANTINOMY

Endings as Beginnings?

Peter J. Katzenstein

At the end of the Great War, which a later generation renamed World War I, W. B. Yeats wrote in "The Second Coming," "Things fall apart; the centre cannot hold."[1] And so it seems again today. Although it has experienced myriad miserable and costly wars, economic calamities, and human rights disasters since 1945, the world has not experienced a truly global conflagration. But as in 1918, the world is living now through a pandemic with unfathomable political effects. Will it weaken political authorities as more or less resilient societies are left to their own devices? Will it strengthen populist movements and authoritarian states? Will it reinvigorate democratic governments and progressive movements? Or will it initiate processes of social and political collapse and political upheaval? At this moment of radical uncertainty, no one can offer plausible answers to any of these pressing questions. In this era of turbocharged mass communication, Arthur Schopenhauer's aperçu remains remarkably timely. Newspapers (and social media) are the second hands of history. But the second hand . . . goes seldom correctly."[2] Rather than struggling with unanswerable questions, this concluding essay argues that each of liberalism's contested and contestable endings is also a new beginning.

"Most abstract terms ending in 'ism,'" Jacob Viner once observed, "inevitably accumulate about them a haze of uncertainty and imprecision."[3] Liberalism is no exception. It does not exist in the singular. In this essay I refer to it as such only for stylistic reasons. Variants, offshoots, and strands of liberalism can be found in all corners of the world. Now painted in nostalgic, autumnal gold, liberalism's past was not the "rule-based liberal order" that Secretary of State Hillary Clinton imagined in a speech she delivered in 2012. And what is true of liberalism is of course true also of embedded liberalism. All isms simplify. They compress complex processes into nouns. Time is conventionally demarcated between Newton's discrete units. In contrast, Einstein's theory of general relativity established that space-time is warped and twisted. In this modern conception, endings and beginnings are connected seamlessly rather than interrupted by clear breaks. And so it is with the endings and beginnings of various strands of liberalisms.

The overlay of endings and beginnings is the red thread that runs throughout this book. John Maynard Keynes's middle way, Jonathan Kirshner argues in chapter 1, proved elusive. A pragmatist and an improviser, Keynes offered an overarching vision, not a fixed set of operating instructions, and Keynesianism's legacy is ambiguous. Mark Blyth shows in chapter 2 how the foundations of American order pivoted three times after 1945: from being embedded in the social purpose of full employment before 1980 to the social purpose of price stability after 1980 and to the absence of any identifiable social purpose in the now-beginning third order that enshrines the centrality of the American dollar without American norms or leadership. Peter Gourevitch and Sheri Berman show in chapters 3 and 4 how Europe's embedded liberalism was based on a historical compromise between right-of-center Christian democracy and left-of-center social democracy. The first putative end of the liberal American century occurred in the interregnum of the pivotal 1970s, when, Francis Gavin suggests in chapter 5, California's phenomenal rise transformed America and the world. In the 1980s and 1990s technocratic political leaders disembedded liberalism, as Rawi Abdelal argues in chapter 6. These leaders followed the advice of economists who favored untrammeled markets and shrinking states, having learned from the miserable 1970s and forgotten the disastrous 1930s and 1940s. With the world ricocheting from one financial crisis to another in the era of financial globalization, the massive financial meltdown of 2008 heralded the beginning of the end of the neoliberal American order. The rise of American, British, and European populism a few years later finished the job. The new incoherence that followed in its wake, Ilene Grabel shows in chapter 7, is a productive interregnum that opens up new possibilities of improvisation and piecemeal reform. Finally, the disembedding of corporate capitalism from national social purpose, John Ruggie shows in chapter 8, has led to a partial reembedding through an incipient social liberalism at the transnational level. Deglobalization in the form of antiliberal pushback and reglobalization in the form of the 2020 pandemic are occurring simultaneously, creating once again liberalism's antinomies of endings and beginnings, for Emmanuel Adler a "'betwixt and between' phase of transition between a liberal international social world order and a nationalist and perhaps authoritarian social international order."[4]

Neoliberalism: *Titanic* and Iceberg

For some, international liberalism since 1945 refers to a rule-governed order overseen by a benevolent, hegemonic United States pursuing its long-term interests. For others it refers to traditional power politics driven by the United States pursuing its narrow national objectives. Is liberalism a *Titanic* sunk by the sharp edges of national and now populist power politics? Or is it an iceberg that sinks other, lifeboat-lacking political orders? In my reading, the story of the *Titanic* (a complicated and coherent piece of engineering) and the iceberg (a simple and incoherent part of nature) are so deeply entangled that the answer to such questions is "both-and" rather than "either-or."

Neoliberalism shares similarities with the *Titanic*. The largest passenger ship in the world embodied the splendors of the Edwardian era at sea. It was the pride of the White Star Line when it commenced its westbound maiden voyage on April 10, 1912, leaving Southampton for New York with about 2,200 passengers and crew on board. Among them were John Jacob Astor, Benjamin Guggenheim, Isidor Straus, and other members of their very own Club Glitterati. About half of all the passengers on the *Titanic* were traveling first class. The luxury of the accommodations surpassed anything afloat; the ship included a French restaurant, electric Turkish baths, a swimming pool, a veranda café, a palm loggia, and squash courts. The *Titanic* embodied the confidence in technology and progress that defined the Edwardian era. In addition, the world's largest ship incorporated the most advanced safety features, making it practically unsinkable. Because it was thought of as its own lifeboat, it had not been equipped with enough lifeboats to carry all passengers and crew members. Two-thirds of the 2,200 people on board drowned in the freezing Atlantic Ocean.

Today's *Titanic*-like neoliberal order is also sinking. The financial crisis of 2008 helped create an iceberg of right-wing, nationalist populism that sank global neoliberalism as we knew it. Anglo-America set the tone, with the 2016 Brexit vote and election of Donald Trump as president of the United States. Both events were full-throated repudiations of the Reagan-Thatcher changes spawned a generation earlier. Now, with Scotland and perhaps Ireland eyeing Europe, the survival of the United Kingdom is no longer assured. And the Labour Party's socialist gambit under Jeremy Corbyn's leadership backfired so badly that battered Conservative prime minister Boris Johnson has a once-in-a-lifetime chance to convert England's heartland into a bastion of working-class Tories. Right-wing populism could transform the frugal and middle-of-the-road Conservative Party into a champion of Little England nationalism propelled by the dream of a new, nimble Singapore fishing for economic advantage off the coast of Europe. And it could leave the Labour Party, dislodged from the Midlands and Scotland, in a disastrously diminished position.

Donald Trump's election of 2016 signaled an even bigger change. His xenophobic Jacksonianism reduced the role of traditional America's political conservatism to that of a silent enabler of far-reaching attacks by the president on the unwritten norms of democratic government.[5] The takeover of the Republican Party by radical conservatism has silenced what used to be a national debate between conservative Republicans and progressive Democrats. The new debate now occurs within the Democratic party, where a progressive alliance of democratic socialists and social democrats battles a coalition of various kinds of moderates and centrists. In this fight, President Trump played the role of great conciliator—an unintended effect of his incendiary rhetoric and polarizing behavior. As a political force, the Democratic Party may still end up following the Republican Party to an extreme of a deeply fractured polity, creating a twenty-first-century installment in America's history of critical realignments dating back to the late nineteenth century.

Elsewhere, nationalist and xenophobic populism on the right and environmental and progressive populism on the left are pushing the decline of traditional center-right and center-left parties. Populism has made strong gains among conservative voters who before had supported moderate center-right parties. Many have lost good jobs and feel that their high-status social positions are threatened by immigrants and refugees, ethnic and racial minorities, and women and gays. Around the world, "true" patriots are defending the "heartland." In America and Europe, the reformist left, led in the 1990s by Bill Clinton, Tony Blair, and Gerhard Schröder, shifted to the center and thus lost much of its traditional strength among workers. Furthermore, urban cosmopolitans supporting multicultural and environmental issues have begun to divide their established parties or moved to support others parties. And autocratic leaders in China, Russia, India, Turkey, Brazil, and Hungary, among others, operate in weak regimes marked by economic, demographic, health, and environmental challenges they do not know how to address, let alone solve. Like the *Titanic*, the international liberal order is sinking.

At the same time, neoliberalism was also the iceberg that sliced open polities that did not live up to its maxims. We know little about the specific iceberg that the *Titanic* hit, except that it was big. The spotter estimated its above-water height to be about fifty to a hundred feet and its length about two hundred to four hundred feet. And only one-third of it was visible above the water line. It had broken off one of Greenland's glaciers one to three years earlier, and its weight and volume shrank by about 90 percent before its fateful collision.[6] On the night of April 14, 1912, that iceberg did to the *Titanic* what a can opener does to a can. It turns out that the *Titanic* had many icebergs to choose from: more than a thousand had made their way so far south that they threatened transatlantic shipping lanes. Collisions between ships and icebergs off the coast of Labrador were not unusual. They were accidents waiting to happen.

Hungary offers an instructive illustration of the neoliberal iceberg hitting a polity. Hungary tried to combat the financial crisis of 2008 and its aftermath with a variety of policy moves taken from the neoliberal playbook.[7] Floating the Hungarian currency in 2008 made exports more competitive and stemmed the collapse of Hungary's foreign trade. It also dramatically increased foreign-denominated mortgage and consumer debts that Hungarians had to repay in forint. This mattered hugely. Nearly 80 percent of Hungary's foreign currency loans and 55 percent of its mortgages were denominated in Swiss francs in the mid-2000s. Delinking from the euro bought Hungary greater policy autonomy. But it also increased the fear of Hungary defaulting on its foreign debt. To combat that fear, in October 2008 the Central Bank raised interest rates by 3 percent. This stalled domestic growth but failed to stop the fall of the forint against the Swiss franc. At the end of 2008, the International Monetary Fund (IMF), World Bank and European Union (EU) put together a $25 billion loan package. This made Hungary the first EU member state to receive an IMF bailout since Britain in 1976. In return, Hungary was compelled to introduce additional austerity measures, including reducing public-sector pay, increasing some taxes, and decreasing spending on social programs. Gross domestic product dropped by more than 6 percent in the next quarter, unemployment rose to about 10 percent, the stock market dropped by more than half compared to the previous year, and exports fell by another 5 percent despite the drastic fall in the value of the forint. At the next election in 2010, disgruntled voters turned to the right and gave Viktor Orbán an overwhelming mandate to carry out economic and political reforms, dialing back neoliberal policies and dealing with domestic corruption, just as he had promised in his campaign.

The ideological seeds of Hungary's backlash were planted long before the crisis of 2008.[8] The crisis simply revealed that imitating western European social purposes and identities had inflicted great economic damage and impaired Hungary's sense of national dignity.[9] The rest is history, as Hungary has become a global model for institutionalizing the kind of illiberal democracy that is now leaving its mark on European and world politics. In response to the 2020 pandemic crisis, Hungary shed all pretenses of democratic rule. Its parliament gave Prime Minister Orbán unlimited power, allowing him to rule by decree for an unspecified but possibly lengthy period. The parliament took this vote (rescinded two months later, after an international outcry) on the same day that an EU COVID-19 investment initiative awarded Hungary €5.6 billion, twice as much as Italy, a country much harder hit by the virus and with a population six times larger than Hungary's.[10] Conscious of the importance of EU subsidies for his country's fiscal health and the financial appetite of his political machine, Orbán may attempt to navigate at the outer edges of what the EU and other international organizations are willing to tolerate. Or his country may be sidelined in the EU or pushed out altogether.

Hungary's experience sheds light on the failings of neoliberalism that sparked the emergence of right-wing populist movements and regimes throughout the world. What happened to Hungary after 2008 was a rerun of the experience of many countries in the Global South. The Mexican debt crisis of 1982 subsequently swept through Latin America before reaching Mexico for a second time in 1994. This was followed by the Asian financial crisis in 1997, Russia's and Argentina's defaults in the late 1990s and early 2000s, Iceland's meltdown in 2008, and the Eurozone and Greek crisis after 2010. In all these cases, speculative money gushed in and out of national markets, wreaking havoc. Malaysia's courageously contrarian policies in 1998–99 enraged American policymakers like Undersecretary of the Treasury Larry Summers, whose unswerving commitment to neoliberal policies and their disastrous consequences is a matter of public record. At the same time, Summers and others are correct in pointing to neoliberalism as the engine that lifted close to eight hundred million people out of poverty and helped create, in India and China, the largest middle classes in the world. It is worth noting of course that economic crisis does not have to end in illiberal democracies. Latin America in the 1980s and Asia in the 1990s experienced democratization instead. In the stories of icebergs and *Titanics*, identifying the victims and victors among tightly coupled actors can be difficult.

The unthinkable sinking of the unsinkable *Titanic* rules the myth market like no other brand. Its news coverage established the *New York Times*'s reputation as the premier newspaper in America. Scores of movies have helped build the legend over the last century. The 2012 centennial was marked by an astonishing range of popular culture products: movies, musicals, magazine articles, museum exhibits, computer games, iPhone apps, requiem masses, memorabilia sales, and more. The *Titanic* has become "an iconic superbrand of the mortality market."[11]

"When the legend becomes fact, print the legend," says reporter Max Scott in the movie *The Man Who Shot Liberty Valance*. Is this true of the story of neoliberalism? In his book *Globalists*, Quinn Slobodian developed an argument that is both related to and divergent from the conventional wisdom.[12] Without denying that neoliberalism succeeded in drastically expanding economic gains by deregulating national markets, he tracked its evolution as the story of insulating capitalism from political intervention at the global level. The collapse of the Hapsburg empire at the end of World War I was a catastrophic experience for central European economies and shaped the outlook of economists who belonged to the Austrian School. After that calamity, all of the small successor states of central and eastern Europe were intent on politicizing the economy. Nationalism was their preferred vehicle. In response, Friedrich Hayek, Ludwig von Mises, and their followers in the Geneva School fanned out throughout the continent and eventually across the Atlantic. Working on the problems of a crisis-ridden world economy, by the late 1930s some of them began calling themselves "neoliberals." The end of empire after 1945 intensified the political interventions of a proliferating number of sovereign states in economic life. Insulating property rights from mass democratic whims became the central mission of neoliberals. Market forces should be permitted to sequester the property of the few from the grasping reach of the many. Protecting markets from overreaching states was important, but less important than designing global governance institutions to isolate markets from democratic politics. In pushing for a vertical scale-shift, neoliberals sought to put their program into practice in a postimperial world.

> The encasement of the market in a spirit of militant globalism is a better way of describing the international dimensions of the neoliberal project than the Polanyian terms of disembedding the economy according to a doctrine of market fundamentalism. . . . The normative neoliberal world is not a borderless market without states but a doubled world kept safe from mass demands for social justice and redistributive equality by the guardians of the economic constitution.[13]

After 1945, decolonization, the Bretton Woods system with capital controls, communist victories in eastern Europe, and Christian democratic and social democratic rule in western Europe all worked against neoliberal programs. The General Agreement on Tariffs and Trade, however, provided a useful platform from which neoliberals could operate. So did the European Community (EC) as it transformed itself from a bloc-like customs union to a multilayered governance system after the European Court of Justice asserted the supremacy of European over national law in the 1960s. The emergence of the American neoliberal intellectual movement centered at the Universities of Chicago and Virginia. Finally, the Reagan and Thatcher political victories helped enormously in spreading the vision of the Geneva School. In the late 1980s unrestricted capital mobility across Europe became one of the EC's governing principles. In fact it was Europe— not the United States—that spread the principle of the free movement of capital across the world. At the insistence of the German government, the EC Council's capital liberalization directive of 1988 was to be applied uniformly to all non-European states.[14] The proliferation of bilateral investment treaties, the structural adjustment programs of the IMF, and the creation of the World Trade Organization completed the implementation of the neoliberal program. For several decades, few states could resist the power of global markets that were politically caged rather than unfettered.

Slobodian took pains to preempt the criticism of a reductionist rendering of a history that put neoliberalism at the center of a global spider web of antidemocratic politics. In fact, neoliberalism generated plenty of criticism all along and, starting in 1999, sometimes massive and at times violent protests. Slobodian's master narrative sticks closely to the ideas of its central protagonists. But for Stephen Wertheim the book "struggles to demonstrate exactly how they influenced particular international rules and institutions . . . how strong a connection exists between the intellectuals he profiles and the developments he credits them with shaping."[15] To give but one example, Hans Tietmeyer, then a state secretary in Germany's finance ministry and a central actor in the creation of the full liberalization of capital movements in Europe, explained the policy in the following terms:

> We saw in full capital liberalization the possibility for a test of the stability of the ERM [European Exchange Rate Mechanism]—a test by the markets of policy credibility. We wanted a test by world markets, not just European markets. That was why the *erga omnes* principle was so crucial. Liberalization *erga omnes* would demonstrate that we had in Europe a stable fixed exchange-rate system with market-proved stability, rather than an artificial stability provided by controls.[16]

As this example illustrates, the motivation of key policymakers was not necessarily informed by the vision of the Geneva School. But the effects of their policies were. Like *Titanic* and iceberg, motivation and effect were deeply entangled.

Varieties of Liberalisms

Liberalism is a plastic concept that we do not seem to be able to do without. It is not a seamless construct that has remained invariant across time and space. It is, rather, a heterogenous, contingent ensemble of ideas and institutionalized practices. One of its leading proponents distinguishes between three versions of liberalism that can be updated like computer programs.[17] Others call international liberalism a myth or a barely concealed kind of balance of power politics.[18] Over time, liberalism's meaning can be tracked best in the multiplicity of its different forms and traditions. As the Swiss historian Jacob Burckhardt feared when he wrote a friend in 1889, everywhere and at all times "terrible simplifiers" make what is plural into a singular.[19]

This view is supported by the different rights-, property-, and analysis-based views of liberalism that scholars of world politics hold to.[20] Ruggie promotes a broad, rights-based view of liberalism.[21] In this view, from the days of John Locke down to the present, liberalism has experienced an enlargement in the meaning of rights, from inalienable property rights and resistance against arbitrary rule in the late seventeenth century to the right of self-identification with different gender categories at the outset of the twenty-first. This enlargement has occurred because liberation movements (women, Black Lives Matter, proponents of gender expansion) tend to invoke natural rights–based claims on behalf of their communities. In contrast, Blyth sees liberalism as an unstable management by capitalists who seek state protection for property rights without wanting to pay for it. Ever since Locke, Adam Smith, and David Hume, this has split liberalism into a reformist camp (John Stuart Mill, John A. Hobson, and Keynes) and a purist camp (Jeremy Bentham, David Ricardo, and contemporary neoliberals). Rights are optional extras, not part of the core model. France, for example, was a liberal country in the first view but not in the second.[22] Finally, Robert Keohane's definition of international liberalism links a broad, rights-based philosophical perspective to an intellectually less capacious methodological individualism and ties this to an ameliorative view of history.[23] All three agree that political change is always marked by struggle. And I suspect that all three would agree that liberals do not believe in destroying their enemies. For Blyth, struggle generates unstable solutions; for Ruggie, in his own words, "a discontinuous invocation of a hypernorm"[24]; for Keohane, a nonlinear arc of liberal amelioration. Instability, discontinuity, and nonlinearity speak to a shared though concealed outlook among the different rights-, property-, and analysis-based perspectives of liberalism.

I share in that outlook. Despite its emotional appeal, a progressive teleology of history or an ameliorative view of liberalism is unconvincing. After Auschwitz, the U-turns in history and prolonged periods of illiberal practices in America condoned in the name of liberalism cannot simply be passed over in silence or interpreted as regrettable speed-bumps on the road of progress. Like nature, as revealed by quantum mechanics, politics is marked by uncertainties, possibilities (for better and for worse), and contingencies. There is no autonomous platform from which to observe the unfolding of long-term trends, and there are no transhistorical forces, as in Newtonian physics.[25] Civilized countries can turn on a dime to commit acts of unimaginable bestiality. Germany did so in a big way in the 1930s and 1940s. Liberal America is not free of its own horror stories. The history of Native American dispossession, slavery, lynching, segregation, and systemic racism in its many contemporary forms illustrate the persistence of deeply illiberal tendencies in America. So does the adoption of torture under the name of "enhanced interrogation" as an acceptable instrument of policy after 2001. At the same time, America is also the center of a dispersed, inchoate, half-formed force that is transforming liberalism while lacking a unifying label. Some call it "left modernism," others "hyper-liberalism," still others "the successor ideology." It is defined more easily by its departures from old progressive liberal ideas than by its agreement on new revolutionary ones.[26] What unites this inchoate force and its incipient ideas is the absence of any identifiable social purpose. Transatlantic translation of these categories is not helped by the fact that in the United States the conventional understanding of liberalism refers to the left, whereas in continental Europe it refers to the right.

Here are two successful examples of providing a historically contextualized approach to the meaning of political liberalism that avoids a teleological or ameliorative worldview. Helena Rosenblatt argued that liberalism is neither a civilizational gift from the West to the world nor the reason for the West's decline.[27] She distinguished the eighteenth- and nineteenth-century French and German emphasis on liberty, rule of law, civil rights, duty, solidarity, patriotism, and self-sacrifice from the twentieth-century American emphasis on democracy, individual rights, and capitalism. Deployed in different contexts, liberalism refers to small government in France and to big government in the United States. The idea that liberalism is a foundational part of America is recent. The protection of individual rights and interests is a product of the wars of the twentieth century, specifically the Cold War. This American adaptation of liberalism differs greatly from the traditional European understanding of it as fostering civic-minded individuals who understand their social connections and support the common good. Insisting on the multiplicity of liberalism and its different forms, Rosenblatt's historical and contextual analysis did not surrender to a purely nominalist definition.

In a similar vein, Duncan Bell tracked Anglo-American political thought from 1850 to 1950.[28] He acknowledged at the outset the manifold and contradictory ways in which this "metacategory of Western political discourse" was construed. Policing its boundaries, telling its history as one of rise and decline, or trying to identify its core constitutive elements, Bell suggested, are all inferior to establishing interpretive protocols as "the sum of arguments that have been classified as liberal, and recognized as such by other self-proclaimed liberals, across time and space."[29] Deploying this strategy, Bell argued that at the turn of the twentieth century, the dominant narrative identified liberalism as a product of the late eighteenth and early nineteenth centuries. By the beginning of the twenty-first century, liberalism had become the product of the mid-seventeenth century or even earlier.[30] Put differently, John Locke became a liberal only after the scope of the liberal tradition greatly expanded during the middle of the twentieth century. Ideological and real wars with fascism and communism transformed different strands of liberal thought into a constitutive ideology of the West—an inheritance we still hold onto and labor under today.

The urge to retroactively extend the contemporary meaning of liberalism diverts attention away from the obvious: liberalism's contested, political, and variegated types and experiences across time and space. In the early twenty-first century, dispositional tolerance, wariness of concentrations of public and private power, freedom of expression and political practice, and the primacy of law over leaders are important definitional traits of liberalism.

The last three-quarters of the twentieth century witnessed broad shifts in both the political meaning and the practice of liberalism. Invented after 1945 as a creative response to the crises of the 1930s and 1940s, welfare-state liberalism was, a short generation later, alleged to be nothing but stultifying state intervention that a reinvigorated market liberalism would correct. Neoliberalism succeeded in freeing markets through privatizing public assets, outsourcing public services, deregulating economic activities, refusing to regulate new financial instruments, weakening antitrust laws, encouraging the explosion of executive compensation, weakening the rights of organized labor, reducing tariffs and other international barriers, creating new global production chains, enabling global financial transactions of once unimaginable scope and scale, and creating global governance arrangements largely shielded from political challenges by states and their citizens. A generation later, after a series of financial crises, backlash nationalism and social communitarianism now target neoliberalism from both the right and the left for having eliminated jobs, weakened the welfare state, eroded communities, produced unsustainable levels of inequality, furthered border-crossing disruptions, and accelerated a global ecological calamity.

The variability in the meaning and practice of liberalism are illustrated by the issue of race in international politics and by America's multiple political traditions.[31] For several centuries, deeply held liberal beliefs and customary practices in the Anglo-American empire were compatible with racial hierarchies both at home and abroad. White supremacy was axiomatic in the late eighteenth century. In the nineteenth century, a single standard of civilization—white, male, Christian—was the core of empire. Classifying the world's population into multiple races was eventually replaced by a binary distinction between white and nonwhite By the end of the nineteenth century, scientific racism made whites the *Herrenvolk*. "Whites only" became a global color line. First used in the state of Mississippi to disenfranchise Black voters, education and literacy tests served as models for immigration restrictions in many countries, including the United States and Nazi Germany.

Race provided a novel foundation for liberal conceptions of an international order that differed sharply from realist ones. Realism holds that the domestic Self is familiar and safe and the international Other is unfamiliar and unsafe. Informed by racial categories, Anglo-American liberalism inverted that conventional understanding in Britain's settler colonies, such as South Africa and Australia. A white external Self was pitted against a nonwhite internal Other. Threats to the Self emanated from domestic rather than international encounters. The identity of the Self was affirmed by a white transnational community. Racial liberalism evolved first into circumscribed political autonomy by the dominions and then eventually into a multiracial Commonwealth. World War II, the Holocaust, and decolonization altered race-based liberal notions. Domestic reforms and transnational oppositional movements created the political space for the recognition of racial equality and human rights. They did not inhere in the principles of liberalism. Instead, they resulted from prolonged political struggle.

Race was very much alive as a political issue in twentieth-century American foreign policy. America contains multiple liberal traditions, typically named after some of its most famous political leaders (Alexander Hamilton, Thomas Jefferson, Andrew Jackson, Woodrow Wilson). Constitutive of America, race plays an important part in all of them. These traditions blend into each other as the good of any one tradition rarely appears without a dose of the bad of another. Wilson, for example, was a man of the South. His views on race shaped his domestic policies and the American approach to world politics. As a man of the South, to the consternation not only of the Japanese delegation, Wilson vetoed the racial equality clause at the Treaty of Versailles. Wilsonian racism also left a deep imprint on America's racism more generally once it had shed Teddy Roosevelt's infatuation with European racist imperialism. For a generation after the end of World War II, legally sanctioned racial segregation in the American South provided the domestic political foundation for a coalition of mainstream Republicans, internationalist Democrats from the Northeast, and segregationist Democrats from the South. The American-led international liberal order was supported by a bipartisan foreign policy grounded on segregation and institutionalized racism.

In the early 2020s, Trumpism illustrates the continuing relevance of race in America.[32] Trumpism emerged from America's multiple traditions, a contemporary offshoot of Jacksonian, common-man populism. Trump is easily stirred. Trumpism is not. It does not want to fight wars in far-flung places. A product of the American heartland, it is antielitist, antiurban, and can easily be aroused by ethnonationalist and racial appeals. With illegal immigration a hot-button issue, appeals to race are once again a staple of contemporary American politics. As a candidate and as president Trump was remarkably frank in making ethnonationalism and race political issues, spreading doubts about President Barack Obama's birth certificate, labeling Mexicans "murderers" and "rapists," equating Islam with ISIS, and calling the COVID-19 virus Chinese. In 2016, American voters were moved by Trump's appeals to racism more than by issues of economic insecurity.[33] In short, America's racist legacy was reactivated politically by the Trump presidency and a conservative Republican Party that had by 2020 more dramatically transformed itself into an illiberal party than any other contemporary, conservative, democratic party; in its programmatic commitments it had moved to the right even of the antidemocratic German Alternative for Germany.[34] At the same time, the many-sided, fierce resistance against the Trump administration and its policies illustrates that multicultural liberalism is alive and well in America. Louis Hartz thus was mistaken in speaking of *the* liberal tradition in America.[35] America's liberalism draws on multiple traditions.

The smallness of Trump the man and the depth of America's multiple traditions stand in marked contrast. But that does not diminish the central point; Trumpism is an indelible part of America's multiple, liberal traditions. American liberalism did not crystallize around immutable values. Its core has remained fluid and thus has created jarring inconsistencies. Walt Whitman recognized this clearly. "Do I contradict myself?" he asked in his poem "Song of Myself." And he answered quickly, "Very well then, I contradict myself, / (I am large, I contain multitudes)."

Liberalism since 1945: Beginnings and Endings

In a seminal article, John Ruggie argued that after 1945, a new order provided for institutional arrangements and understandings that mitigated harmful cross-border effects of unconstrained market forces, most commonly found in the form of costly beggar-thy-neighbor trade policies and harmful unilateral actions during balance-of-payment crises.[36] Ruggie drew his inspiration from Karl Polanyi.[37] In Polanyi's view, the "Great Ditch" separating premodern from modern society was a break in the nature of the social relations of economic production.[38] Speaking of the enclosure movement, Barrington Moore wrote, unforgettably, "sheep ate men."[39] This was a violent and cruel rupture with traditional social norms as the well-to-do abrogated their responsibility for looking after their less-fortunate fellows. In the first part of the nineteenth century, markets were disembedded further from society. Nowhere was this change clearer than in the shift from the Old Poor Laws expressing an ethic of social responsibility to the New Poor Law of 1834 expressing an ethic of individual striving.[40] The institutionalization of a market society thus gradually changed liberalism. Like nineteenth-century liberalism, embedded liberalism was more malleable than Ruggie averred.[41] The architects of Bretton Woods regarded it as not merely offering social security and economic stabilization but also as compatible with active public management of the international economy, state-led development policies in poor countries, and possibly even Soviet-style central planning. Embedded liberalism thus accommodated easily the different welfare-state visions and programs of center-left and center-right after 1945.

What was true of domestic embedded liberalism after 1945 held also for global disembedded neoliberalism after 1980.[42] Like "liberalism," "neoliberalism" refers to many different things as understood by many different people. To be sure, three important neoliberal principles could not be breached: openness to international flows of goods and capital, honoring the strictures of financial-market credibility in the conduct of fiscal policy, and taking account of international competitiveness in the development of domestic growth strategies. But that left considerable leeway to local translators of the global neoliberal script, which they interpreted with reference to their different institutional pasts, their degree of autonomy from the material or symbolic support of global incubators of neoliberal ideas, the political cohesiveness of their national polities, and their differing vulnerabilities to the coercive pressures applied by foreign actors or institutions.

After 1945 the United States created a new international economic order. With a few years of respite in the mid-1920s, 1914–45 was a second Thirty Years' War that enveloped the Great Depression of the 1930s. When Keynes found himself working once again in Treasury in 1942, he wrote, "In 1918 most people's only idea was to get back to pre-1914. No one today feels like that about 1939. That will make an enormous difference when we get down to it."[43] It had, indeed, been a terrible three decades. Nobody wanted to experience anything like it again, ever. Political leaders were seeking out something new and different as they stumbled along uncharted terrain. Keynesianism offered a corrective to the flaws of traditional liberalism, Marxism, fascism, and National Socialism. Markets could not be left to their own devices. Extensive nationalization and a command economy were to be avoided. Keynes argued that in the interest of social stability and economic growth, fiscal and monetary policies were instruments that could and should manage demand and supply. State management of the economy thus was indispensable for the survival of capitalist democracy.

With some local colors added, Europe and Japan painted the same picture. Center-right and center-left haggled. A coalitional politics of "dirty hands" recrafted Christian democracy's religious identity and social democracy's class identity. This made possible a redefinition of conceptions of self-interests that replaced the class war of the interwar years. In addition, national identity was rebuilt in a gradually emerging European context to create a more encompassing solidarity that contained nationalist excess. Importantly, in 1952 the European project developed cartelized market arrangements that tamed the coal and steel core of Germany's war machine. At the same time, civilizational identities were invented to buttress an ideological conflict that pitted a democratic, capitalist West against a totalitarian, communist East. Using instruments beyond fiscal and monetary policy, the small European welfare states eventually became the poster children of embedded liberalism's success. They were particularly adept in buffering their democratic corporatism from the instabilities of liberalizing international markets.[44] Their political experiments since then have continued to be successful. When Dani Rodrik asked whether globalization had gone too far, the small western European states offered an emphatic "No" as an answer.[45]

Eventually, the postwar bargain of Christian democracy and social democracy unraveled because of a confluence of developments.[46] As soon as embedded liberalism was internationalized with full currency convertibility in 1958, the patchiness of Bretton Woods became clear. A rapidly growing, unregulated Euro-dollar market forced the United States in August 1971 to close its gold window, toppling the fixed exchange-rate system. That market was largely created by US policies, most importantly choosing to fight the war in Vietnam and the War on Poverty at the same time. This decision exported homemade US inflation to others rather than incurring the domestic political cost of deflating the US economy.

The 1970s were an era of stagflation. The ugly reality was an unraveling of the Bretton Woods system because of what Blyth (chapter 2) calls several "bugs." High inflation, high unemployment, and anemic growth made this a watershed decade. The collapse of the fixed exchange-rate regime in 1971, inflation, and the oil shocks of 1973 and 1979 created the political coalitions for a reset around price stability as the new social purpose. Other events and factors also contributed to the unraveling of established political patterns and the emergence of new ones: the anti-Vietnam movement and the spring of 1968, which convulsed the political systems on both sides of the Atlantic; and the birth of the women's and environmental movements, heralding the beginning of a new kind of progressive politics.

This Eurocentric narrative conceals liberalism's other endings and beginnings. The loss of the Vietnam war, stagflation, and a domestic constitutional crisis made the 1970s America's lost decade, or so it seemed to East Coast elites and pundits. Meanwhile, as Gavin shows in chapter 5, seismic changes three thousand miles west created in California the foundation for America's and neoliberalism's resurgence. With Ronald Reagan and Margaret Thatcher in the political lead, old economic ideas were dressed up in monetarist and rational expectations garb. Out went Keynesianism and in came the new orthodoxy of deregulation and privatization. Abdelal shows in chapter 6 how center-right and center-left learned their new neoliberal lessons from the miserable 1970s while they forgot the old ones of the disastrous 1930s. After a while, global financialization further undermined the state's capacity to channel the flow of capital and control the exchange rate. In its narrow American meaning, neoliberalism enabled a new beginning of a reinvigorated capitalism, as Gavin shows in chapter 5. The change from the 1970s to the 1980s thus illustrates the antinomy of endings as new beginnings.

The U-turn of France's Socialist president François Mitterrand was similarly decisive. Rather than building socialism in one country, Mitterrand opted for market-friendly social democracy on a European scale. The result was a second founding of Europe in the 1980s, on the basis of a refurbished coalition uniting center-right and center-left and favoring the Anglo-American program of deregulation and market-freeing reforms. The domestic programs of the Third Way initiated by the United States, Britain, and Germany were insufficient to counter the weakening of the political controls that had been at the center of the European welfare state since 1945. Markets and the disruptions they caused were given fuller sway. In particular, liberalization of capital markets and financial services were the cutting edge, with both expected and unexpected political consequences. Economic growth came to depend on ever-more-liquid global financial markets, bilateral investment treaties, and globe-spanning supply chains.

The end of the Cold War eliminated a common external threat. The rise of Asia and Latin America created billions of new customers and killed millions of jobs in what had formerly been the industrial world. And unfettered markets produced increasing domestic inequality in the Global North, rising prosperity and growing inequality in the Global South, and growing equality between north and south. The Asian financial crisis of 1997, the dot.com crash of 2000, and the 2008 financial crisis spurred politicians and policymakers to recover the past, as they had tried to do at the end of World War I, rather than find a new path into a different future, as they had done at the end of World War II. Disembedded global markets thus created their own disjointed opposition at the national, transnational, and global levels. After 1997, China and other Asian states chose to self-insure rather than rely on the politically suspect standby support of the IMF.

By husbanding foreign exchange reserves, Asian states intensified and extended the debt-fueled boom in the United States and left themselves open to a silent expropriation of some of their assets by possible dollar depreciations decided by the unconstrained choices of the US Federal Reserve. In the twenty-first century, varieties of economic nationalism, including America's recent turn to neomercantilism, have filled some of the breach.[47] But no epistemic or normative framework is in sight to permit an orderly redesign of international economic arrangements that would express a new social purpose. Instead, unilateralism as well as overlapping and often competing multilateral and plurilateral arrangements are weakening or replacing existing international institutions. Only the continuing primacy of the dollar in global markets holds the international economy together. If or when that primacy ends, the unraveling of that order will come into full view, as Blyth (chapter 2) and Grabel (chapter 7) argue.

As endings slide into beginnings, we are reminded that at the beginning of the American order, the Cold War created close links between economic and political liberalism in the Atlantic region, though not across the world. In contrast to the New Order of Nazi Germany, those links expressed a social purpose that then defined the American order.[48] Today, with the social purpose of economic and political liberalism in shreds, the world appears like a dark jungle that badly needs the redemptive light of a liberal garden. Liberalism is not tasked with clearing away a few accidental obstacles to have humanity, in the words of Margaret Canovan, "unfold its natural essence. It is more like making a garden in a jungle that is continually encroaching."[49] In its attempt to survive, the garden seeks to conquer the jungle with no apparent justification other than the deep and unshakable belief in universal justice as a natural and fundamental state of affairs. For better and for worse, this liberal mindset has spread its message and practice throughout the world. In the late nineteenth century, it was reflected in landscaping practices that linked imperial centers with their colonial outposts. In the late twentieth century it was mirrored in what Jamie Peck and Adam Tickell called the "jungle law" of neoliberalism.[50] What does the world face now, jungle or garden? The decade of the 1970s was pivotal—for Gavin (in chapter 5), filled with the promise of the sunshine state and for Kurt Andersen, descending into uncharted domains of evil.[51] Without repeating, will the 2020s rhyme with the 1970s?

Endings and Beginnings in an Uncertain World

Varieties of liberalisms have not marched across the stage of history in orderly procession, as Rosenblatt has shown.[52] The same holds for the most recent past, as this book documents. Liberalisms' appearance has been accidental (Blyth), unexpected (Gavin), forgotten and relearned (Abdelal), and experimental (Grabel). Nobody foresaw that the accidental policy moves after 1945 that Blyth discusses in chapter 2 would generate an embedded form of liberalism that lasted several decades. Nobody foresaw, as Gavin shows in chapter 5, the profound disruptions that California would bring to America and the world. And nobody foresaw the end of the Cold War, the disintegration of the Soviet Union, the 2008 financial crisis, or the pandemic of 2020–21. The world does not seek out fictitious points of equilibrium. Novelty and the unexpected are among its defining features, not entropy or unending progress of one political idea. Because human beings are creative bundles of potentialities, not robots enacting fixed programs, situationally specific potential capacities are always waiting to be actualized.[53] This haphazard parade of liberalisms reminds us that the space of reason and predictability must always compete with "the unthinkable or the crazy," and the uncertainty that enfolds it.[54] The constitutive effects of uncertainty create events that blindside the world and thus create the conditions for both endings and beginnings.

The pandemic of 2020–21 is likely to reset politics in unfathomable ways. Pandemics cannot be controlled simply by shutting national borders. The fiasco of all political regimes—autocratic and democratic, liberal and illiberal—to protect their citizens is reflected in the similarity of the curves charting the spread of the pandemic, the failure of containment, the uneven records of mitigation, and the widespread mistrust in all official statistics because of deliberate falsification or unintentional incompleteness. Exemplifying the transformative changes he sees in the offing, the doyen of American realism, Henry Kissinger, wrote about the futility of relying only on nationalist policies and programs and the indispensable need for a "global collaborative vision and program" in order to meet this historic challenge.[55] This aspirational message is fundamentally antithetical to political realism. Yet it sounds utterly realistic, at least to me. Neoliberalism has made the world more flat, interconnected, and fragile.[56] The COVID-19 pandemic, specialists tell us, is child's play compared to the more complicated and deadly ones that may await us. Catastrophic risks that we can fathom at least to some extent differ, after all, from existential ones that we cannot.[57]

At this juncture of history, what should we do and who should be our guide? Niccolò Machiavelli's firemen or Thomas Hobbes's policemen?[58] Firemen contain disasters; policemen maintain order. Firemen are skeptics who react to events as they unfold; policemen are optimistically confident that crazy events can be mastered through reason and force. We give such crazy events different names: "unknown unknowns," "low-probability high-impact events," "ruptures," "black swans," "shocks," or "tipping points." These terms express doubts over the accuracy of our predictions, forecasts, and scenarios for the manipulation of our political future. With multiplying unpredictabilities of various types, resilience and the ability to adapt to the future seem more important than the ability to know it.[59] With the end of neoliberalism, any new incarnation of liberalism will have to engage both deepening national differences and deepening global entanglements. Perhaps it will be a thin, procedural liberalism in an era of nationalism.[60] Perhaps it will be a newly reembedded social liberalism at the global level, as Ruggie suggests in chapter 8. Perhaps it will be a decadent liberalism sustained by the weaknesses of all of its plausible rivals rather than a program of its own.[61] Or, threatened by a global environmental crisis more serious than any pandemic, perhaps it will be an entirely new, ecological liberalism that reaches beyond Enlightenment humanism.[62]

Based on the historical record briefly evoked in this essay, albeit with some hesitation, I dare contradict Alexandre Dumas's reminder that "all generalizations are dangerous, even this one." Liberalism in the singular does not exist—never has, never will. Furthermore, "the end of ideology" and "the end of history," provocative titles of erstwhile bestsellers, continue to be invoked but are no longer read. Ideology and history do not end. And so it is with liberalism. It was risking death in 1943, when Franklin Roosevelt insisted that "Dr. New Deal" had been replaced by "Dr. Win the War."[63] It was risking death in 1969 when my erstwhile, beloved colleague, Theodore Lowi, excoriated America for submitting to the dictates of an interest-group liberalism that traded a robust political philosophy for a sterile proceduralism.[64] It was risking death at the end of the Cold War, together with communism, as Stanley Hoffmann contended.[65] And it is risking death once again, after four years of Trump.[66] Fool me once, shame on you; fool me twice, shame on me. Fool us thrice, shame on all of us. This panicked pandemic and political time is as good as any to put an end to endism. Based on the record of the past, we must acknowledge the obvious; the antinomy of liberalism is as evident as it is paradoxical—its endings are always also new beginnings.

Notes

INTRODUCTION

Note on the epigraph: The full quote is more direct, and perhaps even more apropos: "Let me tell you something. Or watch the fuckin' news. Everything comes to an end." *The Sopranos*, Season 4, Episode 1, "For All Debts Public and Private," September 15, 2002.

1. Franklin D. Roosevelt, State of the Union Address, January 6, 1945, http://www.let. rug.nl/usa/presidents/franklin-delano-roosevelt/state-of-the-union-1945.php.

2. Geir Lundestad, *The United States and Western Europe since 1945: From Empire by Invitation to Transatlantic Drift* (New York: Oxford University Press, 1994).

3. T. J. Pempel, *Uncommon Democracies: The One Party–Dominant Regimes* (Ithaca, NY: Cornell University Press, 1990).

4. See, for example, Richard Rosecrance, ed., *America as an Ordinary Country: US Foreign Policy and the Future* (Ithaca, NY: Cornell University Press, 1976); and Paul Kennedy, *The Rise and Fall of the Great Powers* (New York: Random House, 1987).

5. Susan Strange, "The Persistent Myth of Lost Hegemony," *International Organization* 41, no. 4 (Autumn 1987): 569; see also the (astute) dissent regarding declinism by Samuel P. Huntington, "The US: Decline or Renewal," *Foreign Affairs* 67, no. 2 (Winter 1998–99): 76–96.

6. The Bretton Woods system was rooted in the US commitment to maintaining the convertibility of the dollar to gold at \$35/oz. By the late 1960s undisciplined US macroeconomic policies had undermined the credibility of that link, and President Nixon, when finally confronted with the deflationary measures necessary to shore up the dollar, chose instead to suddenly sever the greenback's ties to gold. See John S. Odell, *US International Monetary Policy: Markets, Power, and Ideas as Sources of Change* (Princeton, NJ: Princeton University Press, 1982); and Joanne Gowa, *Closing the Gold Window: Domestic Politics and the End of Bretton Woods* (Ithaca, NY: Cornell University Press, 1983).

7. Raymond Aron, *In Defense of Decadent Europe* (New Brunswick, NJ: Transaction, [1977] 1996), 193.

8. John Ruggie, "International Regimes, Transactions, and Change: Embedded Liberalism in the Postwar Economic Order," *International Organization* 36, no. 2 (1982): 379–415. See also Eric Helleiner, "The Life and Times of Embedded Liberalism: Legacies and Innovations since Bretton Woods," *Review of International Political Economy* 26, no. 6 (2019): 1112–35.

9. Karl Polanyi, *The Great Transformation* (Boston: Beacon, 1944).

10. Ruggie used the term in his article to refer only to international arrangements and practices.

11. It should be acknowledged that it was much easier for Americans than non-Americans to see more of the liberalism and less of the hypocrisy that characterized US behavior throughout this era.

12. "John Maynard Keynes: Was He a Liberal?," *Economist*, August 18, 2018, 58.

13. Jonathan Kirshner, this volume, chap. 1.

14. Derek Leebaert, *Grand Improvisation: America Confronts the British Superpower, 1945–57* (New York: Farrar, Straus and Giroux, 2018).

15. Leebaert, *Grand Improvisation*; David Mayers, *America and the Postwar World: Remaking International Society, 1945–56* (Abingdon, UK: Routledge, 2018), 3.

16. Peter A. Gourevitch, this volume, chap. 3.

17. Sheri Berman, this volume, chap. 4.

18. Berman, this volume, chap. 4. See also Sheri Berman, *The Primacy of Politics: Social Democracy and the Making of Europe's Twentieth Century* (New York: Cambridge University Press, 2006), 181.

19. Ilene Grabel, *When Things Don't Fall Apart: Global Financial Governance and Developmental Finance in an Age of Productive Incoherence* (Cambridge, MA: MIT Press, 2017), 29–54.

20. James Rosenau, *Along the Domestic Foreign Frontier: Exploring Governance in a Turbulent World* (New York: Cambridge University Press, 1997), 44–52.

21. Ilene Grabel, this volume, chap. 7.

22. Mark Lilla, "No One Knows What's Going to Happen," *New York Times* (Sunday Review), May 24, 2020, 4–5, https://www.nytimes.com/2020/05/22/opinion/sunday/corona virus-prediction-future.html.

23. David E. Sanger, Steven Erlanger, and Roger Cohen, "Biden Tells Allies 'America Is Back,' but Macron and Merkel Push Back," *New York Times*, February 20, 2021, A1.

24. Jonathan Kirshner, *An Unwritten Future: Realism, Uncertainty and World Politics* (Princeton, NJ: Princeton University Press, forthcoming).

25. Peter J. Katzenstein, *A World of Regions: Asia and Europe in the American Imperium* (Ithaca, NY: Cornell University Press, 2005); Peter J. Katzenstein, ed., *Sinicization and the Rise of China: Civilizational Processes beyond East and West* (New York: Routledge, 2012); Peter J. Katzenstein, ed., *Anglo-America and Its Discontents: Civilizational Identities beyond West and East* (New York: Routledge, 2012); Peter J. Katzenstein and Lucia Seybert, eds., *Protean Power: Exploring the Uncertain and Unexpected in World Politics* (Cambridge: Cambridge University Press, 2018).

CHAPTER 1. KEYNES AND THE ELUSIVE MIDDLE WAY

1. For helpful comments and suggestions for this chapter, the author thanks Eric Helleiner, Peter Katzenstein, and all of the participants in this project. The epigraph is from John Maynard Keynes, "Letter to F. A. Hayek," June 28, 1944, in *The Collected Writings of John Maynard Keynes*, ed. Donald Moggridge and Elizabeth Johnson (London: Macmillan, 1971–89) (hereafter *CW*), 27:385, 387. The quotation from the chapter's first sentence is from John Gerard Ruggie, "International Regimes, Transactions, and Change: Embedded Liberalism in The Postwar Economic Order," *International Organization* 36, no. 2 (1982): 379–415.

2. Karl Polanyi, *The Great Transformation: The Political and Economic Origins of Our Time* (Boston: Beacon, [1944] 1980), 57.

3. Polanyi, it should be noted, and very much contra Keynes, was a "steadfast defender of Stalin's regime." Gareth Dale, *Karl Polanyi: A Life on the Left* (New York: Columbia University Press, 2017), 8. As Eric Helleiner noted in his impressive inquest regarding embedded liberalism, "Polanyi had more ambitious socialist goals in mind" and "was explicitly opposed to US postwar international economic plans." Eric Helleiner, "The Life and Times of Embedded Liberalism: Legacies and Innovations since Bretton Woods," *Review of International Political Economy* 26, no. 6 (2019): 1115.

4. "Mother's milk" is from his famous student Joan Robinson, *On Re-reading Marx* (Cambridge: Students' Bookshop, 1953), 6. Keynes extended this metaphor in reference to his break with orthodoxy in correspondence with Dennis Robertson: "You are, so to speak, bent on creeping back into your mother's womb; whilst I am shaking myself like

a dog on dry land." John Maynard Keynes, letter to Dennis Robertson, December 8, 1937, *CW*, 29:165.

5. John Maynard Keynes, "The End of Laissez-Faire," 1925, *CW*, 9:287–88; John Maynard Keynes, "National Self-Sufficiency," 1933, *CW*, 11:239.

6. On the varieties of the reception and practice of Keynesianism, see *The Political Power of Economic Ideas: Keynesianism across Nations,* ed. Peter Hall (Princeton, NJ: Princeton University Press, 1989).

7. Keynes, "Am I A Liberal?," 1926, *CW*, 9:306.

8. Keynes could not have been more explicit about these two points. See John Maynard Keynes, "The General Theory of Employment," *Quarterly Journal of Economics* 51, no. 2 (1937): esp. 122. Frustratingly, and uncharacteristically of Keynes, *The General Theory* is a difficult read and can even invite confusion. See John Maynard Keynes, *The General Theory* 1936, *CW*, vol. 7. This makes "The General Theory of Employment," his only academic article in response to his critics, essential. The best path to understanding *The General Theory* is found here, and in chapter 12 of the book, "The State of Long Term Expectations." Also valuable is "Poverty in Plenty: Is the Economic System Self-Adjusting?" In that article Keynes identified the faith (or lack thereof) that an economy disturbed will always naturally return to a full employment equilibrium as a crucial line of demarcation: "Now I range myself with the heretics." John Maynard Keynes, "Poverty in Plenty: Is the Economic System Self-Adjusting?," 1934, *CW*, 13:489.

9. Armchair psychologists occasionally attribute Keynes's transformation to the death of his great teacher Alfred Marshall in 1924 (giving license to apostasy) or to the grounding effect of his marriage to Lydia Lopokova the following year. Keynes's memorial to Marshall, published less than two months after his death, filled sixty-one pages of the *Economic Journal*. See John Maynard Keynes, "Alfred Marshall, 1842–1924," *Economic Journal* 34 (September 1924): 311–72, reprinted in *CW*, 10), 161–231. Schumpeter called the essay "the most brilliant and profound biography of any scientist the present writer ever read." See Joseph Schumpeter, "Essays in Biography by J. M. Keynes," *Economic Journal* 43 (December 1933): 653. On the marriage, see Judith Mackrell, *Bloomsbury Ballerina: Lydia Lopokova, Imperial Dancer and Mrs. John Maynard Keynes* (London: Weidenfeld & Nicolson, 2008).

10. Keynes, "Poverty in Plenty," 13:487; see also the forcefully phrased defenses of microeconomic efficiency in Keynes, *The General Theory*, e.g., 7:379, 380.

11. Roy Harrod, Keynes's colleague and first biographer, described him as "an individualist to his fingertips." Roy Harrod, *The Life of John Maynard Keynes* (London: Macmillan, 1951), 191; Meade is quoted in D. E. Moggridge, *Maynard Keynes: An Economist's Biography* (London: Routledge, 1992), 710.

12. John Maynard Keynes, "Liberalism and Labour," 1925, *CW*, 9:311; Keynes, "Am I a Liberal?," 9:304; see also Keynes, "The End of Laissez-Faire," 9:290.

13. As for Marxism, Keynes added, "How can I accept a doctrine which sets up as its bible, above and beyond criticism, an obsolete economic textbook which I know to be not only scientifically erroneous but without interest or application for the modern world?" John Maynard Keynes, "A Short View of Russia," 1925, *CW*, 9:257, 258.

14. Keynes, *The General Theory*, 7:380.

15. Keynes, *The General Theory*, 7:372.

16. John Maynard Keynes, "Some Economic Consequences of a Declining Population," 1937, *CW*, 14:132; see also *The General Theory*, 7:372. To Ralph Hawtrey, Keynes wrote that he favored "a scheme of direct taxation in order to redistribute incomes in such a way as to increase the propensity to consume." John Maynard Keynes, letter to Ralph Hawtrey, *CW*, 14:16.

17. John Maynard Keynes, "Liberalism and Industry," 1927, *CW*, 19:639; *The General Theory*, 7:374.

18. John Maynard Keynes, *The Economic Consequences of the Peace*, 1919, *CW*, 2:149; John Maynard Keynes, *A Tract on Monetary Reform*, 1923, *CW*, 4:24 (second and third quotes). In 1937 Keynes would insist that not just prosperity but "the maintenance of . . . civil peace," is "absolutely dependent" on a sufficiently equal distribution of income. See Keynes, "Some Economic Consequences of a Declining Population," 14:32.

19. "Economism" here refers to the evaluation of outcomes—and the measurement of a life well lived more generally—solely by narrowly materialist criteria. This is related to but nevertheless distinct from a common modern usage of the term, which refers to the application of economic analysis to noneconomic problems.

20. Keynes, "A Short View of Russia," 9:266–67.

21. John Maynard Keynes, "My Early Beliefs," 1938, *CW*, 10:445; Robert Skidelsky, *John Maynard Keynes:* vol. 1: *Hopes Betrayed 1883–1920* (London: Macmillan, 1983), 133; Jonathan Kirshner, "Keynes's Early Beliefs and Why They Still Matter," Challenge 58, no. 5 (2015), 398–412. John Maynard Keynes, "Economic Possibilities for Our Grandchildren," 1930, *CW*, 9:328.

22. Joan Robinson, "What Has Become of the Keynesian Revolution?," in *Essays on John Maynard Keynes*, ed. Milo Keynes (Cambridge: Cambridge University Press, 1975), 128.

23. The source for this subsection's epigraph is John Maynard Keynes, "Post-War Currency Policy," Treasury memo, September 8, 1941, *CW*, 25:21–33. As Keynes was drafting plans for the postwar international monetary order, the United States was not yet in the war and German troops, who had been sweeping across the Soviet Union, began the siege of Leningrad.

24. Richard N. Gardner, *Sterling-Dollar Diplomacy in Current Perspective: The Origins and the Prospects of Our International Economic Order*, 3rd ed. (New York: Columbia University Press, 1980); Robert Skidelsky, *John Maynard Keynes*, vol. 3: *Fighting for Freedom* (New York: Viking, 2001). See also the broader account in Eric Helleiner, *Forgotten Foundations of Bretton Woods: International Development and the Making of the Postwar Order* (Ithaca, NY: Cornell University Press, 2014).

25. G. John Ikenberry, "A World Economy Restored: Expert Consensus and the Anglo-American Postwar Settlement," *International Organization* 46, no. 1 (1992): 289–321. In Ruggie's phrasing, there was consensus that "multilateralism would be predicated upon domestic interventionism." Ruggie, "Embedded Liberalism in the Postwar Order," 393.

26. John Maynard Keynes, "Proposals for an International Currency Union," Treasury memo, November 18, 1941, *CW*, 25:185. As Keynes emphasized, "The advocacy of control of capital movements must not be taken to mean that the era of international investment should be brought to an end. On the contrary the system contemplated should greatly facilitate the restoration of international credit" (25:186). Similarly, in subsequently emphasizing in the UK parliament the need for exchange controls, Keynes stressed that the goal was to preserve domestic monetary autonomy, not to inhibit the flow of productive capital. John Maynard Keynes, "House of Lords Debates," May 16, 1944, *CW*, 26:4–6.

27. John Maynard Keynes, *A Treatise on Money*, part 2: *Applied Theory of Money*, 1930, *CW*, 6:256 (conformity), 6:285 (water), 6:270–72, 274, 280, 281. Keynes would become disenchanted with much of the theoretical apparatus of the *Treatise*, moving swiftly to the development of *The General Theory*—but on this essential point he did not waver: "Freedom of capital movements assumes that it is right and desirable to have an equalization of interest rates in all parts of the world." John Maynard Keynes, "Letter to Roy Harrod," April 19, 1942, *CW*, 25:146–51.

28. Keynes, "Post-War Currency Policy," 25:27, 28, 30. With, as always, one eye toward practicality and justice, Keynes also stressed the "social strain" of downward adjustment

(quote at 25:28). See also Ilene Grabel, The Political Economy of 'Policy Credibility': The New-Classical Macroeconomics and the Remaking of Emerging Economies," *Cambridge Journal of Economics* 24, no. 1 (2000): 1–19.

29. Keynes, "The General Theory of Employment," 121; Keynes *The General Theory*, 7:156–58 (on the "beauty contest" analogy regarding collective expectations) and 7:161–62 ("animal spirits"); Hyman Minsky, "The Financial Instability Hypothesis: An Interpretation of Keynes and an Alternative to 'Standard' Theory," 1977, reprinted in Minsky, *Can "It" Happen Again? Essays on Instability and Finance* (New York: M. E. Sharpe, 1982); Charles P. Kindleberger, *Manias, Panics and Crashes* (New York: Basic Books, 1978). See also Mark Blyth, "The Political Power of Financial Ideas: Transparency, Risk and Distribution in Global Finance," in *Monetary Orders: Ambiguous Economics, Ubiquitous Politics,* ed. Jonathan Kirshner (Ithaca, NY: Cornell University Press, 2003), 239–59.

30. As Ruggie argued, although the good times did not roll in the 1970s, the compromise of embedded liberalism would nevertheless endure as long as its normative foundations were shared.

31. This, not debates over the level of the reparations burden, was the key clarion call and enduring contribution of Keynes's *The Economic Consequences of the Peace.*

32. On executive pay and lifestyle, see Margaret M. Blair, "CEO Pay: Why Such a Contentious Issue?," *Brookings Review*, 12, no. 1 (1994): 24 (for 1983 and 1993); Elliot Blair Smith and Phil Kuntz "CEO Pay 1,795-to-1 Multiple of Wages Skirts U.S. Law," *Bloomberg*, April 30, 2013 (for the 1950s), https://www.bloomberg.com/news/articles/2013-04-30/ceo-pay-1-795-to-1-multiple-of-workers-skirts-law-as-sec-delays; Lawrence Mishel and Julia Wolfe, *CEO Compensation Has Grown 940% since 1978* (Washington, DC: Economic Policy Institute, August 14, 2019), p. 4; "How Top Executives Live," *Fortune*, July 1955. On the other side of the coin, see Susan Fleck, John Glaser, and Shawn Sprague, "The Compensation-Productivity Gap: A Visual Essay," *Monthly Labor Review*, January 2011, 62; and Thomas Kochan, "The American Jobs Crisis and the Implications for the Future of Employment Policy," *International Labor Relations Review* 66, no. 2 (2013): 293; Suzanne Mettler, *Soldiers to Citizens: The G.I. Bill and the Making of the Greatest Generation* (Oxford: Oxford University Press, 2005). From 1947 to 1979 productivity and real wages tracked closely together, each growing at a rate of about 2 to 3 percent per year. From 1980 to 2001 productivity grew 86 percent; real hourly wages grew by 7 percent. See Kochan, "The American Jobs Crisis," 294.

33. Mary Dudziak, *Cold War Civil Rights: Race and the Image of American Democracy* (Princeton, NJ: Princeton University Press, 2011).

34. Barry Eichengreen, *Hall of Mirrors: The Great Depression, the Great Recession, and the Uses—and Misuses—of History* (Oxford: Oxford University Press, 2015).

35. I thank Eric Helleiner for bringing this point to my attention. See Eric Helleiner, "National Inequalities and the Political Economy of Global Financial Reform," in *International Policy Rules and Inequality: Implications for Global Economic Governance,* ed. José Antonio Ocampo (New York: Columbia University Press, 2019), 33. On finance, see Benjamin Cohen, "Phoenix Risen: The Resurrection of Global Finance," *World Politics* 48, no. 2 (1996): 268–96.

36. "The pseudo-analogy with the physical sciences leads directly counter to the habit of mind which is most important for an economist to acquire." See John Maynard Keynes, letter to Roy Harrod, July 16, 1938, *CW*, 13:299; see also the similar themes stressed in John Maynard Keynes, letter to Roy Harrod, July 4, 1938, *CW*, 14:297.

37. J. R. Hicks, "Mr. Keynes and the 'Classics': A Suggested Interpretation," *Econometrica* 5, no. 2 (1937): 147–59; Alvin Hansen, *A Guide to Keynes* (New York: McGraw Hill, 1953); Paul Samuelson, *Foundations of Economic Analysis* (Cambridge: Harvard University Press, 1947); Samuelson, *Economics: An Introductions Analysis* (New York: McGraw

Hill, 1948); William Darity Jr. and Warren Young, "IS-LM: An Inquest," *History of Political Economy* 27, no. 1 (1995): 1–41.

38. Joan Robinson, "Has Keynes Failed?," *Annals of Public & Cooperative Economics* 50, no. 1 (1979): 27 (quote).

39. Robinson, "What Has Become of the Keynesian Revolution?," 125, 126.

40. Edmund S. Phelps, "Phillips Curves, Expectation of Inflation, and Optimal Unemployment over Time," *Econometrica* 34, no. 3 (1967): 254–81; Milton Friedman, "The Role of Monetary Policy," *American Economic Review* 53, no. 1 (1968): 1–17; J. Bradford De Long, "America's Peacetime Inflation: The 1970s," in *Reducing Inflation: Motivation and Strategy,* ed. Christina Romer and David Romer (Chicago: University of Chicago Press, 1997): 247–80.

41. In 1952, after losing five straight presidential elections, the Republicans nominated Dwight Eisenhower, a moderate and, crucially, an internationalist, who could have easily run as a centrist Democrat. Under Eisenhower, marginal tax rates on the wealthy remained extremely high, and the United States embarked on massive infrastructure projects. The Federal Aid Highway Act of 1956 was the largest public works project in American history at that time.

42. Noting this incongruity, James Tobin grumbled, "If I had a copyright on who could use the term 'Keynesian' I wouldn't allow them to use it." This observation was in accord (if here with some satisfaction) with Gregory Mankiw's similar assessment: "Keynes might not recognize the new Keynesians as Keynesians at all." Brian Snowdon, Howard Vane, and Peter Wynarczyk, *A Modern Guide to Macroeconomics: An Introduction to Competing Schools of Thought* (Aldershot, UK: Edward Elgar, 1994), 132, 228.

43. Nor for that matter, did the passionate anti-Keynesian Frank Knight, who saw the presence of "true uncertainty," which precludes the possibility that all actors share the same model, as the very engine of capitalism. Frank Knight, *Risk, Uncertainty and Profit* (Chicago: University of Chicago Press, [1921] 1971), 19 (quote). On these issues see also Stephen Nelson and Peter Katzenstein, "Uncertainty, Risk, and the Financial Crisis of 2008," *International Organization* 68, no. 2 (2014): 361–92.

44. Mervyn King, "Monetary Policy—Practice Ahead of Theory," *Bank of England Quarterly Bulletin,* Summer 2005, 4. It ought to have given considerable pause when Thomas Sargent, one of the founders of the movement, reached the conclusion that old-fashioned models that had been dismissed as "discredited" did better in explaining the pattern of inflation in the United States than did rational expectations–based models. Thomas Sargent, *The Conquest of American Inflation* (Princeton, NJ: Princeton University Press, 1999), 133. For more on the "gross empirical failures" of rational expectations theory, see, for example, Roman Frydman and Michael Goldberg, *Beyond Mechanical Markets: Asset Price Swings, Risk, and the Role of the State* (Princeton, NJ: Princeton University Press, 2011), 52.

45. Michael Woodford, "Convergence in Macroeconomics: Elements of the New Synthesis," *American Economic Journal: Macroeconomics* 1, no. 1 (2009): 267–79.

46. Robert Skidelsky, Money and Government: The Past and Future of Economics (New Haven, CT: Yale University Press, 2018), 202–3 (both quotes).

47. These pressures included the collapse of the fixed-exchange-rate Bretton Woods international monetary regime, which made capital controls appear to be less essential for policy autonomy; the growth of international financial markets and the technological innovations that made them more difficult to govern; and the inflation of the 1970s, which undercut the logic of policies like "Regulation Q" in the United States (Regulation Q placed a cap on nominal interest rates, which in a high inflation environment left the real interest rate return for affected institutions negative). For a broader discussion see

Eric Helleiner, *States and the Re-emergence of Global Finance: From Bretton Woods to the 1990s* (Ithaca, NY: Cornell University Press, 1994).

48. Jonathan Kirshner, *American Power after the Financial Crisis* (Ithaca, NY: Cornell University Press, 2014).

49. Greta R. Krippner, *Capitalizing on Crisis: The Political Origins of the Rise of Finance* (Cambridge, MA: Harvard University Press, 2011), 3–4, 28–29; Simon Johnson and James Kwak, *Thirteen Bankers: The Wall Street Takeover and the Next Financial Meltdown* (New York: Pantheon, 2010), 5, 60–61, 115.

50. James Tobin, "On the Efficiency of the Financial System," *Lloyds Bank Review* 153 (July 1984): 1–15; Robert Solow, testimony before the Subcommittee on Investigations and Oversight, "Building a Science of Economics for the Real World," Hearing before the Committee on Science and Technology, House of Representatives, 111th Cong., 2nd sess., July 20, 2012. For a particularly chilling assessment of the phenomenon of financialization, see Rana Foroohar, *Makers and Takers: The Rise of Finance and the Fall of American Business* (New York: Crown, 2016).

51. Keynes, *The General Theory*, 7:159.

52. In this sense, Keynes was right. Except in extreme cases, people hunger for purpose at least as much as for bread. And to date, in the contemporary populist backlash, the mobilizing expressions of grievance (and their manipulation by elites) have largely taken the form of ugly tribalism and nativism, as opposed to concrete measures of economic redistribution—as forcefully illustrated by Abdelal in his contribution to this volume.

53. Keynes, "Economic Possibilities for our Grandchildren," 9:329. A vulgar few, Keynes anticipated, would still mindlessly chase wealth, but the vast majority, liberated from the pressure to assure adequate food, shelter, and comfort, "shall inquire more curiously than is safe today into the true character of this 'purposiveness' with which in varying degrees Nature has endowed almost all of us"; Keynes, "Short View of Russia," 9:268.

54. Keynes, "Short View of Russia," 9:294. "Our experience has demonstrated plainly that these things cannot successfully be carried on if they depend on the motive of profit"; see John Maynard Keynes, "Art and the State," *Listener*, August 26, 1936, *CW*, 28:343, 344, 345, 347, 348; Keynes, "National Self-Sufficiency," 11:241, 242.

55. Warren St John, "Shadows over Central Park," *New York Times*, October 29, 2013, A:29.

56. Candice Jackson, "Jeff Bezos Buying $165 Million Estate, a California Record," *New York Times*, February 15, 2020, B:4; Michael Sainato, "'I'm Not a Robot': Amazon Workers Condemn Unsafe, Grueling Conditions at Warehouse," *Guardian*, February 5, 2020, https://www.theguardian.com/technology/2020/feb/05/amazon-workers-protest-unsafe-grueling-conditions-warehouse.

57. National Commission on the Causes of the Financial and Economic Crisis in the United States, *The Financial Crisis Inquiry Report: Final Report of the National Commission on the Causes of the Financial and Economic Crisis in the United States* (New York: Public Affairs, 2011), 354.

58. Ben S. Bernanke, Timothy Geithner, and Henry Paulson Jr., *Firefighting: The Financial Crisis and Its Lessons* (New York: Penguin, 2019); Martin Wolf, *The Shifts and the Shocks: What We've Learned—and Have Still to Learn—from the Financial Crisis* (New York: Penguin, 2014), 352.

59. As Adam Tooze argues, "The presidential race of 2016 turned out to be more about the financial crisis of 2008 than 2012 had been." Adam Tooze, *Crashed: How a Decade of Financial Crises Changed the World* (New York: Viking, 2018), 566. On the crucial moment of the nominations (as opposed to the general election), see Jonathan Kirshner, "Trump and the End of Everything," *Boston Review*, June 7, 2016.

CHAPTER 2. THE END OF SOCIAL PURPOSE?

1. I think it was a BBC program called *Panorama*, but I have been unable to locate it in the official archive.

2. Mark Blyth, *Great Transformations: Economic Ideas and Institutional Change in the Twentieth Century* (Cambridge: Cambridge University Press, 2002).

3. Donald McKenzie, *An Engine Not a Camera: How Financial Models Shape Markets* (Cambridge, MA: MIT Press, 2006).

4. John Gerard Ruggie, "International Regimes, Transaction, and Change: Embedded Liberalism in the Postwar Economic Order," *International Organization* 36, no. 2 (Spring 1982): 379–415.

5. Karl Polanyi, *The Great Transformation: The Social and Economic Origins of Our Time* (New York: Viking, 1944).

6. Ronald Wannacott and Paul Wannacott, *Economics* (New York: McGraw Hill, 1986).

7. The periodization in *Great Transformations* situates the origins of the new regime in 1980, but 1985 is a reasonable point to start concentrating on regime consolidation, which is the focus here and in the other chapters in this volume.

8. The fact that the two of these literatures were lumped together suggests yet another level of bifurcation, insofar as monetarist theory and rational expectations theory were orthogonal methodologically but were united politically. For a discussion of these issues, see Oddny Helgadottir, "Formal Combat: Scientific Competition and Macroeconomic Paradigms from the Great Depression to the Great Recession" (PhD dissertation, Brown University, 2018).

9. Juliet Johnson, *Priests of Prosperity: How Central Bankers Transformed the Post-Communist World* (Ithaca, NY: Cornell University Press, 2016).

10. Mark Blyth, "Domestic Institutions and the Possibility of Social Democracy," *Comparative European Politics* 3, no. 4 (December 2005): 379–407; Adam Tooze, *Crashed: How a Decade of Financial Crises Changed the World* (New York: Penguin, 2019).

11. Mark Blyth, "Policies to Overcome Stagnation: The Crisis, and the Possible Futures, of All Things Euro," *European Journal of Economics and Economic Policies* 13, no. 2 (2016): 215–28. Many accounts of this issue turn to the politics of race, identity, and status anxiety to explain these phenomena. I find that these explanations do not travel well beyond the United States and tend to be circular when applied there—they explain a rise in racism by reference to a rise in the number of racists, for example. Similarly, they have a hard time explaining left populism. For an excellent discussion of such issues, see Jonathan Hopkin, *Anti-System Politics: The Crisis of Market Liberalism in Rich Democracies* (London: Oxford University Press, 2020); and Martin Sandbu, *An Economy of Belonging* (Princeton, NJ: Princeton University Press, 2020).

12. Hopkin, *Anti-System Politics*; Eric Lonergan and Mark Blyth, *Angrynomics* (New York: Columbia University Press, 2020).

13. Eric Helleiner, *The Forgotten Foundations of Bretton Woods: International Development and the Making of the Postwar Order* (Ithaca, NY: Cornell University Press, 2006).

14. Louis Pauly, *Who Elected the Bankers? Surveillance and Control in the World Economy* (Ithaca, NY: Cornell University Press, 1998).

15. Eric Helleiner, *States and the Reemergence of Global Finance: From Bretton Woods to the 1990s* (Ithaca, NY: Cornell University Press, 1994).

16. Andrew Shonfeld, *Modern Capitalism: The Changing Balance of Public and Private Power* (Oxford: Oxford University Press, 1969).

17. Tony Judt, *Postwar: A History of Europe since 1945* (New York: Penguin, 2006).

18. Blyth, *Great Transformations*; Blyth, "Domestic Institutions."

19. Blyth, *Great Transformations*.

20. Greta Krippner, *Capitalizing on Crisis: The Political Origins of the Rise of Finance* (Cambridge, MA: Harvard University Press, 2012).

21. Michael Piore and Charles Sabel, *The Second Industrial Divide: Possibilities for Prosperity* (New York: Basic Books, 1986).

22. Jonathan Kirshner, *Appeasing Bankers: Financial Caution on the Road to War* (Princeton, NJ: Princeton University Press, 2007).

23. See Peter A. Gourevitch, this volume, chap. 3; and Sheri Berman, this volume, chap. 4.

24. The possible exception is Germany, which has been running a permanent beggar-thy-neighbor devaluation regime to boost its exports, thereby importing rather than generating demand, since 1948. See Lucio Bacarro and Martin Hopner, "The Political and Economic Foundations of Export-Led Growth: The German Case" (working paper, Max-Planck-Institut für Gesellschaftsforschung, 2020).

25. Rudolph Meidner, "Our Concept of the Third Way: Some Remarks on the Sociopolitical Tenets of the Swedish Labor Movement," *Economic and Industrial Democracy* 1, no. 3 (1980): 349.

26. Chalmers Johnson, *MITI and the Japanese Miracle* (Stanford, CA: Stanford University Press, 1982).

27. Mikhal Kalecki, "Political Aspects of Full Employment," *Political Quarterly* 14, no. 4 (Autumn 1943).

28. Krippner, *Capitalizing on Crisis*.

29. Helleiner, *States and the Reemergence*.

30. Michael Bordo, "The Operation and Demise of the Bretton Woods System: 1958 to 1971," NBER Working Paper no. 23189 (Cambridge, MA: National Bureau of Economic Research, 2017).

31. Kalecki, "Political Aspects of Full Employment."

32. Mikhal Kalecki, "Political Aspects of Full Employment," *Political Quarterly* 14, no. 4 (Autumn 1943): 330.

33. Bordo, "The Operation and Demise."

34. I thank Herman Schwartz for impressing on me this side of the story. See Herman Schwartz and Mark Blyth, "Four Galtons and a Minsky," in *The New Politics of Growth and Stagnation,* ed. Lucio Bacarro, Mark Blyth, and Jonas Pontusson (New York: Oxford University Press, forthcoming).

35. Researchers at RAND Corporation estimated that this redistribution constituted $47 trillion transferred from those below the 90th percentile of the US income distribution to those above the 90th percentile over the past forty years. See Carter C. Price and Kathryn Edwards, "Trends in Income from 1975 to 2018" (Santa Monica, CA: Rand Corporation, September 2020).

36. Peter Swenson, *Fair Shares: Unions, Pay and Politics in Sweden and West Germany* (Ithaca, NY: Cornell University Press, 1992); Jonas Pontusson, *The Limits of Social Democracy: Investment Politics in Sweden* (Ithaca, NY: Cornell University Press, 1992).

37. Wolfgang Streeck, *Buying Time: The Delayed Crisis of Democratic Capitalism* (London: Verso, 2014).

38. David Autor, David Dorn, and Gordon Hanson, "The China Shock: Learning from Labor-Market Adjustment to Large Changes in Trade," *Annual Review of Economics* 8 (2016): 205–40.

39. Kathleen Thelen, "The American Precariat: U.S. Capitalism in Comparative Perspective," *Perspectives on Politics* 17, no. 1 (2019): 5–27.

40. Kenneth Rogoff "The Optimal Degree of Commitment to an Intermediate Monetary Target," *Quarterly Journal of Economics* 100, no. 4 (1985): 1169–89.

41. Helgadottir, "Formal Combat."

42. Johnson, *Priests of Prosperity*.

43. Mark Blyth and Richard Katz, "From Catch-All Politics to Cartelization: The Political Economy of the Cartel Party," *Western European Politics* 28, no. 1 (January 2005): 34–61; Hopkin, *Anti-System Politics*.

44. Stephanie Mudge, *Leftism Reinvented: Western Parties from Socialism to Neoliberalism* (Cambridge, MA: Harvard University Press, 2018).

45. Jonathan Hopkin and Mark Blyth, "The Global Economics of European Populism: Growth Regimes and Party System Change in Europe," *Government and Opposition* 54, no. 2 (April 2019): 193–225.

46. Mark Blyth and Simon Tilford, "How the Eurozone Might Split: Could Germany Become a Reluctant Hegemon?" *Foreign Affairs*, https://www.foreignaffairs.com/articles/europe/2018-01-11/how-eurozone-might-split.

47. Timo Fetzer, "Did Austerity Cause Brexit?" *American Economic Review* 109, no. 11 (2018): 3849–86.

48. Mohammed El Erian, *The Only Game in Town: Central Banks, Instability and Avoiding the Next Collapse* (New York: Random House, 2015).

49. Tooze, *Crashed*.

50. Martin Gilens, *Affluence and Influence: Economic Inequality and Political Power in America* (Princeton, NJ: Princeton University Press, 2014).

51. The ongoing COVID-19 crisis seems to have put Austerian debt-mongering arguments to bed for the moment. However, once the crisis passes, we can be sure that these ideas will be back into circulation, with the usual powerful chorus blaring in the ears of postcrisis politicians everywhere. Even when there is less than zero pressure on the government's finances in the form of negative real yields on long-term debt, which pertains to almost all rich country debt, the government of the day must be seen to balance the books, even if that worsens an already shaky economy.

52. Tooze, *Crashed*.

53. Blyth, "Policies to Overcome."

54. Blyth and Tilford, "How the Eurozone."

55. Robert Wade, "From Miracle to Cronyism: Explaining the Great Asian Slump," *Cambridge Journal of Economics* 22, no. 6 (1998): 693–706.

56. Matthias Matthijs and Mark Blyth, eds. *The Future of the Euro* (New York: Oxford University Press, 2015).

57. Herman Schwartz, "American Hegemony: Intellectual Property Rights, Dollar Centrality, and Infrastructural Power," *Review of International Political Economy* 26, no. 3 (2019): 490–519.

58. Schwartz, "American Hegemony."

59. Given the lack of alternatives, dollar dominance is likely threatened only by the move to central bank digital currencies allowing real time settlements bypassing dollar clearance. The fact that the US Fed has its own digital greenback proposal moving forward suggests that the United States is keen to head this off at the pass.

60. Moreover, in a world were exports and surpluses are fetishized by those who hold them, if the United States were to rebalance its accounts by cutting its deficits and paying back its debts, it would destroy the value of offshore dollar assets, which are the national savings of surplus countries. Countries complaining about the United States and its debts and deficits would be crushed if the United States ever decided to really do anything about them, which is a pretty strong incentive to keep the system going.

CHAPTER 3. THE CONSTRUCTION OF COMPROMISE AND THE RISE AND FALL OF GLOBAL ORDERS

1. John Gerard Ruggie, "International Regimes, Transactions, and Change: Embedded Liberalism in the Postwar Economic Order," *International Organization* 36, no. 2 (Spring 1982): 379–415. On the "historical consensus" debate as it applies to the United Kingdom, see Paul Addison, "Consensus Revisited," *Twentieth Century British History* 4,

no. 1 (1993): 91–94; David Dutton, *British Politics since 1945: The Rise, Fall and Rebirth of Consensus*, 2nd ed. (Blackwell, 1997); Dennis Kavanagh and Peter Morris, "Is the 'Postwar Consensus' A Myth?" *Contemporary Record* 2, no. 6 (1989): 14–15; Richard Toye, "From 'Consensus' to 'Common Ground'": The Rhetoric of the Postwar Settlement and Its Collapse" *Journal of Contemporary History* 48, no. 1 (January): 3–23.

2. Gérard Bouchard, "La pensée impuissante: Échecs et mythes nationaux canadiens-français (1850–1960)," *Revue d'histoire de l'Amérique française* 58, no. 3 (Winter 2005): 315–456.

3. Seymour Martin Lipset and Stein Rokkan, *Party Systems and Voter Alignments: Cross-National Perspectives* (New York: Free Press, 1967).

4. Wolfram Kaiser, *Christian Democracy and the Origins of European Union* (Cambridge: Cambridge University Press, 2007); Philip Williams, *Crisis and Compromise: Politics in the Fourth Republic* (New York: Archon, 1964). Kees van Kersbergen, *Social Capitalism: A Study of Christian Democracy and the Welfare State* (London: Routledge, 1995).

5. Williams, *Crisis and Compromise*.

6. Michèle Lamont, *The Dignity of Working Men: Morality and the Boundaries of Race, Class, and Immigration* (New York: Russell Sage Foundation, 2000).

7. Peter A. Hall and David Soskice, eds., *Varieties of Capitalism* (New York: Oxford University Press, 2001); Andrew Shonfield, *Modern Capitalism: The Changing Balance of Public and Private Power* (Oxford: Oxford University Press, 1965).

8. Ronald P. Dore, *British Factory, Japanese Factory: The Origins of National Diversity in Industrial Relations* (Berkeley: University of California Press, 1973); Ronald P. Dore, *Education in Tokugawa Japan* (Berkeley: University of California Press, 1965); Michael Albert, *Capitalism vs. Capitalism: How America's Obsession with Individual Achievement and Short-Term Profit Has Led It to the Brink of Collapse* (New York: Four Walls Eight Windows, 1993).

9. Chalmers A. Johnson, *MITI and the Japanese Miracle: The Growth of Industrial Policy, 1925–1975* (Stanford, CA: Stanford University Press, 1982); Peter J. Katzenstein, Introduction to "Between Power and Plenty: Foreign Economic Policies of Advanced Industrial States," special issue, ed. Peter Katzenstein, *International Organization* 31, no. 4 (1977): 587–606.

10. The phrase comes from Karel Van Wolferen, *The Enigma of Japanese Power: People and Politics in a Stateless Nation* (New York: Vintage, 1990). See also Richard J. Samuels, *The Business of the Japanese State: Energy Markets in Comparative and Historical Perspective* (Ithaca, NY: Cornell University Press, 1987).

11. See the large debate centered around Chalmers Johnson's view of the role of the Japanese state in shaping the rapid revival of Japan after WWII. Johnson, *MITI and the Japanese Miracle*.

12. W. Carl Kester, "American and Japanese Corporate Governance: Convergence to Best Practice?" and Wolfgang Streeck, "Lean Production in the German Automobile Industry: A Test Case for Convergence Theory," in *National Diversity and Global Capitalism*, ed. Suzanne Berger and Ronald P. Dore (Ithaca, NY: Cornell University Press, 1996): 107–37 and 138–70.

13. Peter A. Gourevitch and James Shinn, *Political Power and Corporate Control* (Princeton, NJ: Princeton University Press, 2007).

14. Gourevitch and Shinn, *Political Power and Corporate Control*; Greta R. Krippner, *Capitalizing on Crisis: The Political Origins of the Rise of Finance* (Cambridge, MA: Harvard University Press, 2011).

15. Peter A. Gourevitch, "What Do Corporations Owe Citizens? Pensions, Corporate Governance, and the Role of Institutional Investors," in *What Do We Owe Each Other?*

Rights and Obligations in Contemporary American Society, ed. Howard L. Rosenthal and David J. Rothman (London: Routledge, 2017): 12–18.

16. Peter A. Gourevitch and James Shinn, "The Perplexing Roles of Institutional Investors in a World of Multiple Investing Entities," in *Global Corporate Governance,* ed. Knut Sogner and Andrea Colli (London: Routledge, 2021), 187–205.

17. Reed Hundt, *A Crisis Wasted: Barack Obama's Defining Decisions* (New York: RosettaBooks, 2019).

18. Hundt, *A Crisis Wasted.*

19. Gøsta Esping-Andersen, *The Three Worlds of Welfare Capitalism* (Cambridge: Polity, 1990).

20. Philip Manow, "Welfare State Building and Coordinated Capitalism in Japan and Germany," in *The Origins of Nonliberal Capitalism: Germany and Japan in Comparison,* ed. Wolfgang Streeck and Kozo Yamamura (Ithaca, NY: Cornell University Press, 2001), 94–120; Lane Kenworthy, *Social Democratic Capitalism* (New York: Oxford University Press, 2019); Kathleen Thelen, *How Institutions Evolve: The Political Economy of Skills in Germany, Britain, the United States, and Japan* (Cambridge: Cambridge University Press, 2004); Hall and Soskice, *Varieties of Capitalism.*

21. Streeck is among the leading critics of the simple policy transfer model. Streeck, "Lean Production."

22. Peter F. Cowhey, "The Future Trade and Investment Order of the Pacific Rim: ASEAN, NAFTA, and APEC in the Context of Japanese and U.S. Diplomacy," in Peter A. Gourevitch, Takashi Inoguchi, and Courtney Parrington, eds., *U.S.-Japan Relations and International Institutions after the Cold War* (La Jolla: Graduate School of International Relations and Pacific Studies, University of California, San Diego, 1995), 183–226.

23. James P. Womack, Daniel T. Jones, and Daniel Roos, *The Machine That Changed the World* (New York: Free Press, 2007).

24. Hall and Soskice, *Varieties of Capitalism;* Adam Tooze, *Crashed: How a Decade of Financial Crises Changed the World* (New York: Viking, 2018). Peter A. Gourevitch, "Yet More Hard Times? Reflections on the Great Recession in the Frame of Earlier Hard Times," afterword to Miles Kahler and David A. Lake, eds., *Politics in the New Hard Times: The Great Recession in Comparative Perspective* (Ithaca, NY: Cornell University Press, 2013).

25. Yanis Varoufakis, *Adults in the Room: My Battle with the European and American Deep Establishment* (New York: Farrar, Straus and Giroux, 2017).

26. Kenworthy, *Social Democratic Capitalism;* J. Lawrence Broz, Jeffry Frieden, and Stephen Weymouth, "Populism in Place: The Economic Geography of the Globalization Backlash," *SSRN,* September 2019, https://doi.org/10.2139/ssrn.3501263.

27. Thomas Frank, *Listen, Liberal* (New York: Picador, 2016); Robert Kuttner, *Can Democracy Survive Global Capitalism?* (New York: W. W. Norton, 2018).

28. Hundt, *A Crisis Wasted.*

29. Diana C. Mutz, "Status Threat, Not Economic Hardship, Explains the 2016 Presidential Vote," *PNAS* 115, no. 9 (May 8, 2018): E4330–E4339, https://doi.org/10.1073/pnas.1718155115; Marisa Abrajano and Zoltan L. Hajnal, *White Backlash: Immigration, Race, and American Politics* (Princeton, NJ: Princeton University Press, 2017).

30. Arlie Russell Hochschild, *Strangers in Their Own Land* (New York: New Press, 2016).

31. George Lakoff, *Moral Politics: What Conservatives Know that Liberals Don't* (Chicago: University of Chicago Press, 1996).

32. Jens Hainmueller and Daniel J. Hopkins, "Public Attitudes toward Immigration," *Annual Review of Political Science* 17, no. 1 (May 2014): 232, https://doi.org/10.1146/annurev-polisci-102512-194818.

33. John H. Goldthorpe et al., *The Affluent Worker in the Class Structure* (Cambridge: Cambridge University Press, 1969).

34. Mattei Dogan, "Political Change and Social Stratification in France and Italy," in *Party Systems and Voter Alignments*, ed. S. M. Lipset and Stein Rokkan (New York: Free Press, 1967): 184–93.

35. Hainmueller and Hopkins, "Public Attitudes."

36. Robert Kuttner, *Can Democracy Survive Global Capitalism?* (New York: Norton, 2018); Autor et al., "Importing Political Polarization?"; Thomas Piketty, *Capital and Ideology* (Cambridge: Harvard University Press, 2020); Thomas Piketty, "Brahmin Left vs. Merchant Right: Rising Inequality & the Changing Structure of Political Conflict," WID. world Working Paper series no. 2018/7 (March 2018).

37. Peter B. Clark and James Q. Wilson, "Incentive Systems: A Theory of Organizations," *Administrative Science Quarterly* 6, no. 2 (September 1961): 129–66.

CHAPTER 4. THE SOCIAL DEMOCRATIC ORDER AND
THE RISE AND DECAY OF DEMOCRACY IN WESTERN EUROPE

1. Larry Diamond, Marc F. Plattner, and Christopher Walker, *Authoritarianism Goes Global: The Challenge to Democracy* (Baltimore: Johns Hopkins University Press, 2016); R. S. Foa and Y. Mounk, "The Danger of Deconsolidation," *Journal of Democracy* 27, no. 3 (2016): 5–17; R. S. Foa and Y. Mounk, "The Signs of Deconsolidation," *Journal of Democracy* 33, no. 1 (2017): 5–16.

2. Marc Santora and Helene Bienvenu, "Secure in Hungary, Orban Readies for Battle with Brussels," *New York Times*, May 11, 2018, https://www.nytimes.com/2018/05/11/world/europe/hungary-victor-orban-immigration-europe.html.

3. By any reasonable definition, this is also true of the United States, where of course up through the Civil War a significant part of the country was a tyrannical oligarchy and up through the 1960s and before civil rights legislation the government was unable or unwilling to ensure the most basic political rights of a significant number of American citizens.

4. Sheri Berman, *Democracy and Dictatorship in Europe: From the Ancien Régime to the Present Day* (New York: Oxford University Press, 2019).

5. Tony Judt, *Postwar* (New York: Penguin, 2005), 13–14; Donald Bloxham and Robert Gerwarth, *Political Violence in Twentieth Century Europe* (New York: Cambridge University Press, 2011); Keith Lowe, *Savage Continent* (New York: St. Martin's, 2011), 13–17; Ian Buruma, *Year Zero: A History of 1945* (New York: Penguin, 2014).

6. Judt, *Postwar*, 13–14.

7. William Hitchcock, *The Bitter Road to Freedom* (New York: Free Press, 2008), 190.

8. Hitchcock, *The Bitter Road*, 3.

9. Judt, *Postwar*, 20; Lowe, *Savage Continent*, 51.

10. Giles Macdonogh, *After the Reich* (New York: Basic Books, 2007).

11. Judt, *Postwar*, 21–22; Hitchcock, *The Bitter Road*, 99, 111; and Lowe, *Savage Continent*, 41ff.

12. Richard Bessel, *Germany 1945* (New York: Harper, 2010), 11.

13. Macdonogh, *After the Reich*; Bessel, *Germany 1945*; and the primary source collection Manfred Malzahn, ed., *Germany 1945–1949* (New York: Routledge, 1990).

14. Mark Mazower, *Dark Continent: Europe's Twentieth Century* (New York: Vintage, 2000), 213.

15. Ralf Dahrendorf, *Society and Democracy in Germany* (New York: W. W. Norton, 1979); Nancy Kogan, "Fascism as a Political System," in S. J. Woolf, ed., *The Nature of Fascism* (London: George Weidenfeld & Nicolson, 1968); and David Schoenbaum, *Hitler's Social Revolution* (New York: W. W. Norton, 1967).

16. Andreas Wimmer, *Nationalist Exclusion and Ethnic Conflict* (New York: Cambridge University Press, 2002); and Norman Naimark, *Fires of Hatred: Ethnic Cleansing in Twentieth-Century Europe* (Cambridge, MA: Harvard University Press, 2002).

17. Mazower, *Dark Continent*, 218.

18. Thomas Macaulay, *Complete Writings*, 27:263 quoted in Adam Przeworski, *Crises of Democracy* (New York: Cambridge University Press, 2019).

19. Writings on the Paris Commune, 198; and Przeworski, *Crises of Democracy*.

20. Friedrich Sterky, quoted in Herbert Tingsten, *The Swedish Social Democrats: Their Ideological Development* (London: Bedminster, 1973), 361.

21. Or, to put it another way, many came to accept (echoing the insights of T. H. Marshall) that without certain social and economic rights, neither political nor civil liberties could be truly realized. T. H. Marshall, *Class, Citizenship and Social Development* (Garden City, NY: Anchor, 1965); and Thomas Meyer, *The Theory of Social Democracy*, with Lewis Hinchman (Cambridge: Polity, 2007).

22. In the first postwar elections, communists won 12 percent of the vote in Norway and Denmark, 13 percent in Belgium, 19 percent in Italy, 23.5 percent in Finland, and 28.8 percent in France (in the November 1946 election). Lowe, *Savage Continent*, 278.

23. John Gerard Ruggie, "International Regimes, Transactions, and Change: Embedded Liberalism in the Postwar Economic Order," *International Organization* 36, no. 2 (Spring 1982): 386.

24. Sheri Berman, *The Primacy of Politics: Social Democracy and the Making of Europe's Twentieth Century* (New York: Cambridge University Press, 2006).

25. Berman, *The Primacy of Politics*, and James Kloppenberg, *Uncertain Victory* (New York: Oxford University Press, 1988).

26. Donald Sassoon, *One Hundred Years of Socialism* (New York: New Press, 1998), 140.

27. G. John Ikenberry, "A World Economy Restored," *International Organization* 46, no. 1 (Winter 1992): 289–321 and Ethan Kapstein, "Workers and the World Economy," *Foreign Affairs*, 75, no. 3 (May/June 1996): 16–37.

28. Philip Armstrong, Andrew Glyn, and John Harrison, *Capitalism since 1945* (New York: Basil Blackwell, 1991); and Stephen Marglin and Juliet Schor, eds., *The Golden Age of Capitalism* (New York: Clarendon, 1991).

29. Robert Skidelsky, "The Political Meaning of Keynesianism," in Peter Hall, ed., *The Political Power of Economic Ideas* (Princeton, NJ: Princeton University Press, 1989), 35–36.

30. Adam Przeworski, *Capitalism and Social Democracy* (New York: Cambridge University Press, 1985), 207.

31. Gøsta Esping-Andersen, *Politics against Markets: The Social Democratic Road to Power* (Princeton, NJ: Princeton University Press, 1985).

32. C. A. R. Crosland, *The Future of Socialism* (London: Fletcher and Son, 1967), 98.

33. The best statement of this probably remains T. H. Marshall, *Citizenship and Social Class* (New York: Cambridge University Press, 1950).

34. Charles de Gaulle, quoted in Andrew Shennan, *Rethinking France: Plans for Renewal 1940–1946* (Oxford: Clarendon, 1989), 251.

35. Simon Schama, *A History of Britain: The Fate of Empire, 1776–2000* (New York: Hyperion, 2002), 529.

36. Lowe, *Savage Continent*, 66–67.

37. Martin Pugh, *State and Society. British Political and Social History* (London: Bloomsbury, 2012), 228ff; and T. O. Lloyd, *Empire, Welfare State, Europe* (New York: Oxford University Press, 1993).

38. Spencer Di Scala, *Italy: From Revolution to Republic* (Boulder, CO: Westview, 1998), 283; Harold James, *Europe Reborn* (New York: Longman, 2003), 257.

39. Simon Reich, *The Fruits of Fascism* (Ithaca, NY: Cornell University Press, 1990).

40. Wolfgang Streeck, "Beneficial Constraints: On the Economic Limits of Rational Voluntarism," in *Contemporary Capitalism: The Embeddedness of Institutions*, ed. J. Hollingsworth and R. Boyer (Cambridge: Cambridge University Press, 1997): 197–219.

41. Lars Trädgårdh, "Statist Individualism: On the Culturality of the Nordic Welfare State," in *The Cultural Construction of Norden*, ed. Bo Stråth (Gothenburg, Sweden: Gothenburg University Press, 1990), 261; and Korpi, *The Working Class in Welfare Capitalism* (London: Routledge & Kegan Paul, 1978), esp. 48–49.

42. Gunnar Adler-Karlsson, *Functional Socialism* (Stockholm: Prisma, 1967), 18.

43. Magnus Ryner, *Capital Restructuring, Globalisation and the Third Way* (London: Routledge, 2002), 85.

44. Evelyn Huber and John Stephens, *Development and Crisis of the Welfare State* (Chicago: University of Chicago Press, 2001), 103; Esping-Andersen, *Politics against Markets*; and Gøsta Esping-Andersen, *The Three Worlds of Welfare Capitalism* (Princeton, NJ: Princeton University Press, 1990).

45. German residents polled in the American zone after World War II expected that it would take at least twenty years for the country to recover. De Gaulle had similarly informed French citizens that would take twenty-five years of "furious work" before France would be back on its feet again; Judt *Postwar*, 105, 89.

46. Charles Maier, "The Two Postwar Eras," *American Historical Review* 86, no. 2 (April 1981): 327–52.

47. Maier, "The Two Postwar Eras," 237.

48. Sheri Berman, "Taming Extremist Parties: The Lessons from European Communism," *Journal of Democracy* 18, no. 5 (January 2008): 5–18.

49. Claus Offe, "Competitive Party Democracy and the Keynesian Welfare State: Factors of Stability and Disorganization," *Policy Sciences* 15 (1983): 225–26.

50. See Rawi Abdelal, this volume, chap. 6.

51. Milton Friedman, *Capitalism and Freedom* (Chicago: University of Chicago Press, 1982), ix.

52. Robert Lucas, "Macroeconomic Priorities," American Economic Review 93, no. 1 (March 2003): 1–14.

53. Binyamin Applebaum, *The Economists' Hour* (New York: Little, Brown, 2019).

54. Patrick Wintour, "Clinton, Blair, Renzi: Why We lost, and How to Fight Back," *Guardian*, November 22, 2018, https://www.theguardian.com/world/2018/nov/22/clinton-blair-renzi-why-we-lost-populists-how-fight-back-rightwing-populism-centrist; Sheri Berman, "The Specter Haunting Europe: The Lost Left," Journal of Democracy 27, no. 4 (October 2016): 69–76. https://www.theguardian.com/politics/2002/mar/12/speeches.labour.

55. Stephanie Mudge, *Leftisim Reinvented* (Cambridge, MA: Harvard University Press, 2018).

56. Sheri Berman and Maria Snegovaya, "Populism and the Decline of Social Democracy," *Journal of Democracy* 30, no. 3 (2019): 5–19.

57. Sheri Berman and Hans Kundnani, "Convergence and Democratic Dysfunction," *Journal of Democracy* 32, no. 1 (2021): 22–36.

58. Hanspeter Kriesi et al., "Globalization and the Transformation of the National Political Space: Six European Countries Compared," *European Journal of Political Research* 45 (October 2006): 921–56; Ronald Inglehart and Pippa Norris, "Trump and the Populist Authoritarian Parties: *The Silent Revolution* in Reverse," *Perspectives on Politics* 15 (June 2017): 443–54; and Christoffer Green-Pedersen, "The Growing Importance of Issue Competition: The Changing Nature of Party Competition in Western Europe," *Political Studies* 55 (October 2007): 607–28.

59. Wolfgang Merkel, "Is Capitalism Compatible with Democracy?" *Zeitschrift für Vergleichende Politikwissenschaft* 8 (July 2014): 109–28; and Wolfgang Streeck and Armin Schäfer, *Politics in the Age of Austerity* (New York: Polity, 2013).

60. Wolfgang Streeck, "The Crisis of Democratic Capitalism," *New Left Review* 71 (September–October 2011): 5–29.

61. Bhaskar Sunkara, *The Socialist Manifesto* (New York: Basic Books, 2019); and Joseph Schwartz and Jason Schulman, "Toward Freedom: Democratic Socialist Theory and Practice" (n.p.: Democratic Socialists of America, December 21, 2012), https://www.dsausa.org/strategy/toward_freedom/.

62. Will Wilkinson, "How Libertarian Democracy Skepticism Infected the American Right" (Washington, DC: Niskanen Center, November 3, 2017), https://www.niskanencenter.org/libertarian-democracy-skepticism-infected-american-right/; David Van Reybrouck, *Against Elections* (London: Random House, 2016); Jason Brennan, *Against Democracy* (Princeton, NJ: Princeton University Press, 2016); and David Harsanyi, *The People Have Spoken (And They Are Wrong)* (New York: Regnery, 2014).

63. Ed Luce, "Why Billionaires Are Backing Trump," *Financial Times*, November 25, 2019, https://www.ft.com/content/9d682f68-0f12-11ea-a7e6-62bf4f9e548a?desktop=true.

64. Eefje Steenvoorden and Eelco Harteveld, "The Appeal of Nostalgia: The Influence of Societal Pessimism on Support for Populist Radical Right Parties," *West European Politics* 41, no. 1 (2018): 28–52; and Bruce Stokes, "Populism: It's Not Just Views on the Economy," accessed at Populist views in Europe: It's not just the economy (Washington, DC Pew Research Center, July 19, 2018), https://www.pewresearch.org/fact-tank/2018/07/19/populist-views-in-europe-its-not-just-the-economy.

CHAPTER 5. CALIFORNIA DREAMING

1. J. G. Ruggie, "International Regimes, Transactions, and Change: Embedded Liberalism in the Postwar Economic Order," *International Organization* 36, no. 2 (1982): 379–415.

2. For three excellent works reexamining the significance of the 1970s, see Thomas Borstelmann, *The 1970s: A New Global History from Civil Rights to Economic Inequality* (Princeton, NJ: Princeton University Press, 2011); Niall Ferguson, Charles S. C Maier, Erez Manela, and Daniel J. Sargent, *The Shock of the Global: The 1970s in Perspective* (Cambridge, MA: Belknap, 2011); and Bruce J. Schulman, *The Seventies: The Great Shift in American Culture, Society, and Politics* (Cambridge, MA: De Capo, 2002).

3. An outstanding analysis that looks at American foreign policy through a more traditional lens can be found in Daniel Sargent, *A Superpower Transformed: The Remaking of American Foreign Relations in the 1970s* (New York: Oxford University Press, 2015).

4. This was well understood in Hollywood, where ideas and stories from around the world were captured, repurposed, and commercialized.

5. For an account that takes a more skeptical view of the shifts in the United States in the 1970s, see Kurt Andersen, *Evil Geniuses: The Unmaking of America; A Recent History* (New York: Random House, 2020). For an outstanding insight into the mixed legacy as it affected Southern California, see Mike Davis's classic, *City of Quartz: Excavating the Future in Los Angeles* (New York: Verso, 2006).

6. For the important shifts that made California the ideal place for the revolution in information technology, see AnnaLee Saxenian, *Regional Advantage: Culture and Competition in Silicon Valley and Route 128* (Cambridge, MA: Harvard University Press, 1994); AnnaLee Saxenian, "Inside-Out: Regional Networks and Industrial Adaptation in Silicon Valley and Route 128," *Cityscape: A Journal of Policy Development and Research* 2, no. 2

(May 1996). For the consequences of the shift from the Fordist, mass-industrialized economies to more flexible, adaptable arrangements that were reflected in many parts of California's economy, see Michael Piore and Charles Sabel, *The Second Industrial Divide* (New York: Basic Books, 1984).

7. Daniel T. Rodgers, *Age of Fracture* (Cambridge, MA: Harvard University Press, 2011).

8. Peter J. Katzenstein, Stephen C. Nelson, and Lucia A. Seybert, "Slumdog versus Superman," in *Protean Power: Exploring the Uncertain and Unexpected in World Politics,* ed. Peter J. Katzenstein and Lucia A. Seybert (Cambridge: Cambridge University Press, 2018), 210.

9. See Jonathan Kirshner's framing of these two orders and the transition the 1970s represented in this volume, chap. 1.

10. Far and away the best historian of California is Kevin Starr. See Kevin Starr, *California: A History* (New York: Modern Library, 2007).

11. Margaret O'Mara, *The Code: Silicon Valley and the Remaking of America* (New York: Penguin, 2019), 1–7.

12. Marc Levinson, *The Box: How the Shipping Container Made the World Smaller and the World Economy Bigger* (Princeton, NJ: Princeton University Press, 2006).

13. For a compelling view that laments this change in Hollywood's orientation, see Jonathan Kirshner, *Hollywood's Last Golden Age: Politics, Society and the Seventies Film in America* (Ithaca, NY: Cornell University Press, 2012).

14. James Conaway, *Napa* (New York: Avon, 1990).

15. George M. Taber, *The Judgement of Paris: California vs. France and the Historic 1976 Paris Testing That Revolutionized Wine* (New York: Scribner, 2005).

16. Patrick Bromley, "History of Standup Comedy in the 1970s: The Birth of Modern Stand-Up," *ThoughtCo,* February 2019, https://www.liveabout.com/history-of-stand-up-comedy-in-the-1970s-801532; Richard Zoglin, *Comedy at the Edge: How Stand-Up in the 1970s Changed America* (New York: Bloomsbury, 2009).

17. Alice Waters, *Coming to My Senses: The Making of a Countercultural Cook* (New York: Penguin, 2017).

18. David Davis, "Sex, Steroids, and Arnold: The Story of the Gym That Shaped America," *Deadspin,* August 21, 2018, https://deadspin.com/sex-steroids-and-arnold-the-gym-that-shaped-america-1828228786.

19. For a sense of this, see Rawi Abdelal's insightful analysis in this volume, chap. 6.

20. Although the notions of human rights and global citizenship had powerful beginnings in the late 1940s, recent historical work identifies the 1970s as the crucial decade for their development as shared norms. See Samuel Moyn, *The Last Utopia: Human Rights in History* (Cambridge, MA: Harvard University Press, 2010); and Sarah Snyder, *From Selma to Moscow: How Human Rights Activists Transformed US Foreign Policy* (New York: Columbia University Press, 2018).

21. Ilene Grabel offers a compelling counterpoint to some of this optimism in this volume, chap. 7.

22. For the key role of central banks, and in particular the remarkable efforts of the US Federal Reserve during and after the 2008–10 economic collapse, see Adam Tooze, *Crashed: How a Decade of Financial Crises Changed the World* (New York: Penguin, 2018); for similar but even more dramatic departures from past practice among central bankers, see Adam Tooze, "The World's Central Bankers Are Starting to Experiment: But What Comes Next?," *Guardian,* September 9, 2020, https://www.theguardian.com/commentis free/2020/sep/09/central-banks-deflation-covid-19-world-economy.

23. This sense of incoherence and disarray are well captured by Mark Blyth and Ilene Grabel in this volume, chaps. 2 and 7, respectively.

24. John M. Keynes, *The Economic Consequences of the Peace* (London: Macmillan, 1919), 4–5.

25. Daniel Walker Howe, *What Hath God Wrought: The Transformation of America, 1815–1848* (New York: Oxford University Press, 2007), 821–22.

CHAPTER 6. OF LEARNING AND FORGETTING

1. John Gerard Ruggie, "International Regimes, Transactions, and Change: Embedded Liberalism in the Postwar Economic Order," *International Organization* 36, no. 2 (1982): 379–416.

2. Rawi Abdelal, *Capital Rules: The Construction of Global Finance* (Cambridge, MA.: Harvard University Press, 2007); Rawi Abdelal and Sophie Meunier, "Managed Globalization: Doctrine, Practice, and Promise," *Journal of European Public Policy* 17, no. 3 (2010): 350–67; and Dani Rodrik, "The Abdication of the Left," *Project Syndicate*, July 11, 2016. https://www.project-syndicate.org/commentary/anti-globalization-backlash-from-right-by-dani-rodrik-2016-07.

3. Mark Blyth, *Great Transformations: Economic Ideas and Institutional Change in the Twentieth Century* (New York: Cambridge University Press, 2002).

4. Sheri Berman, this volume, chap. 4.

5. Stephanie L. Mudge, "What's Left of Leftism? Neoliberal Politics in Western Party Systems, 1945–2004," *Social Science History* 35, no. 3 (2011): 337–80; Stephanie L. Mudge, *Leftism Reinvented: Western Parties from Socialism to Neo-Liberalism* (Cambridge, MA: Harvard University Press, 2018); Mark Bovens and Anchrit Wille, *Diploma Democracy: The Rise of Political Meritocracy* (New York: Oxford University Press, 2017); and Robert Kuttner, *Can Democracy Survive Global Capitalism?* (New York: W. W. Norton, 2018), chaps. 6–7.

6. On the overlapping international, regional, and domestic orders that composed both the postwar and the contemporary orders, see Berman, this volume, chap. 4.

7. Peter A. Gourevitch, this volume, chap. 3.

8. Karl Polanyi, *The Great Transformation: The Political and Economic Origins of Our Times* (repr. Boston: Beacon, [1944] 1957), 25.

9. See Tony Judt, *Ill Fares the Land* (New York: Penguin, 2011).

10. Jonathan Kirshner, this volume, chap.1.

11. John Gerard Ruggie, this volume, chap. 8.

12. Abdelal, *Capital Rules*, chap. 8.

13. Ilene Grabel, "The Rebranding of Capital Controls in an Era of Productive Incoherence," *Review of International Political Economy* 22, no. 1 (2015): 7–43; and Ilene Grabel, *When Things Don't Fall Apart: Global Financial Governance and Developmental Finance in an Age of Productive Incoherence* (Cambridge, MA: MIT Press, 2017).

14. Jonathan Kirshner, *American Power after the Financial Crisis* (Ithaca, NY: Cornell University Press, 2014).

15. Ilene Grabel, this volume, chap. 7.

16. Mark Blyth, this volume, chap. 2. Also see Eric Lonergan and Mark Blyth, *Angrynomics* (Newcastle, UK: Agenda, 2020).

17. See, for example, Sheri Berman and Maria Snegovaya, "Populism and the Decline of Social Democracy," *Journal of Democracy* 30, no. 3 (2019): 5–19; and Berman, this volume, chap. 4.

18. Gourevitch, this volume, chap. 3.

19. It has in fact become more difficult to describe these new populist movements and politics in terms of the traditional left-right continuum. See Liesbet Hooghe, Gary Marks, and Carole J. Wilson, "Does Left/Right Structure Party Positions on European

Integration?," *Comparative Political Studies* 35, no. 8 (2002): 965–89; and Liesbet Hooghe and Gary Marks, "Cleavage Theory Meets Europe's Crises," *Journal of European Public Policy* 25, no. 1 (2018): 109–35.

20. Ruggie, this volume, chap. 8.

21. On the place of capital controls in the embedded liberal compromise, see Eric Helleiner, *States and the Reemergence of Global Finance* (Ithaca, NY: Cornell University Press, 1994); Jonathan Kirshner, "Keynes, Capital Mobility, and the Crisis of Embedded Liberalism," *Review of International Political Economy* 6, no. 3 (1999): 313–37; and Jonathan Kirshner, "The Inescapable Politics of Money," in *Monetary Orders,* ed. Jonathan Kirshner (Ithaca, NY: Cornell University Press, 2003), 3–24.

22. Rawi Abdelal and John Gerard Ruggie, "The Principles of Embedded Liberalism: Social Legitimacy and Global Capitalism," in *New Perspectives on Regulation,* ed. David Moss and John Cisternino (Cambridge, MA: Tobin Project, 2009), 151–62.

23. Among many examples, see Economic, Financial, and Transit Department, League of Nations, *International Currency Experience: Lessons of the Inter-War Period* (Geneva, Switzerland: League of Nations, 1944); Ragnar Nurkse, *Conditions of Monetary Equilibrium,* Princeton Essays in International Finance no. 4 (Princeton, NJ: Princeton University Press, 1945); Arthur I. Bloomfield, "Postwar Control of International Capital Movements," *American Economic Review* 36, no. 2 (1946): 687–709; and Richard N. Gardner, *Sterling-Dollar Diplomacy* (Oxford: Clarendon, 1956), 76.

24. Abdelal, *Capital Rules,* 58–64.

25. Abdelal, *Capital Rules,* 64–71.

26. Rawi Abdelal, "Le consensus de Paris," *Critique internationale,* no. 28 (2005): 87–115.

27. On the putatively neoliberal Geneva consensus in Europe, see Quinn Slobodian, *Globalists: The End of Empire and the Birth of Neoliberalism* (Cambridge, MA: Harvard University Press, 2018), chap. 6.

28. Abdelal, *Capital Rules,* chap. 4.

29. Abdelal, *Capital Rules,* chap. 5.

30. Abdelal, *Capital Rules,* chap. 6.

31. Mudge, *Leftism Reinvented,* chaps. 6 and 8. Also see Dani Rodrik, "The Left's Choice," *Project Syndicate,* January 8, 2019. https://www.project-syndicate.org/commentary/reviving-the-left-means-reintegrating-economies-by-dani-rodrik-2019-01.

32. Tony Blair, *The Third Way: New Politics for a New Century* (London: Fabian Society, 1998).

33. Tony Blair and Gerhard Schröder, *The Third Way: Die Neue Mitte* (London: Labor Party and Sozialdemokratische Partei Deutschlands).

34. Peter A. Hall, "The Comparative Political Economy of the 'Third Way,'" in *The Third Way Transformation of Social Democracy,* ed. Oliver Schmidtke (Farnham, UK: Ashgate, 2002), 26–54.

35. Anthony Giddens, *Beyond Left and Right* (Cambridge: Polity, 1994); Anthony Giddens, *The Third Way* (Cambridge: Polity, 1998).

36. Mudge, "What's Left of Leftism?," 340.

37. Peter J. Katzenstein, *A World of Regions: Asia and Europe in the American Imperium* (Ithaca, NY: Cornell University Press, 2005), 1.

38. See also Kirshner, this volume, chap. 1; and Grabel, this volume, chap. 7.

39. Abdelal, *Capital Rules,* chap. 8; Rawi Abdelal and Adam Segal, "Has Globalization Passed Its Peak?," *Foreign Affairs* 86, no. 1 (2007): 103–14.

40. Kirshner, *American Power.* Also see Grabel, this volume, chap. 7.

41. See, for example, Miles Corak, "Income Inequality, Equality of Opportunity, and Intergenerational Mobility," *Journal of Economic Perspectives* 27, no. 3 (2013): 79–102.

42. See Raj Chetty et al., "The Fading American Dream: Trends in Absolute Income Mobility since 1940," *Science* 356, no. 6336 (2017): 398–406.

43. Gourevitch, this volume, chap. 3.

44. Rawi Abdelal, "Dignity, Inequality, and the Populist Backlash: Lessons from America and Europe for a Sustainable Globalization," *Global Policy* 11, no. 4 (2020): 492–500. On the connections between dignity, class, and race in France and elsewhere, see Michèle Lamont, *The Dignity of Working Men: Morality and the Boundaries of Race, Class, and Immigration* (New York: Russell Sage; and Cambridge, MA: Harvard University Press, 2000). On the connection between "hard work" and "dignity" in the resentments that fuel the resurgence of contemporary American nationalism and populism, see Frances Fukuyama, *Identity: The Demand for Dignity and the Politics of Resentment* (New York: Farrar, Straus and Giroux, 2018), 88–90. On social status and social integration as essential elements of the populist backlash, see Noam Gidron and Peter A. Hall, "The Politics of Social Status: Economic and Cultural Roots of the Populist Right," *British Journal of Sociology* 68, no. S1 (2017): 57–84; and Noam Gidron and Peter A. Hall, "Populism as a Problem of Social Integration," *Comparative Political Studies*, forthcoming. Also see Dani Rodrik, "Tackling Inequality from the Middle," *Project Syndicate*, December 10, 2019, https://www.project-syndicate.org/commentary/tackling-inequality-from-the-middle-by-dani-rodrik-2019-12; Cecilia L. Ridgeway, "Why Status Matters for Inequality," *American Sociological Review* 79, no. 1 (2014): 1–16; and Simone M. Schneider, "Why Income Inequality Is Dissatisfying: Perceptions of Social Status and the Inequality-Satisfaction Link in Europe," *European Sociological Review* 35, no. 3 (2019): 409–30. This is a modern notion of dignity rooted in the evolution of capitalism. See, for example, Christine Dunn Henderson, "On Bourgeois Dignity," in *Dignity: A History*, ed. Remy Debes (Oxford: Oxford University Press, 2017), 269–90.

45. Rogers Brubaker, "Why Populism?," *Theory and Society* 46, no. 5 (2017): 357–85. Also see Pippa Norris and Ronald Inglehart, *Cultural Backlash: Trump, Brexit, and Authoritarian Populism* (Cambridge: Cambridge University Press, 2019), chap. 1.

46. Arlie Russell Hochschild, *Strangers in their Own Land: Anger and Mourning on the American Right* (New York: New Press, 2016).

47. Brubaker, "Why Populism?"

48. Christophe Guilluy, *Twilight of the Elites: Prosperity, the Periphery, and the Future of France* (New Haven, CT: Yale University Press, 2019), chap. 4.

49. Brubaker, "Why Populism?," 371.

50. Berman and Snegovaya, "Populism and the Decline of Social Democracy," 6.

51. Peter A. Hall and Georgina Evans, "Representation Gaps: Changes in Popular Preferences and Party Positions over the Longer Term in the Developed Democracies" (unpublished manuscript, February 4, 2019, Harvard University Department of Government. Also see Suzanne Berger, "Populism and the Failures of Representation," *French Politics, Culture & Society* 35, no. 2 (2017): 21–31. For a similar argument about populism and the disintermediation of traditional political parties, see Nadia Urbinati, *Me the People: How Populism Transforms Democracy* (Cambridge, MA: Harvard University Press, 2019).

52. See, for example, Rogers Brubaker, "Populism and Nationalism," *Nations and Nationalism* 26, no. 1 (2020): 44–66; and Rogers Brubaker, "Between Nationalism and Civilizationism: The European Populist Moment in Comparative Perspective," *Ethnic and Racial Studies* 40, no. 8 (2017): 1191–1226. On the cultural fissures that have replaced traditional left-right divides, see Norris and Inglehart, *Cultural Backlash*. On the proglobalization versus antiglobalization fissure, see John L. Campbell, *American Discontent: The Rise of Donald Trump and the Decline of the Golden Age* (New York: Oxford University Press, 2018).

53. Yann Algan, Elizabeth Beasley, Daniel Cohen, and Martial Foucault, "The Rise of Populism and the Collapse of the Left-Right Paradigm: Lessons from the 2017 French Presidential Election," Discussion Paper no. 13103 (London: Center for Economic Policy Research, August 2018).

54. Rawi Abdelal, Dante Roscini, and Elena Corsi, "The Rise of Populism and Italy's Electoral 'Tsunami,'" Harvard Business School Case no. 719–042 (Boston, MA: Harvard Business Publishing, 2019).

55. "EU: In or Out?" Sky News, June 3, 2016.

56. Rawi Abdelal and Ulrich Krotz, "Dis-Atlanticism: The West in an Era of Global Fragmentation," in *Key Controversies in European Integration*, third edition, ed. Hubert Zimmerman and Andreas Dür (London: Macmillan, forthcoming). Also see Rawi Abdelal and Ulrich Krotz, "Disjoining Partners: Europe and the American Imperium," in *Power in a Complex Global System*, ed. Louis W. Pauly and Bruce W. Jentleson (London: Routledge, 2014), 131–47. On the effects of US unilateral, extraterritorial sanctions on the fraying, fragile transatlantic relationship, see Rawi Abdelal and Aurélie Bros, "Sanctions and the End of Trans-Atlanticism: Iran, Russia, and the Unintended Division of the West," *Notes de l'Ifri*, January 23, 2020.

CHAPTER 7. POST-AMERICAN MOMENTS IN CONTEMPORARY GLOBAL FINANCIAL GOVERNANCE

1. For invaluable comments on the chapter, I thank George DeMartino; participants at a February 2020 seminar at Brown University's Rhodes Center for Economics and Finance; Erin Lockwood, the chapter's discussant at the June 2020 book workshop, as well as all of the other participants at the workshop; Jonathan Kirshner and Peter Katzenstein; and two anonymous referees. I also thank Rachel Epstein for guidance on literature on embedded liberalism; and Kaylin McNeil, Daniel Rinner, and Suraj Thapa for excellent research assistance. On embedded liberal ideas and practices, see John Gerard Ruggie, "International Regimes, Transactions, and Change: Embedded Liberalism in the Postwar Economic Order," *International Organization* 36, no. 2 (1982): 379–415; John Gerard Ruggie, "Embedded Liberalism Revisited: Instiutions and Progress in International Economic Relations," in *Progress in Postwar International Relations,* ed. Emanuel Adler and Beverly Crawford (New York: Columbia University Press, 1991), 201–34.

2. Peter J. Katzenstein and Jonathan Kirshner, introduction to this volume; Mark Blyth, this volume, chap. 2; Jonathan Kirshner, this volume, chap. 1. I follow Katzenstein and Kirshner, this volume, in using the term "embedded liberalism" to refer to international and domestic aims.

3. Compromise and consensus are frequent descriptors of this order. Although these terms capture important attributes of the first order (especially in comparison with later periods) they conceal contestation, not least by actors from the Global South and East and those in the Global North excluded from the rewards associated with what many see as the golden age of capitalism. (On contestation and exclusion of actors from the Global South and East, see e.g., Eric Helleiner, *Forgotten Foundations of Bretton Woods* (Ithaca, NY: Cornell University Press, 2014) and Vincent Bevins, "The 'Liberal World Order' Was Built with Blood," *New York Times*, May 31, 2020. On racism and exclusion in the Global North, see Richard Rothstein, *The Color of Law: A Forgotten History of How Our Government Segregated America* (New York: W. W. Norton, 2017) and Ira Katznelson, *When Affirmative Action Was White: An Untold History of Racial Inequality in Twentieth-Century America* (New York: W. W. Norton, 2005).

4. Mark Blyth, "Global Trumpism," *Foreign Affairs*, November 15, 2016. https://www.foreignaffairs.com/articles/2016-11-15/global-trumpism.

5. Not all social scientists celebrate fastidiousness. Most notably, Albert Hirschman embraced messiness, experimentation, and rejected grand plans and narratives, as I argue below and in Ilene Grabel, *When Things Don't Fall Apart: Global Financial Governance and Developmental Finance in an Age of Productive Incoherence* (Cambridge, MA: MIT Press, 2017), chap. 2. See George F. DeMartino, "Harming Irreparably: On Neoliberalism, Kaldor-Hicks, and the Paretian Guarantee," *Review of Social Economy* 73, no. 4 (2015): 315–40. On fastidiousness in economics, see George F. DeMartino and Ilene Grabel "Irreparable Ignorance, Protean Power, and Economics," *International Theory* 12, no. 3 (2020): 435–48.

6. However, it is a safe bet to say that whatever emerges will be less centripetal, tidy, and coherent, as well as less centered on the United States. This is a theme that cuts across most chapters in this volume. Blyth, this volume, chap. 2, is an exception insofar as he argues that the order taking shape is of uncertain contours, but will nonetheless remain American because the dollar is hardwired into the global financial system.

7. Grabel, *When Things Don't Fall Apart.*

8. For example, see Ruchir Sharma, "The Comeback Nation: U.S. Economic Supremacy Has Repeatedly Proved Declinists Wrong," *Foreign Affairs* 99, no. 3 (2020), https://www.foreignaffairs.com/articles/united-states/2020-03-31/comeback-nation.

9. On this concept, see Grabel, *When Things Don't Fall Apart*, 15–17.

10. Quinton Hoare and Geoffrey Nowell-Smith, eds., *Selections from the Prison Notebooks of Antonio Gramsci* (London: Lawrence and Wishart, 1971), 278.

11. The current period is unique in its particulars, but it is not without historical antecedents. Other interregna are the interwar period and the 1970s. The latter is treated widely in this volume. The 1970s and the present are marked by contestation; a high degree of uncertainty; and what Charles Lindblom referred to as "muddling through" on the part of policymakers. See Charles Lindblom, "The Science of 'Muddling Through,'" *Public Administration Review* 19, no. 2 (1959): 79–88; Charles Lindblom, "Still Muddling, Not Yet Through," *Public Administration Review* 39, no. 6 (1979): 517–26. Today's interregnum is different in several respects, including the absence of competing isms; a messy ideational and institutional landscape; and, as noted above, the rejection of expertise.

12. On the latter point, see George F. DeMartino, Editor's Introduction: Forum for Social Economics Papers and Proceedings, Symposium on "The Democratic Crisis and Responsibility of Economics," special issue, *Forum for Social Economics* 47, no. 2 (2018): 153–57; DeMartino and Grabel, "Irreparable Ignorance, Protean Power." Also see Rawi Abdelal, this volume, chap. 6.

13. Blyth, "Global Trumpism."

14. The failed response to the COVID-19 crisis in the United States is a perfect illustration of destructive incoherence. Balanced-budget rules for state and municipal governments constrain their fiscal capacity and cancel out much of the effects of federal expansionism. At the same time, the absence of federal leadership in implementing closures and openings of schools and workplaces and in securing ventilators and personal protection equipment led to damaging deficiencies in constraining the virus. (Destructive incoherence played out even after vaccines became widely available in countries of the Global North. This incoherence involved conflicts over and the absence of consistent strategies toward masking and vaccine mandates.) Nonetheless the US government and the Fed implemented expansive economic and social protection programs, such as the extension of unemployment compensation to "self-employed" gig economy workers, some features of which are consistent with embedded liberalism and which may stick long after the pandemic has passed. National governments in many European contexts went much further in the direction of expansive, universal social protection.

15. Grabel, *When Things Don't Fall Apart.*

16. Grabel, *When Things Don't Fall Apart*, chap. 2.

17. John Gerard Ruggie (this volume, chap. 8) echoes Hirschmanian themes, highlighting gradual, uneven evolution as concerns transnational norms and evolving standards.

18. Grabel, *When Things Don't Fall Apart*.

19. The concept of productive incoherence—and Hirschman's key commitments, as outlined above—resonate with Lindblom's muddling through. Indeed, Hirschman and Lindblom coauthored an essay that highlights the overlapping nature of their approaches to policy. See Albert O. Hirschman and Charles Lindblom, "Economic Development, Research and Development and Policy Making: Some Converging Views," in *A Bias for Hope: Essays on Development and Latin America*, ed. Albert O. Hirschman (New Haven, CT: Yale University Press, [1962] 1971), 63–84. Productive incoherence also resonates with John Kingdon's "garbage can theory of politics," in which ideas that have been in the ether for some time can become influential when windows of opportunity occasionally open. See John Kingdon, *Agendas, Alternative, and Public Policies*, second edition (New York: Harper/Collins, 1995). Some may incorrectly see in productive incoherence an echo of Joseph Schumpeter's "creative destruction" (Joseph Schumpeter, *Capitalism, Socialism, and Democracy* (New York: Harper & Bros., 1942). Creative destruction is embedded in a neoliberal, Darwinian mindset that suggests an impulse and mechanism toward progress, whereas productive incoherence suggests no such trajectory.

20. Peter J. Katzenstein and Lucia A. Seybert, eds., *Protean Power: Exploring the Uncertain and Unexpected in World Politics* (Cambridge: Cambridge University Press, 2018).

21. It bears mention that rearticulations of embedded liberalisms are occurring on the intrastate level. For example, in the United States many states and cities have made commitments to the Paris Climate Accord and living wages. Other examples include Medicare programs in Massachusetts; protective policies enacted by US states and municipalities during the COVID-19 crisis; and policies on immigration, the environment, and private prisons in California. On California, see Francis J. Gavin, this volume, chapter 5. Note that much of the New Deal architecture was modeled on successful state-level initiatives (see James K. Galbraith, "Can Sanders Do It?," *Project Syndicate*, January 31, 2020).

22. Albert O. Hirschman, "The Search for Paradigms as a Hinderance to Understanding," *World Politics* 22, no. 3 (1970): 329–43.

23. Neil Brenner, Jamie Peck, and Nik Theodore, "Variegated Neoliberalization: Geographies, Modalities, Pathways," *Global Networks* 10, no. 2 (2010): 182–222; Helleiner, *Forgotten Foundations of Bretton Woods*; Eric Helleiner, "The Life and Times of Embedded Liberalism: Legacies and Innovations since Bretton Woods," *Review of International Political Economy* 26, no. 6 (2019): 1112–35. Treatments of embedded liberalism in Sheri Berman, this volume, chap. 4; and Peter A. Gourevitch, this volume, chap. 3; and of the first American order in Blyth, this volume, chap. 2, underscore the messiness, contestation, and contingency that is underappreciated in most accounts.

24. Grabel, *When Things Don't Fall Apart*, chap. 3.

25. European SBAs after 2008 had similar effects on remaining vestiges of embedded liberalism.

26. Grabel, *When Things Don't Fall Apart*, chaps. 3, 7; Ilene Grabel, "Averting Crisis? Assessing Measures to Manage Financial Integration in Emerging Economies," *Cambridge Journal of Economics* 27, no. 3 (2003): 317–36.

27. Ilene Grabel, "Not Your Grandfather's IMF: Global Crisis, 'Productive Incoherence' and Developmental Policy Space," *Cambridge Journal of Economics* 35, no. 5 (2011): 805–30.

28. Grabel, *When Things Don't Fall Apart*, chap. 5.

29. Grabel, *When Things Don't Fall Apart*, chap. 4; Eric Helleiner, "Legacies of the 2008 Crisis for Global Financial Governance," *Global Summitry* 2, no. 1 (2016): 1–12. Jonathan

Luckhurst too uncriticially identifies these networks, especially the G20, as a space for "ad hoc embedded liberalism." See Luckhurst, "The G20 and Ad Hoc Embedded Liberalism: Economic Governance Amid Crisis and Dissensus," *Politics & Policy* 40, no. 5 (2012): 740–82.

30. The issue of how to think about the nature of economic integration today is complex when it comes to China. I return to this matter later.

31. Discussion in this section draws on Grabel, *When Things Don't Fall Apart*, chaps. 3–7; Ilene Grabel, "The Upside of a Messier Global Financial Architecture," *Current History* 117, no. 802 (2018): 321–24; Ilene Grabel, "Continuity, Discontinuity and Incoherence in the Bretton Woods Order: A Hirschmanian Reading," *Development and Change* 50, no. 1 (2019): 46–71. The argument that elements of embedded liberalism might be resurrected can be understood as a process of "bricolage," by which is meant taking already existing (and, in some instances, dormant) ideational and institutional bits and pieces and recombining them in novel ways to create something new that still echoes the past. There are elements of bricolage in the analysis by Berman, this volume, chap. 4. On the concept of bricolage, see Mary Douglas, *How Institutions Think* (Syracuse, NY: Syracuse University Press, 1986); and for a discussion of its application to the institutional landscape see James H. Mittleman, "Global Bricolage: Emerging Market Powers and Polycentric Governance," *Third World Quarterly* 34, no. 1 (2013): 23–37.

32. Jonathan Kirshner, *American Power after the Financial Crisis* (Ithaca, NY: Cornell University Press, 2014).

33. Miriam Campanella, "Far-Reaching Consequences of US Financial Sanctions," Robert Triffin International (Turin, Italy: Centro Studi Sul Federalismo, June 2019), http://www.triffininternational.eu/images/RTI/articles_papers/RTI-CSF_Consequences-of-US-Financial-Sanctions_June2019.pdf; Henry Farrell and Abraham Newman, "Chained to Globalization: Why It's Too Late to Decouple," *Foreign Affairs* 99, no. 1 (2020), https://www.foreignaffairs.com/articles/united-states/2019-12-10/chained-globalization.

34. Experimentalism is a key feature of Chinese policy. See discussion in Grabel, *When Things Don't Fall Apart*, 44. On experimentalism in regards to poverty-reduction strategies, see Yuen Yuen Ang, *How China Escaped the Poverty Trap* (Ithaca, NY: Cornel University Press, 2016).

35. Paola Subacchi, *The People's Money: How China Is Building a Global Currency* (New York: Columbia University Press, 2017).

36. Daniela Gabor, "Goodbye (Chinese) Shadow Banking, Hello Market-Based Finance," *Development and Change* 49, no. 2 (2018): 394–419.

37. Gregory Chin, "China's Rising Monetary Power," in Eric Helleiner and Jonathan Kirshner, eds., *The Great Wall of Money* (Ithaca, NY: Cornell University Press, 2014), 184–263; Jonathan Kirshner, "Meet the New Twenties—Same as the Old Twenties?," paper presented at the workshop "Monetary Conflict and Disorder in the New Age of Uncertainty," Cornell University, Government Department, May 18, 2018, 16–17n46.

38. The dollar, however, benefited from Trumpian chaos and the COVID-19 crisis just as it did in late 2008 as the United States emerged as the epicenter of the global crisis. Carla Norloff et al., "Global Monetary Order and the Liberal Order Debate," *International Studies Perspectives* 21, no. 2 (2020): 109–53; Brad Setser, "Did the Dollar's Position as the Leading Reserve Currency Help Hold Treasury Yields Down This Spring?," *Follow the Money* blog (Council on Foreign Relations), May 27, 2020, https://www.cfr.org/blog/did-dollars-position-leading-reserve-currency-help-hold-treasury-yields-down-spring.

39. "Dethroning the Dollar: America's Aggressive Use of Sanctions Endangers the Dollar's Reign," *Economist*, January 18, 2020. Russia is developing an alternative to SWIFT that will connect to CIPS, and India might connect with Russia's platform. See Dipanjan Roy Chaudhury, "India-Russia-China Explore Alternative to SWIFT Payment Mechanism,"

Economic Times, November 14, 2019. The CIPS is still in its infancy—in all of 2018 it processed less than SWIFT did in a day. This is not surprising given that it is new and the dollar enjoys numerous incumbency and structural advantages ("Dethroning the Dollar"). Moreover, Europe has built a new clearing house called Instex, though it has not yet been used. See "The Search to Find an Alternative to the Dollar," *Economist*, January 18, 2020. Europe's officials are playing the long game, seeing Instex as a ten- to twenty-year project ("Dethroning the Dollar").

40. Chris Giles, "Mark Carney Calls for a Global Monetary System," *Financial Times*, August 23, 2019.

41. Giles, "Mark Carney Calls."

42. Islamic finance takes many forms, but all prohibit speculation and prioritize the real-sector and productive investment.

43. Always dependable, the Bundesbank remained doggedly committed to fighting the ghost of inflations past during the global crisis. This was not the case early in the COVID-19 crisis. Note that the US Fed moved to an average-inflation-targeting regime in the fall of 2020. Soon thereafter the ECB's president, Christine Lagarde, indicated interest in studying this matter, which unsurprisingly triggered a statement of concern by Bundesbank officials and the ECB's policymaking governing council. See Ferdinando Giugliano, "Lagarde's Mixed Report Card after One Year at European Central Bank," *Bloomberg Businessweek*, October 13, 2020, https://www.bloomberg.com/news/articles/2020-10-14/christine-lagarde-slipped-up-on-italian-bonds-but-held-ecb-together-amid-covid; Francesco Canepa and Balazs Koranyi, "ECB's Policymakers Wary of Following Fed's Route on Inflation Target," Reuters, October 12, 2020, https://www.reuters.com/article/us-ecb-policy-inflation-exclusive/exclusive-ecb-policymakers-wary-of-following-feds-route-on-inflation-target-sources-say-idUSKBN26X25B.

44. Ahmet Benlialper and Hasan Cömert, "Central Banking in Developing Countries after the Crisis: What Has Changed?," IDEAS Working Paper Series, Working Paper No. 1 (New Delhi, India: International Development Economics Associates (2016). https://www.networkideas.org/ideas-publications/ideas-working-papers/2016/01/central-banking-in-developing-countries-after-the-crisis-what-has-changed.

45. Brendan Greeley, "Central Bankers Rethink Everything at Jackson Hole," *Financial Times*, August 25, 2019.

46. Christopher Condon, "Fed's Powell Says Central Banks Must Help Address Climate Change," *Bloomberg Businessweek*, November 12, 2020, https://www.bloomberg.com/amp/news/articles/2020-11-12/fed-s-powell-says-central-banks-must-help-address-climate-change; Jana Randow, "Largarde Leverages Virus to Press for Greener Monetary Policy," *Bloomberg Businessweek*, September 14, 2020, https://www.bloomberg.com/news/articles/2020-09-15/christine-lagarde-fights-climate-change-through-monetary-policy-despite-covid.

47. Larry Elliot, "Tackling Climate Change Is What We Should Be Doing, Says New IMF Boss, *Guardian*, November 30, 2019, https://www.theguardian.com/business/2019/nov/30/imf-boss-kristalina-georgiva-climate-crisis-financial-crash-economics.

48. Jeanna Smialek, "Fed Chair Powell Warns Pandemic Downturn Could Widen Inequalities," *New York Times*, June 16, 2020. In this respect central bankers are certainly reflecting the contemporary zeitgeist, and their commitment to racial justice may erode as attention shifts to other matters. But I think it's also reasonable to consider that some have come to see that their work cannot be entirely divorced from the major challenges of our time, such as inequality, racism, climate change, and the fallout of the COVID-19 crisis.

49. Ilene Grabel, "The Rebranding of Capital Controls in an Era of Productive Incoherence," *Review of International Political Economy* 22, no. 1 (2015): 7–43; Ilene Grabel, "Capital Controls in a Time of Crisis," in *Financial Liberalisation: Past, Present and Future,*

ed. Philip Arestis and Malcolm Sawyer (Basingstoke, UK: Palgrave Macmillan, 2017), 177–223; Grabel, *When Things Don't Fall Apart*, chap. 7.

50. Jonathan D. Ostry, Atish R. Ghosh, Karl Habermeier, Marcos Chamon, Mahvash S. Qureshi, and Dennis B. S. Reinhardt. "Capital Inflows: The Role of Controls," IMF Staff Position Note No. 4. Washington, DC: International Monetary Fund, February 19, 2010. https://www.imf.org/external/pubs/ft/spn/2010/spn1004.pdf.

51. Gita Gopinath, "A Case for an Integrated Policy Framework," paper presented at Jackson Hole Economic Policy Symposium, Jackson Hole, WY, August 24, 2019.

52. A parallel line of rethinking is emerging in new IMF research on industrial policy, which recently caught up with decades of work in the developmental-state tradition. See Reda Cherif and Fuad Hasanov, "The Return of the Policy That Shall Not Be Named: Principles of Industrial Policy," IMF Working Paper no. 19/74 (Washington, DC: International Monetary Fund, March 2019).

53. Chang Yong Rhee, "COVID-19 Pandemic and the Asia-Pacific Region: Lowest Growth since the 1960s," *IMFBlog*, April 15, 2020. https://blogs.imf.org/2020/04/15/covid-19-pandemic-and-the-asia-pacific-region-lowest-growth-since-the-1960s.

54. On a global Green New Deal, see United Nations Conference on Trade and Development, *Trade and Development Report* (New York: United Nations, 2019). Capital controls are also a feature of progressive COVID-19 economic recovery proposals. See, e.g., Ilene Grabel, "Enabling a Permissive Multilateralisms Approach to Global Macroeconomic Governance to Support Feminist Plans for Sustainability and Social Justice," United Nations Women Think Piece, Series on Feminist Ideas for a Post-COVID World (New York: United Nations Women, 2021, https://www.unwomen.org/-/media/headquarters/attachments/sections/library/publications/2021/think-piece-enabling-a-permissive-mul tilateralisms-approach-to-global-macroeconomic-governance-en.pdf?la=en&vs=2840).

55. Keith Johnson, "Will David Malpass Run the World Bank or Ruin It?," *Foreign Policy*, February 5, 2019, https://foreignpolicy.com/2019/02/05/will-david-malpass-run-the-world-bank-or-ruin-it.

56. Larry Elliot, "World Bank Chief's Davos Snub Dashes Hopes of Climate Consensus," *Guardian,* January 23, 2020, https://foreignpolicy.com/2019/02/05/will-david-mal pass-run-the-world-bank-or-ruin-it.

57. "Quota Reform Impasse Likely as IMF Faces Legitimacy Crisis," *Bretton Woods Observer*, July 30, 2019, https://www.brettonwoodsproject.org/2019/07/quota-reform-impasse-likely-as-imf-faces-legitimacy-crisis.

58. Under existing rules, 70 percent of new SDRs would go to G20 members, most of which do not need them. But those countries could lend the new SDRs to poor countries (or could transfer some of their idle SDRs to the IMF for its use), providing large pools of liquidity to developing economies, especially the poorest among them. See Barry Herman, "The Looming Developing Country Debt Crisis and the Fear of Imposed Austerity" (New York: New School India-China Institute, October 15, 2020), https://www.indiachi nainstitute.org/2020/10/15/the-looming-developing-country-debt-crisis-and-the-fear-of-imposed-austerity/. The US crisis response has been inconsistent even as concerns multilateralism. The first of the disaster recovery packages in the United States, the CARES Act, included increased funding for the BWIs, e.g., by authorizing continued and expanded US participation in the IMF's New Arrangements to Borrow.

59. International Monetary Fund, "IMF Governors Approve a Historic US$650 Billion SDR Allocation of Special Drawing Rights," International Monetary Fund Press Release No. 21/235, August 2, 2021. https://www.imf.org/en/News/Articles/2021/07/30/pr21235-imf-governors-approve-a-historic-us-650-billion-sdr-allocation-of-special-drawing-rights.

60. The Trump administration went so far as to defund a US nongovernmental organization doing vitally important research on coronaviruses in China. See Nurith Aizenman,

"Why the US Government Stopped Funding a Research Project on Bats and Coronaviruses," *NPR*, April 29, 2020.

61. There is evidence of declining US influence in other multilateral organizations along with the attempt to dismantle them. For instance, in 2018 the International Organization of Migrants rejected President Trump's choice for executive director. See Nick Cumming-Bruce, "Migration Agency Picks a New Leader, and Sends Trump a Message," *New York Times*, June 29, 2018. https://www.nytimes.com/2018/06/29/world/europe/iom-trump-migration-ken-isaacs.html.

62. On changes in the institutional landscape, see Grabel, *When Things Don't Fall Apart*, chap. 6.

63. Elinor Ostrom, "Polycentricity, Complexity, and the Commons," *Good Society* 9, no. 2 (1999): 37–41.

64. Wolfram Elsner, "Complexity Economics as Heterodoxy: Theory and Policy," *Journal of Economic Issues* 11, no. 4 (2017): 939–78. For some, pluripolar systems induce instability and aggravate uncertainty. See Daniel Drezner, "The Tragedy of the Global Institutional Commons," unpublished paper (Medford, MA: Tufts University, 2010). http://danieldrezner.com/research/InstitutionalProliferation.pdf. Strong versions of this argument reflect the gravitational pull that coherent systems have on social scientists. These arguments also underestimate the benefits of pluripolarity, such as the bargaining power offered to smaller countries, competitive pressures on legacy institutions, and the potential of complex systems to enhance antifragility, as per Nassim Nicholas Taleb, *Anti-Fragile: Things That Gain from Disorder* (New York: Random House, 2012), especially if rules of engagement are negotiated outside of a crisis context. The benefits of complex, pluripolar systems might be greater during moments of heightened instability when new challenges present themselves, particularly if traditional respondents do not have the capacity and/or cannot be counted on to respond consistently. See discussion of complex systems in Mauro F. Guillén, *The Architecture of Collapse: The Global System in the 21st Century* (Oxford: Oxford University Press, 2015).

65. "A New Study Tracks the Surge in Chinese Loans to Poor Countries," *Economist*, July 13, 2019, https://www.economist.com/finance-and-economics/2019/07/13/a-new-study-tracks-the-surge-in-chinese-loans-to-poor-countries.

66. Sebastian Horn, Carmen Reinhart, and Christoph Trebesch, "China's Overseas Lending," Kiel Working Paper no. 2132, Kiel, Germany, June 2019.

67. "Will China's Belt and Road Initiative Outdo the Marshall Plan?," *Economist*, March 8, 2018, https://www.economist.com/finance-and-economics/2018/03/08/will-chinas-belt-and-road-initiative-outdo-the-marshall-plan.

68. "Will China's Belt and Road."

69. "Will China's Belt and Road."

70. Xi Jingpin, speech at Opening Plenary Session, World Economic Forum, Davos, Switzerland, January 17, 2017.

71. "Countries Team Up to Save the Liberal Order from Donald Trump," *Economist*, August 2, 2018, https://www.economist.com/international/2018/08/02/countries-team-up-to-save-the-liberal-order-from-donald-trump.

72. Barry Eichengreen, "Globalization with Chinese Characteristics," *Project Syndicate*, August 10, 2018, https://www.project-syndicate.org/commentary/globalization-chinese-characteristics-by-barry-eichengreen-2018-08.

73. Daniel Drezner, "China Plays Forum Shopping Game," *Washington Post*, June 25, 2014, https://www.washingtonpost.com/posteverything/wp/2014/06/25/china-plays-the-forum-shopping-game; Ana Palacio, "Europe on a Geopolitical Fault Line," *Project Syndicate*, November 12, 2019, https://www.project-syndicate.org/commentary/europe-international-order-china-great-fracture-by-ana-palacio-2019-11.

74. The D10 aims to increase cooperation among a small number of strategic-minded and capable states.

75. Instead of a federal response to the COVID-19 crisis there was propaganda, denial, and chaos. See Grabel, *When Things Don't Fall Apart*, chap. 8 on the threats associated with incoherence.

76. Much the same will likely be said about the manner and speed with which tent poles are removed after the COVID-19 crisis subsides.

77. Hirschman, *A Bias for Hope*; Albert O. Hirschman, "Political Economics and Possibilism," in *The Essential Hirschman*, ed. Jeremy Adelman (Princeton, NJ: Princeton University Press, [1971] 2013), 1–34.

78. Albert O. Hirschman, "Obstacles to Development: A Classification and a Quasi-Vanishing Act," *Economic Development and Cultural Change* 13, no. 4 (1965): 385–93; Albert O. Hirschman, *The Rhetoric of Reaction: Perversity, Futility, Jeopardy* (Cambridge, MA: Harvard University Press, 1991); Albert O. Hirschman, *Journeys toward Progress: Studies of Economic Policy-Making in Latin America* (New York: Norton Library, Twentieth Century Fund, [1963] 1973), 247–49.

79. We might contrast Hirschmanian possibilism with readings that necessarily associate anarchy and perpetual instability with aperture and decentralization. This latter view might be understood as "impossibilism," or what Hirschman referred to as "futilism" (Hirschman, "Political Economics and Possibilism"). Wolfgang Streeck, *How Will Capitalism End? Essays on a Failing System* (London: Verso, 2017) is an important work in the futilist tradition. Notwithstanding this critical divergence in *weltanschauung*, I share with Streeck the view that the future is uncertain, not least because there is no ism or system on standby.

80. See corrective accounts, e.g., Bevins, "The 'Liberal World Order'"; Rothstein, *The Color of Law*; Katznelson, *When Affirmative Action*.

81. "Embedded populism" refers to a rejection of political liberalism—universal recognition of equality, appreciation of difference, equal participation, and tolerance—combined with continued economic protections, now severely circumscribed by factors such as citizenship, nationality, ethnicity, race, and gender. In contrast, "disembedded populism" would be a rejection of political liberalism and a full-bore dismantling of social protections from market processes and outcomes—neoliberal authoritarianism, perhaps best represented by Augusto Pinochet. Totalitarianism versus authoritarianism in Hayek might map onto the distinction between embedded populism versus disembedded populism. (Friedrich Hayek, *The Road to Serfdom*. (London, Routledge, [1944 (2014)].

82. As of this writing, it is an open question whether the Joe Biden–Kamala Harris administration will succeed in its vision of restoring, modernizing, and multilateralizing the US role in international affairs, or whether it will founder in nostalgia for a moment that, thankfully, has passed. See a cautionary treatment of this matter in Peter Beinhart, "Biden Wants America to Lead the World," *New York Times*, December 2, 2020, https://www.nytimes.com/2020/12/02/opinion/biden-foreign-policy.html.

83. Dani Rodrik, *The Globalization Paradox: Democracy and the Future of the World Economy* (New York: W. W. Norton, 2011), 205–6, 280.

CHAPTER 8. CORPORATE GLOBALIZATION AND THE LIBERAL ORDER

Earlier versions of this chapter were delivered as the Milton R. Konvitz Memorial Lecture, School of Industrial & Labor Relations, and in the Distinguished Speaker Series, Einaudi Center for International Studies, Cornell University, September 26, 2019; and as the Frank Irvine Lecture, Cornell Law School, September 27, 2019. For their helpful comments, I am grateful to the editors and the other contributors to this volume; Eric

Helleiner, who led the discussion of the chapter at our book workshop; and Doug Cassel, Rachel Davis, Caroline Rees, and Mary Ruggie.

1. John Gerard Ruggie, "International Regimes, Transaction, and Change: Embedded Liberalism in the Postwar Economic Order," *International Organization* 36, no. 2 (1982): 379–415.

2. See, for example, Melvyn Krauss, *The New Protectionism: The Welfare State and International Trade* (New York: New York University Press, 1978), 36.

3. Ruggie, "International Regimes, Transaction, and Change," 413.

4. John Braithwaite, *Regulatory Capitalism* (Cheltenham, UK: Edward Elgar, 2008); Colin Crouch, *The Strange Non-Death of Neoliberalism* (Cambridge: Polity, 2011); Quinn Slobodian, *Globalists: The End of Empire and the Birth of Neoliberalism* (Cambridge, MA: Harvard University Press, 2018).

5. William Allen, "Our Schizophrenic Conception of the Business Corporation," *Cardozo Law Review* 14, no. 2 (1992): 261–82.

6. Legally, the commonly used term "multinational corporation" is a misnomer, as explained later. Therefore, the term I use is "multinational enterprise" or "firm"—or simply "the multinational." The Organization for Economic Cooperation and Development (OECD) *Guidelines for Multinational Enterprises*, first adopted in 1976, employ a minimalist definition: "They usually comprise companies or other entities established in more than one country and so linked that they may coordinate their operations in various ways." OECD, *Guidelines for Multinational Enterprises* (Paris: OECD, 2011). For the sake of simplicity, I also include nonequity relationships between buyers (such as retailers) and their suppliers, as well as contract-based production networks (as for parts and assembly of consumer electronics and automobiles).

7. Kofi Annan, "Kofi Annan's Address to World Economic Forum in Davos," (February 1, 1999), https://www.un.org/sg/en/content/sg/speeches/1999-02-01/kofi-annans-address-world-economic-forum-davos. All subsequent Annan quotations are from this speech.

8. Business Roundtable, "Business Roundtable Redefines the Purpose of a Corporation to Promote 'An Economy That Serves All Americans.'" (August 19, 2019), https://www.businessroundtable.org/business-roundtable-redefines-the-purpose-of-a-corporation-to-promote-an-economy-that-serves-all-americans.

9. Larry Fink, "A Fundamental Reshaping of Finance," 2019, https://www.blackrock.com/corporate/investor-relations/larry-fink-ceo-letter.

10. "King Warren of the Roundtable," *Wall Street Journal*, editorial, October 6, 2019, https://www.wsj.com/articles/king-warren-of-the-roundtable-11570395953.

11. Lucian A. Bebchuk and Roberto Tallarita, "The Illusory Promise of Stakeholder Governance," The Harvard Law School Forum on Corporate Governance (March 2, 2020), https://corpgov.law.harvard.edu/2020/03/02/the-illusory-promise-of-stakeholder-governance/.

12. Quoted in Alan Murray, "America's CEOs Seek a New Purpose for the Corporation," *Fortune*, August 19, 2019, https://fortune.com/longform/business-roundtable-ceos-corporations-purpose/. Adding to the skepticism, signatories of the BR statement included the CEOs of Boeing, whose corporate culture the *New York Times* described as "broken," as revealed by the 737 Max crisis, "with senior executives having little regard for regulators, customers and even co-workers"; as well as Johnson & Johnson, which an Oklahoma judge had just ordered to pay the state $572 million for carrying out "false, misleading, and dangerous marketing campaigns," fueling the opioids crisis and causing "exponentially increasing" rates of addiction and deaths. David Gelles, "'I Honestly Don't Trust Many People at Boeing': A Broken Culture Exposed," *New York Times*, January 10, 2020. https://www.nytimes.com/2020/01/10/business/boeing-737-employees-messages.html; and Jan

Hoffman, "Johnson & Johnson Ordered to Pay $572 Million In Landmark Opioid Trial," *New York Times*, July 26, 2019, https://www.nytimes.com/2019/08/26/health/oklahoma-opioids-johnson-and-johnson.html.

13. Raymond Vernon, *In the Hurricane's Eye: The Troubled Prospects of Multinational Enterprises* (Cambridge, MA: Harvard University Press, 1998), vii–viii.

14. Fernand Braudel, *The Wheels of Commerce: Civilization and Capitalism 15th–18th Century* (New York: Harper and Row, 1982), 28.

15. UNCTAD, *World Investment Report 2002* (Geneva: United Nations Conference on Trade and Development, 2002), 7.

16. "Basic Facts about TNCs," *Cool Geography*, n.d., http://www.coolgeography.co.uk/GCSE/Year11/EconomicGeog/Industry/TNCs/basic_facts_about_tncs.htm; and UNCTAD, *World Investment Report 2010* (Geneva: UNCTAD, 2010), xviii.

17. UNCTAD, *World Investment Report 2013* (Geneva: UNCTAD, 2013), 135.

18. ILO, *Decent Work in Global Supply Chains* (Geneva: International Labor Organization, 2016), https://www.ilo.org/wcmsp5/groups/public/---ed_norm/---relconf/documents/meetingdocument/wcms_468097.pdf.

19. ILO, *World Employment and Social Outlook* (Geneva: International Labor Organization, 2015).

20. Emily Blanchard, "Trade Wars in the Global Value Chain Era," VoxEU, June 20, 2019, https://voxeu.org/article/trade-wars-global-value-chain-era; Austin Hufford and Bob Tita, "Manufacturers Move Supply Chains out of China," *Wall Street Journal*, July 14, 2019, https://www.wsj.com/articles/manufacturers-move-supply-chains-out-of-china-11563096601; Gavyn Davies, "Global Policy Adjusts to the Surprising Effects of Trade Wars," *Financial Times* July 28, 2019, https://www.ft.com/content/ab213fb0-a891-11e9-984c-fac8325aaa04.

21. John Gerard Ruggie, "Multinationals as Global Institutions: Power, Authority and Relative Autonomy," *Regulation & Governance* 12, no. 2 (2018): 317–37.

22. For nearly two decades beginning in 1996, US federal courts allowed foreign plaintiffs to bring civil suits against multinationals, whether US-based or not, under the Alien Tort Statute. This is a provision of the Judiciary Act of 1789, granting US federal courts jurisdiction for human rights abuses in violation of international law or a US treaty. Plaintiffs and multinationals had settled several cases before the US Supreme Court in 2013 ruled that a presumption against extraterritoriality applies to the act, which can be displaced only if a claim touches and concerns the territory of the United States "with sufficient force"—a term the court did not define. *Kiobel v. Royal Dutch Petroleum Co.*, 569 US 108 (2013).

23. Amy Qin, "Can You Say 'Hakuna Matata' in Mandarin?," *New York Times*, June 17, 2016, https://www.nytimes.com/2016/06/18/theater/the-lion-king-disneyland-shanghai.html.

24. Gus Van Harten, "Private Authority and Transnational Governance: The Contours of the International System of Investor Protection," *Review of International Political Economy* 12, no. 4 (2005): 600–23; Peter T. Muchlinski, *Multinational Enterprises and the Law*, second ed. (Oxford: Oxford University Press, 2007); Surya P. Subedi, *International Investment Law: Reconciling Policy and Principle* (Oxford: Hart, 2008).

25. José E. Alvarez, "The Evolving BIT," *Transnational Dispute Management* 1 (2010): quotation on 5–6, www.transnational-dispute-management.com.

26. Catharine Titi, "Embedded Liberalism and International Investment Agreements: The Future of the Right to Regulate," in *The Future of International Economic Integration: The Embedded Liberalism Compromise Revisited*, ed. Gillian Moon and Lisa Toohey (Cambridge: Cambridge University Press, 2018), 122–36.

27. Nicholas Lemann, *Transaction Man: The Rise of the Deal and the Decline of the American Dream* (New York: Farrar, Straus and Giroux, 2019), 67.

28. I say "resurged" because it had been the dominant form when the main players were natural persons who came together for the purpose of capital formation, before corporations expanded nationally to the point of requiring professional managers and sourcing capital from dispersed investors.

29. Milton Friedman, "The Social Responsibility of Business Is to Increase its Profits," *New York Times Magazine,* September 13, 1970, https://www.nytimes.com/1970/09/13/archives/a-friedman-doctrine-the-social-responsibility-of-business-is-to.html.

30. J-P Robé has expressed Friedman's error most succinctly: "After the process of incorporation, shareholders have no right of access to the assets of the corporation; they do not enter into any contract in its name. No liability can arise for them from the corporate activity. They do not run the corporation and do not own it." J-P Robé, "Being Done with Milton Friedman," *Accounting, Economics and Law* 2, no. 1 (2012): 8 (emphases in original).

31. Michael C. Jensen and William H. Meckling, "Theory of the Firm: Managerial Behavior, Agency Costs and Ownership Structure," *Journal of Financial Economics* 3, no. 4 (1976): 305–60.

32. Henry Hausman and Reinier Kraakman, "The End of History for Corporate Law," *Georgetown Law Journal* 89 (2001): 439–68.

33. Lynn Stout, *The Shareholder Value Myth: How Putting Shareholders First Harms Investors, Corporations, and the Public* (San Francisco: Barret-Koehler, 2012), 19–21.

34. Ronen Palan, *The Offshore World: Sovereign Markets, Virtual Places, and Nomad Millionaires* (Ithaca, NY: Cornell University Press, 2003), 157.

35. OECD, "International Collaboration to End Tax Avoidance," www.oecd.org/tax/beps/.

36. Gabriel Zucman, *The Hidden Wealth of Nations: The Scourge of Tax Havens* (Chicago: University of Chicago Press, 2018).

37. Ronen Palan, Richard Murphy, and Christian Chavagneux, *Tax Havens: How Globalization Really Works* (Ithaca, NY: Cornell University Press, 2010).

38. Palan, Murphy, and Chavagneux, *Tax Havens,* 5.

39. Zucman, *The Hidden Wealth of Nations,* 195.

40. Quoted in Eduardo Porter, "Tax Tactics Threaten Public Funds," *New York Times,* October 1, 2014. https://www.nytimes.com/2014/10/02/business/economy/multinational-tax-strategies-put-public-coffers-at-risk.html.

41. Gay W. Seidman, "Monitoring Multinationals: Lessons from the Anti-Apartheid Era," *Politics & Society* 31, no. 3 (2003): 381–406; Susan K. Sell and Aseem Prakash, "Using Ideas Strategically: The Contest between Business and NGO Networks in Intellectual Property Rights," *International Studies Quarterly* 48, no. 1 (2004):143–75; Suerie Moon, "Embedding Neoliberalism: Global Health and the Evolution of the Global Intellectual Property Regime (1995–2009)" (PhD dissertation, John F. Kennedy School of Government, Harvard University, 2010); Margaret E. Keck and Kathryn Sikkink, *Activists beyond Borders: Advocacy Networks in International Politics* (Ithaca, NY: Cornell University Press, 1998).

42. Quoted in John Cushman, "Nike Pledges to End Child Labor and Apply US Rules Abroad," *New York Times,* May 13, 1998, https://www.nytimes.com/1998/05/13/business/international-business-nike-pledges-to-end-child-labor-and-apply-us-rules-abroad.html#:~:text=Nike%20said%20it%20would%20raise,underage%20workers%20already%20in%20place.

43. Simon Zadek, "The Path to Corporate Responsibility," *Harvard Business Review,* no. 82, December 2004, 125–32.

44. Quoted in Bronwen Manby, *The Price of Oil: Corporate Responsibility and Human Rights Violations in Nigeria's Oil Producing Communities* (New York: Human Rights Watch, 1999).

45. Sir Mark Moody-Stuart, *Responsible Leadership: Lessons from the Front Line of Sustainability and Ethics* (Sheffield, UK: Greenleaf, 2014).

46. This is not to say that Shell subsequently has always lived up to its business principles and CSR commitments.

47. Geert Demuijnck and Björn Fasterling, "The Social License to Operate." *Journal of Business Ethics* 136 (2016): 675–85.

48. John Gerard Ruggie, "Reconstituting the Global Public Domain: Issues, Actors, and Practices," *European Journal of International Relations* 10, no. 4 (2004): 519.

49. Andrew Crane, Abagail McWilliams, Dirk Matten, Jeremy Moon, and Donald S. Siegel, eds., *The Oxford Handbook of Corporate Social Responsibility* (Oxford: Oxford University Press, 2008), 3.

50. United Nations, "Human Rights Policies and Management Practices: Results from Questionnaire Surveys of Governments and Fortune Global 500 Firms," *Report of the Special Representative of the Secretary-General on the Issue of Human Rights and Transnational Corporations and Other Business Enterprises: John Ruggie.* UN Document A/HRC/4/35/Add.3 (February 28, 2007); Krista Bondy, Jeremy Moon, and Dirk Matten, "An Institution of Corporate Social Responsibility (CSR) in Multinational Corporations (MNCs): Form and Implications," *Journal of Business Ethics* 111, no. 2 (2012): 281–99.

51. Thomas Donaldson and Thomas W. Dunfee, *Ties That Bind: A Social Contracts Approach to Business Ethics* (Cambridge, MA: Harvard Business School Press, 1999).

52. For contemporaneous accounts that make this clear, see John Gerard Ruggie, "global_governance.net: The Global Compact as Learning Network," *Global Governance* 7, no. 4 (2001): 371–78; John Gerard Ruggie, "The Theory and Practice of Learning Networks: Corporate Social Responsibility and the Global Compact," *Journal of Corporate Citizenship* 5 (Spring 2002): 27–36; Georg Kell and John Gerard Ruggie, "Global Markets and Social Legitimacy: The Case of the Global Compact," in *The Market or the Public Domain: Global Governance and the Asymmetry of Power,* ed. Daniel Drache (London: Routledge, 2003).

53. "A New Global Compact?," *Christian Science Monitor,* September 8, 2000, https://www.csmonitor.com/2000/0908/p10s1.html.

54. Norwegian Nobel Committee (2001), http://nobelpeaceprize.org/en_GB/laureatel/laureates-2001/press-2001/.

55. DNV-GL, *The United Nations Global Compact: Transforming Business, Changing the World* (2015), 15, https://www.unglobalcompact.org/library/1331.

56. For examples, see Rebecca Henderson, *Reimaging Capitalism in a World on Fire* (New York: Public Affairs, 2020); and Myriam Sidibe, *Brands on a Mission* (London: Routledge, 2020). Although increasingly widespread among leading firms, these steps do not yet constitute mainstream practices.

57. Andreas Rasche, "'A Necessary Supplement': What the Global Compact Is and Is Not," *Business & Society* 48, no. 4 (2009): 511–37.

58. Steven Lydenberg, *Corporations and the Public Interest: Guiding the Invisible Hand* (San Francisco: Berrett-Koehler, 2005).

59. https://www.unepfi.org/fileadmin/events/2004/stocks/who_cares_wins_global_compact_2004.pdf.

60. Darren Fonda, "The Trump Bump and Sustainable Investing," *Barron's,* June 23, 2018. In fact, the Trump administration subsequently issued rules that pension funds must be managed exclusively for "pecuniary purposes;" Rachel Koning Beals, "Trump Labor Department's Rule Discouraging ESG investing in Retirement Plans Is Finalized over Swell of Objections," *Market Watch,* October 31, 2020, https://www.marketwatch.com/story/trumps-labor-rule-discouraging-esg-investing-in-retirement-plans-is-finalized-over-swell-of-objections-11604089492. The rules were challenged in the courts and have been reversed by the Biden administration.

61. Chris Flood, "Record Sums Deployed into Sustainable Investment Funds," *Financial Times,* January 19, 2020, https://www.ft.com/content/2a6c38f7-4e4b-411b-b5e6-96b36e597cfc.

62. Patrick Temple-West, "'Monstrous' Run for Responsible Stocks Stokes Fears of a Bubble," *Financial Times,* February 20, 2020, https://www.ft.com/content/73765d6c-5402-11ea-90ad-25e377c0ee1f.

63. Morningstar UK, "How Does European Sustainable Funds' Performance Measure Up?," June 2020, https://www.morningstar.com/en-uk/lp/European-Sustainable-Funds-Performance.

64. Patrick Temple-West, "ESG Shines in the Crash" *Financial Times,* March 13, 2020, https://www.ft.com/content/dd47aae8-ce25-43ea-8352-814ca44174e3. Establishing causality remains elusive. ESG funds tend have higher exposure to technology stocks and less to fossil fuels, which accounts for part of the variation. But some have also hypothesized that firms with high ESG ratings are simply better managed, incorporating a wider range of information into their decision-making. For a more detailed discussion, see John Gerard Ruggie, "Corporate Purpose in Play: The Role of ESG Investing," in *Sustainable Investing: A Path to a New Horizon,* ed, Andreas Rasche, Herman Bril, and Georg Kell (London: Routledge, 2020).

65. Sandra Flow, Caroline Hailey, and Ahsan Sayed, "Navigating the ESG Landscape," The Harvard Law School Corporate Governance Forum, January 31, 2020, https://corpgov.law.harvard.edu/2020/01/31/navigating-the-esg-landscape/.

66. John Gerard Ruggie and Emily K. Middleton, "Money, Millennials and Human Rights: Sustaining 'Sustainable Investing,'" *Global Policy* 10, no. 1 (2019): 144–50.

67. Attracta Mooney, "BlackRock Pushes for Global ESG Standards," *Financial Times,* October 29, 2020, https://www.ft.com/content/2a8d7fac-5ab6-43e5-9e04-8e9b3adfd195; Carlos Tornero, "IFRS Foundation Throws Hat in the ESG Ring with a 'Sustainability Standards Board,'" *Responsible Investor,* September 30, 2020, https://www.responsible-investor.com/articles/ifrs-foundation-throws-hat-in-the-esg-ring-with-a-sustainability-standards-board; Carlos Tornero, "EU to Launch Single Platform for Sustainability and Financial Data," *Responsible Investor,* September 25, 2020, https://www.responsible-investor.com/articles/eu-to-launch-single-platform-for-sustainability-and-financial-data.

68. Steven R. Ratner, "Introduction to the Symposium on Soft and Hard Law on Business and Human Rights," *American Journal of International Law Unbound* 114 (July 2020): 163–64, https://www.cambridge.org/core/journals/american-journal-of-international-law/article/introduction-to-the-symposium-on-soft-and-hard-law-on-business-and-human-rights/1532C4E20155F5A925EF1D9F24948BD8. For some of the theoretical underpinnings of the UNGPs, see Ruggie, "The Social Construction of the UN Guiding Principles on Business and Human Rights," in *Research Handbook on Business and Human Rights,* ed. Surya Deva and David Birchall (Cheltenham, UK: Edward Elgar, 2020).

69. United Nations, *Guiding Principles on Business and Human Rights* (2011), https://www.business-humanrights.org/en/un-guiding-principles.

70. "Soft law" refers to international instruments that derive their normativity from broad political consensus but do not in themselves have legally binding force.

71. Karin Buhmann, "The Development of the 'UN Framework': A Pragmatic Process towards a Pragmatic Output," in *The UN Guiding Principles on Business and Human Rights,* ed. Radu Mares (Leiden, The Netherlands: Martinus Nijhoff, 2012); Karin Buhmann, "Business and Human Rights: Analysing Discursive Articulation of Stakeholder Interests to Explain the Consensus-Based Construction of the 'Protect, Respect, Remedy UN Framework,'" *International Law Research* 1, no. 1 (2012): 88–101.

72. For an in-depth discussion, see John Gerard Ruggie, *Just Business: Multinational Corporations and Human Rights* (New York: W. W. Norton, 2013).

73. United Nations, "Responsibilities of Transnational Corporations and Related Business Enterprises with Regard to Human Rights," UN. Doc. E/CN.4/DEC/2004/116 (2004).

74. Rebecca Henderson and Nien-he Hsie, "Putting the Guiding Principles into Action: Human Rights at Barrick Gold (A)," Harvard Business School Case 315–108 (March 2015), 9.

75. José E. Alvarez. "Are Corporations 'Subjects' of International Law?," *Santa Clara Journal of International Law* 1 (2011): 2–36.

76. For example, a body affiliated with China's Ministry of Commerce issued an advisory report to Chinese mining companies operating overseas, stating that they should "ensure that all operations shall be in line with the UN Guiding Principles on Business and Human Rights during the entire life-cycle of the mining project." China Chamber of Commerce of Metals, Minerals & Chemicals, "Guidelines for Social Responsibility in Outbound Mining Investments" (2015), https://www.emm-network.org/wp-content/uploads/2015/03/CSR-Guidelines-2nd-revision.pdf.

77. For example, the OECD incorporated the UNGPs' Pillar II into its *Guidelines for Multinational Enterprises*, which had lacked a human rights chapter, and extended the due-diligence provisions to other elements of the *Guidelines*—which have the only intergovernmental complaints mechanism for the conduct of multinationals.

78. Ratner, "Introduction to the Symposium," 163.

79. In addition to its corruption problems, FIFA was under great pressure from advocacy groups, commercial sponsors, and workers organizations over the use of essentially bonded labor from South and Southeast Asia to construct facilities for the 2222 World Cup in Qatar. FIFA commissioned me to produce a human rights risk profile and make recommendations. See John Gerard Ruggie, "'For the Game. For the World.' FIFA and Human Rights," Corporate Responsibility Initiative Report no. 68 (Cambridge, MA: John F. Kennedy School of Government, Harvard University, 2016). Together with its local affiliate and the Building and Woodworkers' International, FIFA has used its leverage with Qatari authorities to improve migrant-worker conditions. Building and Woodworkers' International, "2019 Report on Joint Inspections" (2020), https://www.bwint.org/cms/news-72/2019-bwi-sc-jwg-report-on-joint-inspections-in-qatar-released-1641.

80. The European Parliament has recommended a draft law to this effect to the European Commission. It is not binding on the Commission, but as it was adopted by the overwhelming majority of 504-79, it sends a strong signal. For a more extensive discussion of these developments, see John Gerard Ruggie, Caroline Rees and Rachel Davis, "Ten Years After: From UN Guiding Principles to Multi-Fiduciary Obligations," *Business and Human Rights Journal* 6, no. 2 (2021): 1–19.

81. Milton Friedman, *Capitalism and* Freedom, second ed. (Chicago: University of Chicago Press, 1982), xviii–xiv.

82. G. John Ikenberry, *Liberal Leviathan: The Origins, Crisis, and Transformation of the American World Order* (Princeton, NJ: Princeton University Press, 2011).

CHAPTER 9. LIBERALISM'S ANTINOMY

1. I would like to thank the participants of a seminar at Columbia University, Robert Keohane, all the discussants at the book workshop (Eric Helleiner, Peter Hall, and Erin Lockwood), and all the authors in this volume for helpful comments and criticisms of an earlier draft of this chapter.

2. Ernest Belfort Bax, *Selected Essays of Arthur Schopenhauer: With a Biographical Introduction and Sketch of His Philosophy* (London: George Bell and Sons), 312.

3. Jacob Viner, "The Economist in History," in Douglas A. Irwin, ed., *Jacob Viner: Essays on the Intellectual History of Economics* (Princeton, NJ: Princeton University Press, 1991), 227.

4. Emmanual Adler, *World Ordering: A Social Theory of Cognitive Evolution* (New York: Cambridge University Press, 2018), 154.

5. Jean-François Drolet and Michael C. Williams, "Radical Conservatism and Global Order: International Theory and the New Right," *International Theory* 10, no. 3 (2018): 285–313.

6. Richard Litell, "Icebergs Still Menace Ships," *Science News-Letter* 77, no. 10 (March 1960): 154; Lane Wallace, "No, the Moon Did Not Sink the Titanic," *Atlantic*, March 12, 2012, https://www.theatlantic.com/technology/archive/2012/03/no-the-moon-did-not-sink-the-titanic/254291/.

7. Harvard Business School, *Hungary: Economic Crisis and a Shift to the Right*, Case no. 9–711–051 (June 22, 2016), 4–6.

8. Aron Buzogány and Mahai Varga, "The Ideational Foundations of the Illiberal Backlash in Central and Eastern Europe: The Case of Hungary," *Review of International Political Economy* 25, no. 6 (2018): 811–28; Maria Csanádi, "Paths to Political Capture and Institutionalized Corruption in Hungary 2010–2020," in *Winners Take All: Dynamics of Political Capture and Redistribution in Hungary*, ed. Maria Csanádi (Centre for Economic and Regional Studies, Institute of Economics, Budapest, forthcoming). Alen Toplišek, "The Political Economy of Populist Rule in Post-Crisis Europe: Hungary and Poland," *New Political Economy* 25, no. 3 (2020): 388–403.

9. Ivan Krastev and Stephen Holmes, *The Light That Failed: Why the West Is Losing the Fight for Democracy* (New York: Pegasus, 2020).

10. Sam Fleming, Valerie Hopkins, and James Shotter, "For the EU, Deciding How to Fund the Recovery Is Only Half the Battle," *Financial Times*, April 20, 2020, https://www.ft.com/content/2e5ba35b-d3fd-4095-8aad-4d01349c89e5.

11. Stephen Brown and Pierre McDonagh, "Titanic: Consuming the Myths and Meanings of an Ambiguous Brand," *Journal of Consumer Research* 40, no. 4 (2013): 595.

12. Quinn Slobodian, *Globalists: The End of Empire and the Birth of Neoliberalism* (Cambridge MA: Harvard University Press, 2018).

13. Slobodian, *Globalists*, 16.

14. Rawi Abdelal, *Capital Rules: The Construction of Global Finance* (Cambridge, MA.: Harvard University Press, 2007), 67–71.

15. Stephen Wertheim, "A World Safe for Capital: How Neoliberalism Shaped the International System," *Foreign Affairs* 98, no. 3 (May/June 2019): 181.

16. Abdelal, *Capital Rules*, 70.

17. G. John Ikenberry, "Liberal Internationalism 3.0: America and the Dilemmas of Liberal World Order," *Perspectives on Politics* 7, no. 1 (2009): 71–87.

18. Nazneen Barma, Ely Ratner, and Steven Weber, "The Mythical Liberal Order," *National Interest* Issue #124 (March/April 2013): 56–67; Randall Schweller, *Maxwell's Demon and the Golden Apple: Global Discord in the New Millennium* (Baltimore: Johns Hopkins University Press, 2014).

19. Quoted in Harold Brackman, "Trump and 'The Terrible Simplifiers,'" *Jewish Journal* (March 2, 2016), https://jewishjournal.com/commentary/blogs/183012/trump-and-the-terrible-simplifiers.

20. I would like to thank Marc Blyth, Robert Keohane, and John Ruggie for their clarifying correspondence on this point.

21. John Gerard Ruggie, email correspondence, July 9, 2020.

22. Mark Blyth, *Austerity: The History of a Dangerous Idea* (New York: Oxford University Press, 2013), 85–106.

23. I would like to thank Robert Keohane for his critical comments and helpful suggestions on this point. See also Robert O. Keohane, *Power and Governance in a Partially Globalized World* (New York: Routledge, 2002), 45.

24. John Gerard Ruggie, email correspondence, July 8, 2020.

25. Peter J. Katzenstein, "Worldviews in World Politics" in *Uncertainty and Its Discontents: Worldviews in World Politics,* ed. Peter J. Katzenstein (New York: Cambridge University Press, forthcoming).

26. Ross Douthat, "The Tom Cotton Op-Ed and the Cultural Revolution," *New York Times,* June 12, 2020, https://www.nytimes.com/2020/06/12/opinion/nyt-tom-cotton-oped-liberalism.html.

27. Helena Rosenblatt, *The Lost History of Liberalism: From Ancient Rome to the Twenty-First Century* (Princeton, NJ: Princeton University Press, 2018).

28. Duncan Bell, "What Is Liberalism?," *Political Theory* 42, no. 6 (2014): 683.

29. Bell, "What is Liberalism?," 685, 689-99.

30. Bell, "What is Liberalism?," 692.

31. Robert Vitalis, *White World Order, Black Power Politics: The Birth of American International Relations* (Ithaca, NY: Cornell University Press, 2015). See also Peter J. Katzenstein, ed., Anglo-America and Its Discontents: Civilizational Identities beyond West and East (New York: Routledge, 2012); Peter J. Katzenstein and Christopher Hemmer, "Why Is There No NATO in Asia? Collective Identity, Regionalism and the Origins of Multilateralism," *International Organization* 56, no. 3 (Summer 2002): 575-607.

32. Peter J. Katzenstein, "Das Problem heisst nicht Donald Trump: Die lange Vorgeschichte der amerikanischen Gegenwart," *WZB-Nachrichten,* no. 164 (June 2019): 7-9.

33. Ashley Jardina, *White Identity Politics* (New York: Cambridge University Press, 2019).

34. Julian Borger, "Republicans Closely Resemble Autocratic Parties in Hungary and Turkey," *Guardian,* October 26, 2020, https://www.theguardian.com/us-news/2020/oct/26/republican-party-autocratic-hungary-turkey-study-trump; *Der Spiegel,* October 30, 2020, 18.

35. Louis Hartz, *The Liberal Tradition in America* (New York: Harcourt, Brace and World, 1955).

36. John G. Ruggie, "International Regimes, Transactions, and Change: Embedded Liberalism in the Postwar Economic Order," *International Organization* 36, no. 2 (1982): 379-415.

37. Karl Polanyi, *The Great Transformation* (Boston: Beacon, 1944).

38. Polanyi also explored two other Great Ditches: the emergence of a commercial society grounded in exchange relations and the division of labor and technological change in industrial society. Charting the course of modern history requires traversing all three Great Ditches, as Polanyi understood only too well. See Gareth Dale, *Karl Polanyi: A Life on the Left* (New York: Columbia University Press, 2016), 5-7.

39. Barrington Moore, *Social Origins of Dictatorship and Democracy: Lord and Peasant in the Making of the Modern World* (Boston: Beacon, 1966), 12.

40. The economic implications of the Old Poor Laws and their replacement by the Poor Law Amendment Act of 1834 continue to be debated by economic historians. With respect to that debate, one historian suggested, mischievously, that history repeats itself because "historians repeat each other." See Mark Blaug, "The Myth of the Old Poor Law and the Making of the New," *Journal of Economic History* 23, no. 2: 152.

41. Eric Helleiner, "The Life and Times of Embedded Liberalism: Legacies and Innovations since Bretton Woods," *Review of International Political Economy* 26, no. 6 (2019): 1114, 1123-25.

42. Cornel Ban, *Ruling Ideas: How Global Neoliberalism Goes Local* (New York: Oxford University Press, 2016); Stephen Nelson, "'Critical Dialogue,'" *Perspectives on Politics* 16, no. 3 (2018): 785–87.

43. Martin Wolf, "Why So Little Has Changed since the Financial Crash," *Financial Times*, September 3, 2018, https://www.ft.com/content/c85b9792-aad1-11e8-94bd-cba 20d67390c.

44. Peter J. Katzenstein, *Small States in World Markets: Industrial Policy in Europe* (Ithaca, NY: Cornell University Press, 1985); and Peter J. Katzenstein, *Corporatism and Change: Austria, Switzerland, and the Politics of Industry* (Ithaca, NY: Cornell University Press, 1984).

45. Dani Rodrik, *Has Globalization Gone Too Far?* (Washington, DC: Institute for International Economics, 2007); Peter J. Katzenstein, "*Small States* and Small States Revisited," *New Political Economy* 8, no. 1 (2003): 9–30.

46. Carlo Invernizzi Accetti, *What Is Christian Democracy? Politics, Religion and Ideology* (New York: Cambridge University Press, 2019); and Udi Greenberg, "Can Christian Democracy Save US?," *Boston Review*, October 22, 2019, http://bostonreview.net/philos ophy-religion/udi-greenberg-christian-democracy.

47. Eric Helleiner and Andreas Pickel, eds., *Economic Nationalism in a Globalizing World* (Ithaca, NY: Cornell University Press, 2005); Eric Helleiner, "Varieties of American Neomercantilism: From the First Years of the Republic to Trumpian Economic Nationalism," *European Review of International Studies* 6, no. 3 (2019): 7–29.

48. Ruggie, "International Regimes, Transactions, and Change."

49. Margaret Canovan, "On Being Economical with the Truth: Some Liberal Reflections," *Political Studies* 38, no. 1 (1990): 26.

50. Jamie Peck and Adam Tickell, "Jungle Law Breaks Out: Neoliberalism and Global-Local Disorder," *Area* 26, no. 4 (1994): 317–26.

51. Kurt Andersen, *Evil Geniuses: The Unmaking of America; A Recent History* (New York: Penguin Random House, 2020).

52. Rosenblatt, *The Lost History of Liberalism.*

53. Peter J. Katzenstein, "The Second Coming? Reflections on a Global Theory of International Relations," *Chinese Journal of International Politics* 11, no. 4 (2018): 374–75.

54. Patchen Markell, "Power, Attention and the Tasks of Critical Theory" (unpublished manuscript, University of Chicago, May 2017), 3.

55. Henry Kissinger, "The Coronavirus Pandemic Will Forever Alter the World Order," *Wall Street Journal*, April 4, 2020, A17.

56. Thomas L. Friedman, "How We Broke the World," *New York Times*, May 31, 2020, SR 4–5.

57. "What's the Worst That Could Happen? The World Should Think Better about Catastrophic and Existential Risks," *Economist*, June 27–July 3, 2020, 13–16, https://www. economist.com/briefing/2020/06/25/the-world-should-think-better-about-catastrophic-and-existential-risks.

58. Joshua Foa Dienstag, "Pessimistic Realism and Realistic Pessimism," in *Political Thought and International Relations: Variations on a Realist Theme,* ed. Duncan Bell (Oxford: Oxford University Press, 2009), 171–72.

59. Peter J. Katzenstein, "Fractures and Resilience of Liberal International Orders," in *From Western-Centric to a Post-Western World: In Search of an Emerging Global Order in the 21st Century,* ed. Chuan Chu (New York: Routledge, 2020), 146–65.

60. Ernst Haas, *Nationalism, Liberalism, and Progress,* vol. 2: *The Dismal Fate of New Nations* (Ithaca, NY: Cornell University Press, 1997), 322–52, 411–54.

61. Ross Douthat, "The Crisis of the Liberal Zombie Order," *New Statesman*, March 18, 2020.

62. Katzenstein, "Worldviews in World Politics."

63. Timothy Noah, "The L Word," *New York Times*, Sunday Book Review, October 6, 2019, 12.

64. Theodore J. Lowi, *The End of Liberalism: Ideology, Policy, and the Crisis of Public Authority* (New York: Norton, 1969).

65. Stanley Hoffman, "The Crisis of Liberal Internationalism," *Foreign Policy*, no. 98 (Spring, 1995): 159.

66. Adam Gopnik, *A Thousand Small Sanities: The Moral Adventures of Liberalism* (New York: Basic Books, 2019); James Traub, *What Was Liberalism? The Past, Present, and Promise of a Noble Idea* (New York: Basic Books, 2019); Mark Lilla, *The Once and Future Liberalism: After Identity Politics* (New York: Harper Collins, 2017).

Contributors

Rawi Abdelal is the Herbert F. Johnson Professor of International Management at Harvard Business School, Faculty Co-Chair of the Bloomberg Harvard City Leadership Initiative, and Director of Harvard University's Davis Center for Russian and Eurasian Studies. His books include *Capital Rules: The Construction of Global Finance.*

Sheri Berman is Professor of Political Science, Barnard College, Columbia University. Her most recent book is *Democracy and Dictatorship in Europe: From the Ancien Régime to the Present Day.*

Mark Blyth is the William R. Rhodes '57 Professor of International Economics and Director of the Center for International Economics and Finance at the Watson Institute for International and Public Affairs at Brown University. His most recent book is *Angrynomics* (with Eric Lonergan).

Francis J. Gavin is the Giovanni Agnelli Distinguished Professor and Director of the Henry A. Kissinger Center for Global Affairs, Johns Hopkins School of Advanced International Studies. His most recent book is *Nuclear Weapons and American Grand Strategy.*

Peter A. Gourevitch is Founding Dean of the School of Global Policy and Strategy (GPS), University of California, San Diego, and Distinguished Professor Emeritus of Political Science. His most recent book is the coedited volume *The Credibility of Transnational NGOs.*

Ilene Grabel is Distinguished University Professor at the Josef Korbel School of International Studies, University of Denver. Her most recent book, *When Things Don't Fall Apart: Global Financial Governance and Developmental Finance in an Age of Productive Incoherence*, won awards from the International Studies Association, the British International Studies Association, and the European Association for Evolutionary Political Economy.

Peter J. Katzenstein is the Walter S. Carpenter Jr. Professor of International Studies at Cornell University. He has served as President of the American Political

Science Association and is the recipient of the 2020 Johan Skytte Prize. His most recent book is *Uncertainty and Its Discontents: Worldviews in World Politics*.

Jonathan Kirshner is Professor of Political Science and International Studies at Boston College, and the Stephen and Barbara Friedman Professor of International Political Economy Emeritus in the Department of Government, Cornell University. His books include *American Power after the Financial Crisis*.

John Gerard Ruggie was the Berthold Beitz Research Professor in Human Rights and International Affairs at the John F. Kennedy School of Government, Harvard University. He also served as the Dean of the School of International and Public Affairs at Columbia University, and in several senior United Nations posts, including Assistant Secretary General for Strategic Planning. His books include *Just Business: Multinational Corporations and Human Rights*.

Index

Page numbers with an f indicate figures. Page numbers with a t indicate tables.

225